BANNED IN BOSTON

Banned in Boston

The Watch and Ward Society's Crusade against
Books, Burlesque, and the Social Evil

NEIL MILLER

Beacon Press, Boston

Beacon Press
25 Beacon Street
Boston, Massachusetts 02108-2892
www.beacon.org

Beacon Press books
are published under the auspices of
the Unitarian Universalist Association of Congregations.

13   12   11   10   8   7   6   5   4   3   2   1

This book is printed on acid-free paper that meets the uncoated paper
ANSI/NISO specifications for permanence as revised in 1992.

Text design and composition by Wilsted and Taylor Publishing Services

Library of Congress Cataloging-in-Publication Data
Miller, Neil.
Banned in Boston : the Watch and Ward Society's crusade against books,
burlesque, and the social evil / Neil Miller.
    p. cm.
Includes bibliographical references and index.
ISBN 978-0-8070-5112-2 (hardcover : alk. paper)
1. Watch and Ward Society (Boston, Mass.)—History. 2. Vigilance
committees—Massachusetts—Boston—History. 3. Social control—
Massachusetts—Boston—History. 4. Corruption—Massachusetts—
Boston—History. 5. Censorship—Massachusetts—Boston—History.
6. Sex-oriented businesses—Massachusetts—Boston—History. 7. Boston
(Mass.)—Social conditions—19th century. 8. Boston (Mass.)—Social
conditions—20th century. 9. Boston (Mass.)—Moral conditions. I. Title.
HV6795.B7M55 2010
363.409744'61—dc22   2010007770

For Paul Brouillette

CONTENTS

The Battle of Brimstone Corner, April 1926

IT WAS A PROVERBIAL MATCH OF THE TITANS. In one corner was H. L. Mencken, the most prominent editor in America, the great iconoclast and savage and sharp-tongued foe, in his words, of all "preposterous Puritans," "malignant moralists," and "Christians turned cannibals." In the other corner was the Reverend J. Frank Chase, Boston's reigning censor and moral policeman, secretary of the powerful New England Watch and Ward Society, scourge of small-time gamblers, burlesque promoters, and writers who trafficked in "hells" and "goddamns" and anything that smacked of frankness in terms of sex. The scene was Brimstone Corner, just off the Boston Common, in front of the Park Street Church, a block from the gilded dome of the State House. It was at the Park Street Church where the Watch and Ward Society (then called the New England Society for the Suppression of Vice) was originally established in 1878.

A week before, Chase, whose word was law to Massachusetts booksellers and magazine vendors, had ordered the banning of the April 1926 issue of Mencken's magazine, the *American Mercury*. It contained a vignette called "Hatrack," a tale of prostitution and hypocrisy in a small Missouri town that Chase contended was obscene. Across the river in Cambridge, the proprietor of a Harvard Square newsstand had been arrested for selling a copy of the magazine to a Watch and Ward agent.

Mencken had taken the train up to Boston from his hometown of Baltimore on April 5, 1926, for the purpose of challenging the Watch and Ward Society by selling Chase a copy of that very issue. Henry Louis Mencken was a small man, with "a plum pudding of a body and a square head stuck on it with no intervening neck," as British journalist Alistair Cooke described him. He parted his hair in the middle, and his eyes, so small that you could see the whites above the irises, gave him "the earnestness of a gas jet when he talked, an air of resigned incredulity when he listened, and a merry acceptance of the human race and all its foibles when he grinned." He usually dressed "like the owner of a country hardware store," noted Cooke. On ceremonial occasions, however, he dressed "like a plumber got up for church." This day was one of the latter.

More than a thousand curiosity-seekers—largely Harvard undergraduates—turned out for the spectacle on the Common. Some hung off trees and out of windows. Mencken's lawyer, Arthur Garfield Hays, lately a counsel for the defense at the Scopes "monkey" trial in Dayton, Tennessee, arrived first, at about 1:50 in the afternoon. He mounted the steps of the Park Street Church carrying a bundle of fifty copies of the *American Mercury*, clothed in its famous green cover, to sell just in case Chase declined to show up at the last minute. The crowd, impatient to snap up copies of the magazine, rushed towards him, holding out dollar bills. When Mencken stepped from a taxicab a few minutes later, accompanied by a *Baltimore Sun* reporter and an Alfred A. Knopf book salesman, he found no place to move or even stand. It was *that* crowded. Traffic officers tried unsuccessfully to disperse the mob as the editor and his lawyer pushed their way across Park Street to the Common, where they could barely gain their footing.

A man claiming to represent Chase approached Mencken and offered to buy a copy of the *Mercury*. Mencken waved him away. It was Chase he was waiting for. And then, amidst cries of "Here he is!" the superintendent of police, Michael H. Crowley, cleared a path for the Watch and Ward secretary. He was accompanied by Captain George W. Peterson, chief of Boston's Vice Squad, and a young plainclothes officer named Oliver Garrett, later to become a notorious character in Boston.

"Are you Chase?" demanded Mencken.

"I am," replied a solidly built man with glasses and a walrus mustache.

"And do you want to buy a copy of the *Mercury?*"

"I do," came the reply.

Chase offered Mencken a silver half-dollar, and, in a theatrical moment that delighted the throng, the editor took the coin and bit the end of it to make sure that it was genuine. Then he handed over a copy of the magazine.

"Officer, arrest that man!" commanded Chase, addressing Captain Peterson. The Boston police and the Watch and Ward had had their differences over the years—sometimes the vice organization's agents had acted as if they *were* the Boston police—but this time the police were more than happy to do the Watch and Ward's bidding. Garrett, the plainclothes officer, tapped Mencken on the arm.

Mencken still had three copies of the *Mercury* in his hand. "Throw them away," his lawyer counseled.

Mencken tossed the magazines into the air. There was a scramble, and, in the rush to get a copy, the crowd ripped the magazines to pieces. Chase handed his over to Peterson.

Then Mencken, hat low on his head and trademark cigar in hand, accompanied by Hays and followed by several hundred onlookers, was marched up Tremont Street to police headquarters at Pemberton Square, four blocks away. He was led to the second floor and booked on a charge of violating Chapter 272, Section 28, of the Public General Laws of Massachusetts. The charge was clear—that he, Mencken, "did sell to one Jason F. Chase certain obscene, indecent, and impure printing . . . manifestly tending to corrupt the morals of youth." After that, Mencken was taken to the Central Municipal Court and formally arraigned. A hearing was set for 10 a.m. the following day, April 6. Mencken was released on his own recognizance, with a surety bond fixed at $500.

Chase had won round one.

PART I

Early Days

CHAPTER 1

Founding Fathers, 1878

HALF A CENTURY EARLIER, on a late May afternoon in 1878, some 400 to 500 men gathered at the vestry of Boston's Park Street Church to found the New England Society for the Suppression of Vice. The historic church, with its brick facade and white New England spire, designed by Christopher Wren to rise ten feet higher than the State House dome, was, in many respects, the natural spot for such a gathering. The spire was, after all, as a Boston guidebook put it, "a heaven-pointing finger at the very center of Boston life." And the church itself exemplified the two sides of the organization that would soon change its name to the New England Watch and Ward Society. Park Street Church was an institution with a passion for reform, where William Lloyd Garrison launched his anti-slavery campaign in 1829, and where the American Education Society, the Prison Reform Society, and the American Temperance Society were established. At the same time, the Congregational church was historically one of the most rigid in Boston. Its early minister, Edward Dorr Griffin, who gave Brimstone Corner its name, is said to have sprinkled sulfur on the sidewalks on Sunday mornings to entice visitors to his hell-and-damnation sermons.

That afternoon, women were barred from the meeting, although some twenty-five of them stood at the entrance of the vestry, clamoring to be admitted. "If this is a meeting for the suppression of vice, why can't we go in?" a female voice demanded above the din. But the discussion was deemed unfit for the delicate ears of Boston womanhood, and the women were compelled to remain outside.

The main speaker was Anthony Comstock, founder and secretary of the New York Society for the Suppression of Vice, the first organization of its kind in the country. The New England society was to be its first branch. (By 1888, ten years later, there were "kindred societies" in Cincinnati, St. Louis, Chicago, Louisville, and San Francisco.) The thirty-four-year-old Comstock was already well known as an anti-vice and anti-obscenity crusader. A Union Army veteran, Comstock had moved from his native Connecticut to New York City in 1867 with $3.50 in his pocket, becoming a salesman of ladies' laces, ribbons, and embroideries in a dry goods house. When he discovered that two of his fellow employees were reading erotic books, he bought one as evidence and had the dealer arrested. In May 1873, he founded the New York Society for the Suppression of Vice, an outgrowth of a YMCA committee.

In the first annual report of his organization, Comstock claimed to have seized 130,000 pounds of bound books, 194,000 "bad" pictures and photos, 5,500 indecent playing cards, and 3,150 pills and powders used by abortionists. Two years before his death in 1913, Comstock boasted, "In the forty-one years I have been here, I have convicted persons enough to fill a passenger train of sixty-one coaches, containing sixty passengers each and the sixty-first almost full. I have destroyed 160 tons of obscene literature."

The 1873 federal Comstock Law—his brainchild—granted the U.S. Postal Service the power to ban from the mails any items deemed to be "obscene, lewd, or lascivious" or "of indecent character." This edict included birth control material. That same year, Comstock had received a commission from the postmaster general to serve as a special agent of the Post Office, giving him new authority to fight vice. His name entered the language when playwright George Bernard Shaw retorted with the word "Comstockery!" after Comstock described him as "this Irish smut dealer" during a campaign against Shaw's play about prostitution, *Mrs. Warren's Profession*. As Comstock biographer Heywood Broun noted, by changing the proper name of the vice crusader into a proper noun, "It was Shaw who conferred on the Connecticut farmer boy his best chance for immortality." *Comstockery* became a term of ridicule, a synonym for Puritanism, censorship, and general moral squeamishness.

More than anything, Comstock was, as H. L. Mencken pointed out, a showman, "a sort of Barnum. A band always followed him, playing in time to his yells. He could not undertake even so banal a business as raiding a dealer in abortifacient [abortion-inducing] pills without giving it the melodramatic air of a battle with a brontosaurus."

Comstock was no stranger to Boston. Three years earlier, he had come to the city to talk at a meeting of the Morning Ministers. That group funded his travels to Boston to arrest various dealers of indecent literature. More recently, in his capacity as postal inspector, he had swept into a New England Free Love Society convention at Nassau Hall in Boston and arrested Ezra Heywood—anarchist, anti-marriage advocate, and fierce opponent of the Comstock Law—on a charge of sending obscene material through the mail. The obscene material in question was a sociological treatise containing Heywood's views on love and marriage that also strongly criticized Comstock; Heywood was sentenced to two years at hard labor but pardoned by President Rutherford B. Hayes after serving six months.

Comstock was a large man, known for his trademark ginger side whiskers, and possessing "Atlas shoulders of tremendous breadth and squareness" and a chest of "prodigious girth, surmounted by a bull-like neck," as his semi-official biographer, Charles Gallaudet Trumbull, described him. At the Park Street Church that afternoon, attired as was his custom in a black suit, stiffly starched shirt, and black bow tie—he never dressed in colors—the vice crusader quickly warmed to his subject. He touted the number of people he had arrested and the pounds of "villainous" materials he had destroyed. Turning to Boston, he noted that sixteen persons engaged in the business of distributing obscene publications in the city had recently been arrested through his efforts, and thirteen of those were convicted. But some of the most illicit publications were still being published in Massachusetts, he said, and there was no law in the commonwealth to shut them down. That was something he hoped the Park Street Church gathering would address.

Anthony Comstock had his enemies. His moral crusades, his penchant for vicious hyperbole, his harassment of liberals and free thinkers like the anarchist Heywood and the feminist Victoria Woodhull, and his often questionable tactics—use of entrapment, for example—antagonized many. Mencken wrote, "He did more than any other man to ruin Puritanism in the United States. When he began his long, brilliant career of unwitting sabotage, the essential principles of comstockery were believed in by practically every reputable American." Five decades later, in large measure due to Comstock's overreaching, those principles were "at best, laughable . . . at worst, revolting."

And not unexpectedly, one of his opponents was in the crowd on that day in Boston. Comstock explained to the audience that this man attended every event that he took part in, and whenever Comstock spoke, the man would stare at him and sneer. The crowd began to shout, "Put him out! This is no place for him!" But Comstock insisted that he remain. As if it were all a staged moment, the culprit rose, pointed at Comstock, and shouted, "That man is a liar!"

Later, during the question-and-answer phase of the gathering, a clergyman rose and asked permission to ask three questions. "Did you ever use decoy letters or false signatures?" he demanded. "Did you ever sign a woman's name when writing a letter? Did you ever try to make a person sell you forbidden wares and then, when you had succeeded, use the evidence thus obtained to convict him?" The questions were an unmistakable allusion to Comstock's entrapment of Madame Restell (Ann Tro Lohman), a well-known New York City abortionist. He had contacted her, using a false name, and, telling her of his family's supposed desperate poverty—if they had another child, they would face financial disaster—asked her for birth control material for his wife. Comstock answered "yes" to all three questions, explaining that that was the only way he could obtain legal evidence. The clergyman replied, "Mr. Comstock has done what would be pronounced disgraceful in a policeman in a Boston Court." Many in the audience were undoubtedly aware that, just a month before, shortly after her arrest, the sixty-seven-year-old Madame Restell slit her own throat with a carving knife in the bathtub, one of many enemies of Comstock who met an untimely end. "A bloody end to a bloody life," pronounced Comstock unrepentantly.

Comstock's tactics did not seem to concern the overwhelming majority of those present at Park Street that afternoon. Once he finished his talk, the gathering approved a resolution thanking him for his work, and then put forth another resolution. "Be it resolved," it went, "that we recommend the formation of a New England Society for the Suppression of Vice; that the annual payment of any sum, not less than five dollars shall constitute the donor as a member of this society." Eight distinguished Bostonians were named to an executive committee. Anthony Comstock looked on, a proud father.

———

Four years after Comstock's visit, the Boston branch split off from the New York society to follow its own path, taking on all six New England states as its territory. The Bostonians were apparently hesitant to accede to Comstock's demand that they send increased funds to support his New York work. In 1891, they officially changed the organization's title to the New England Watch and Ward Society, adopting the name of an unofficial police force of the Massachusetts Bay Colony that patrolled the lanes and byways of Boston and other towns from sundown to sunrise. The society's crest, inscribed with the Latin phrase *Manu Forti* ("With a strong hand"), featured an illustration of a hand clutching a snake that was coiled and ready to strike.

In the post–Civil War period, the city of Boston, like much of the rest of the nation, was undergoing vast changes. Just fifty years before, Boston was "a large, pretty country town, where stage-coaches still clattered in from the country," as Edward Everett Hale described it in his book *A New England Boyhood*. At that time, there were nine blocks of buildings in the town, Hale wrote, and "all the other buildings stood with windows or doors on each of the four sides, and in most instances with trees, or perhaps little lanes, between; as all people will live when the Kingdom of Heaven comes."

The city was expanding rapidly, with entire new areas—the Back Bay, the South End—springing up, and suburbs being absorbed: Roxbury in 1868, Dorchester in 1874, and Brighton, Charlestown, and West Roxbury four years later. However, "expansion did not mean cosmopolitanism," wrote S. Foster Damon in his essay, "The Genesis of Boston," published in the *Atlantic* in 1935. "The Brahmins still lived on the water side of Beacon Street or the sunny side of Commonwealth Avenue; they still dined at two and had 'tea' at six; they read the *Atlantic* and the *Transcript*, held four receptions a year, escaped the Egyptian heat of summer by moving to the North Shore; sent their sons to Harvard and their dead to Mt. Auburn. Their exclusiveness, as Russell Sturgis noted, was 'as by a law of nature.' "

But if their traditions remained, Boston's wealthier and educated classes were increasingly feeling they were losing control of their city. The Massachusetts economy was in decline, especially in the economic depression following the Panic of 1873. New England industries like shipbuilding and textiles had trouble competing in the post–Civil War

period against the gigantic corporate structures of the "Robber Barons."
And the increasing materialism of the period was disquieting as well.
"In an age dominated more and more by material forces and secular phi-
losophies, Puritan Christianity's old moral concepts seemed alarmingly
out of place," Boston historian Thomas H. O'Connor writes. "Many of
the old Boston families viewed the postwar period as completely alien,
in contrast to the prewar society in which they had lived and flourished.
Traditional moral principles, ethical practices, and cultural standards
seemed to have completely degenerated."

Their sense of alienation was heightened by the large numbers of
immigrants who were transforming the city—first the Irish and later
Italians, Jews, Eastern Europeans, and Chinese. By 1890, 68 percent of
Boston's population were first- and second-generation immigrants. Most
of the old families had come to the city before 1812, and some, by the
1890s, became active in the formation of the Immigration Restriction
League. Dr. Oliver Wendell Holmes reportedly told a friend that a New
Englander felt far more at home "among his own people" in London than
"in one of our seaboard cities."

Political power had passed from the Unitarian and Congregationalist
"Brahmins" to the Catholic Irish, and, in the city proper, from Republicans to Democrats. (The state as a whole remained strongly Republican,
however.) Hugh O'Brien became the city's first Irish mayor in 1884. His
comment that Boston had become "the most Catholic city in the country"
did not endear him to the city's old families, nor did his decision to close
the public library on St. Patrick's Day. In fact, Boston was the most Catholic city in the country—73 percent by the 1920s—and ethnic conscious-
ness and ethnic divisions continued to be the center of the city's politics
and social life for many years.

The breakdown of traditional structures was worrisome. Young men
—and sometimes young women—were living alone in large numbers in
crowded urban neighborhoods. Boarding houses grew up, and parts of
the city like Scollay Square and the North End became home to all kinds
of less-than-respectable activities: burlesque shows, penny arcades, tattoo parlors, and cafés that were really fronts for houses of prostitution
("the social evil," in the euphemism of the day). Pool rooms for register-
ing bets, "policy shops" that were essentially lotteries, and faro banks,
where young men would bet a week's wages over a game of cards, were
rampant. The police and corrupt city officials turned a blind eye to what

was going on around them. To the old families, the Kingdom of Heaven seemed farther away by the year.

Despite all this, Boston was still "the Athens of America," the most educated, cultured, and cultivated city in the country, with a long tradition of reform. Amidst the economic decline of the 1870s, a large number of social welfare organizations emerged—settlement houses, hospitals, missions, and other charitable institutions—in which Boston's elites tried to assimilate the newcomers and ameliorate the effects of poverty and disease.

If the charitable organizations took care of the physical needs of the city, an organization was required to address the moral needs as well. The result was the New England Watch and Ward Society, in part a reaction to the perceived moral decline of a materialistic age, in part an extension of the reforming impulses and Puritan conscience that were long the heart and soul of Boston.

In an address to the twentieth-anniversary meeting of the Watch and Ward Society in 1898, Dr. Francis Peabody, a Harvard professor known for his course in social ethics, compared the society to the engineers who monitored the city's system of sewers and drains. "We see the great city on the surface with all its works and buildings, and streets and businesses," he said. "And then we remember that under our feet and unseen are miles and miles of pipes from which at any minute there may come up into our faces some pestiferous gas which may creep into our very homes and infect our very dearest with its poison. All the time, therefore, while we go about our daily avocations the engineers of the city are watching all these pipes, cleansing the sewers, warding the public health." That, as Peabody saw it, was the role of the Watch and Ward—"quietly, unobtrusively working underground, guarding us from the pestiferous evil which at any time may come up into our faces, into our homes, into our children's lives."

In New York, Anthony Comstock was the public face of that city's vice crusaders. Comstock made arrests personally and was involved in a number of violent fights. Early on, a book dealer whom he was taking to a courtroom slashed his face with a bowie knife; Comstock covered up his scar with the side whiskers that became his trademark (and the delight of generations of cartoonists). He exulted at the death of his enemies, such as Madame Restell. When five publishers of obscene books died of various causes shortly after brushes with Comstock, their deaths, along with the numbers of obscene books and pictures destroyed, were included in statistics of his yearly accomplishments.

Although it took many of its cues and tactics from Comstock, the New England Watch and Ward Society's image was more genteel. Its version of Comstockery was very much in keeping with the culture and traditions of Boston. The first agent in charge of day-to-day operations, Henry Chase, hired on January 1, 1882, was a former teacher, librarian, school principal, and state representative. Chase (no relation to later secretary J. Frank Chase) took the Watch and Ward position at age fifty-nine and served until he was well into his eighties. The society's president for twenty-six years spanning the late nineteenth and early twentieth centuries was the Reverend Frederick Baylies Allen, a Congregationalist minister who converted to the Episcopal church and became the assistant minister at Boston's prestigious Trinity Church in 1879, in part because the Trinity elders were impressed by his organizational work at the Watch and Ward. He was later chief administrator of the Episcopal City Mission for many years, transforming it into one of Boston's major social service organizations, which cared for vast swaths of the city's poor and underprivileged, with programs ranging from sailors' havens and shelters for the destitute to summer "fresh air" programs for mothers and children. In equal parts moralist and social worker, Allen was characterized by his son and biographer, the historian Frederick Lewis Allen, as "the most beloved man in Boston."

The early leaders of the Watch and Ward came from the highest social strata of the city, were members of the clergy in many cases, and were deeply involved in the social reform movements of their day. One of the first vice presidents was Edward Everett Hale, the Unitarian minister and author of the The Man Without a Country, the classic Civil War–era story of an army officer who curses the United States and is condemned to perpetual physical and spiritual exile. When the twentieth century arrived, it was Hale who was chosen to read the Ninetieth Psalm from the balcony of the State House to a great, silent crowd that assembled below on the Boston Common during the final hour of December 31, 1899; he was later chaplain of the U.S. Senate. Another vice president was Phillips Brooks, passionate opponent of slavery and rector of Trinity Church, who was widely regarded as the most eloquent preacher of his day. (Among other things, he was renowned for speaking 213 words a minute.) He made Trinity the leading church in Boston in the 1870s, moving it from the South End and overseeing the building of the magnificent Romanesque Copley Square edifice, designed by H. H. Richardson. It was largely Brooks's influence that led the senior Allen to leave his Congregational ministry and become an Episcopal priest, serving under Brooks and focusing on parish work for which the spellbinding preacher had little taste. Both Hale and Brooks were revered and beloved figures—the most prominent ministers in Boston—and considered to be progressive and enlightened. Brooks was later canonized.

Members of the original 1878 executive committee included Homer P. Sprague, an educator and the headmaster of Girls' High School, later president of Mills College and the University of South Dakota. Another was Trinity Church stalwart Robert Treat Paine, a wealthy philanthropist who built a hundred suburban dwellings that workingmen were encouraged to buy on easy terms, and who was a founder and, for many years, president of Associated Charities of Boston. (In the 1890s, Paine co-founded the Immigration Restriction League.) In 1886, the society's vice presidents included the presidents of Dartmouth, Amherst, Brown, Colby, and the University of Vermont—Protestant ministers all. This religious makeup—liberal Protestantism—would continue until the 1920s, when the society included a Catholic and Jew among its directors for the first time.

Behind the public faces were the dues-paying members, "almost a roll call of the Brahmin aristocracy," as Paul S. Boyer notes in his book *Purity in Print.* The Watch and Ward contributors list for 1889, a year that Boyer picked at random, contained names like Coolidge, Forbes, Lawrence, Lodge, Lowell, Peabody, Saltonstall, and Weld. (That year's subscriptions amounted to $2,411.50, most of them in $5, $10, and $20 sums, of which $1,500 went to pay agent Chase's salary.) In the twentieth century, its treasurer for forty years was Godfrey Lowell Cabot, whose Brahmin credentials were impeccable and his wealth immense. A study of the male contributors to society from 1885 to 1892 by sociologist Nicola Beisel found that 92.3 percent were members of the upper classes. It was the "old guard on guard," as Cleveland Amory put it in his book *The Proper Bostonians.*

Each year, the society would hold large public meetings, with well-known speakers like the Reverend Endicott Peabody, headmaster of the elite Groton School (and later a Watch and Ward vice president), and Julia Ward Howe, composer of "The Battle Hymn of the Republic"; its annual reports detailed its accomplishments and finances and enumerated the criminal convictions obtained by the society.

———

In its earliest years, the Watch and Ward had two main preoccupations: indecency in books, pictures, and performances, and gambling.
Later, prostitution and drugs were added to the list, although alcohol
largely was not (that was left to others). The society did not have an anti-
immigrant tinge to it—certainly not in its rhetoric—but a great deal
of what it perceived as vice was associated at the time with immigrant
groups—gambling with the Irish, for example, and opium with the Chinese. For Boston's old families who were losing political influence and
felt that their city was slipping away from them in many respects, the
Watch and Ward offered something else: moral power.

"Commercialized vice" was the Watch and Ward's primary target.
"We are not merely fighting evil and sin," noted the Reverend Frederick B. Allen, in a February 1903 address to the public meeting of the
society in which he reprised its first twenty-five years. "A thousand forces
are already engaged in that common object. We are especially antago-
nizing *organized* evil. It is when sin endeavors to extend its sway and is
aggressive, when money has been invested in special forms of temptation, especially against the young, that our Society, supported by the better sense and earnestness of the community, has undertaken to make a
vigorous fight against these sources of temptation."

But its purview was wide. Nothing seemed too small or unimpor-
tant to engage the Watch and Ward's interest: "immodest" paintings and
photographs in shop windows at Christmas "pandering to man's lowest tastes"; theatrical posters considered obscene even if the shows they
were advertising were perfectly respectable; phonographs on Nantasket
Beach, on Boston's South Shore, that uttered "the most profane and obscene language"; a fad for collar and inscription buttons that featured
double entendres and what the newspapers referred to as "sensational
language"; and especially anything that even faintly smacked of a raffle
or lottery, from the lowliest church bazaar to the most obscure agricultural fair. Then, there was the matter of young boys hanging around the
police courts, idealizing and admiring criminals and making each court
a "school of vice." In 1881, the society obtained the passage of a law making it illegal for a minor to be allowed in a courtroom unless called as a
witness.

The first official action of the Watch and Ward—or rather, the New
England Society for the Suppression of Vice—concerned newsstands at
railroad stations and on the trains themselves where "immoral and sen-

sational papers and books" were sold. At its very first meeting, on May 31, 1878, the society's executive committee prepared a petition asking the railroads to suppress such material; 270 of Boston's leading citizens signed it. The railroads immediately complied, and did so "cheerfully," according to the society's annual report.

It was relatively easy to crack down on blatantly obscene books and magazines like those sold at the railways because Massachusetts law banned printed material that "contained language obscene, indecent, or impure." What was harder to control was literature that, although it didn't contain an indecent word or sentence, was able, through more subtle means, to "excite the imagination and inflame the passions, thereby corrupting the morals and debasing the life," as the society's 1897–98 report put it. Books of that category did the most harm, in the society's view, and they were found on newsstands everywhere, often in the guise of "realistic fiction" that made a life of "sensuality, vice, and crime" appear desirable. No law covered such reading material. So, in 1880, the society secured an amendment to the obscenity statute that added the vague and elastic phrase "or manifestly tending to the corruption of the morals of youth" to widen the scope of the law. Almost anything could fall into that category, depending on your viewpoint.

When the general statutes of Massachusetts were revised in 1882, the "or" in the obscenity statue somehow vanished, nullifying the effect of the change. The "or" was crucial to going after that less obvious class of pernicious books. The society worked hard to restore it, involving the organization in a lengthy legislative fight. But it took until 1890 for the legislature to restore the missing preposition. Now the law read clearly that it was illegal to publish or sell books and other printed matter containing "obscene, indecent, or impure language, or manifestly tending to the corruption of the morals of youth." The society finally had back the legal language that it required, setting the stage for years of battles to suppress books, magazines, and performances that it considered immoral. The Watch and Ward, as it became known the following year, would make the expression "Banned in Boston" a national catchphrase. And Boston was the "Athens of America," after all. What was banned in Boston mattered.

CHAPTER 2

First Forays into Censorship, 1881–1898

In 1881, when Boston publisher James Osgood approached Walt Whitman about issuing a definitive, one-volume edition of the poet's great work, *Leaves of Grass*, "the good gray poet" was quick to agree. Osgood was a prominent publisher, after all—he had issued works by Emerson, Hawthorne, Twain, and Dickens—and, since its original publication in 1855, *Leaves of Grass* had had a somewhat checkered history. Because of the erotic nature of some of the poems, Whitman had mostly wound up publishing the work himself. So the poet had one caveat, as he wrote in a letter to Osgood: "Fair warning on one point the sexuality odes about which the original row was started and kept up so long are all retained and must go in the same as ever." Osgood assured him that nothing would be removed or changed in any way. By the end of the year, the book was out and selling nicely.

Meanwhile, the New England Society for the Suppression of Vice had just declared its independence from its New York founders and appointed Henry Chase as its agent. It was eager to make its mark. Anthony Comstock himself strongly disapproved of *Leaves of Grass*. "Another 'classic' for which exemption is named, is an attempt by an author of our own time to clothe the most sensual thoughts, with the flowers and fancies of poetry, making the lascivious conception only more insidious and demoralizing," he wrote. New England Society executive committee member the Reverend Frederick Baylies Allen felt similarly; so did its president, Homer P. Sprague. At the New England group's February 6, 1882, meeting, the executive committee voted that Chase should consult with the assistant state attorney general regarding the prosecution of three books—the Italian writer Giovanni Boccaccio's *Decameron*, the French novelist Honoré de Balzac's *Droll Stories*, and *Leaves of Grass*. At its next monthly meeting, the committee voted unanimously that Whitman's poems tended to corrupt the morals of the young. It decided to appeal to the publisher either to withdraw the book from circulation or to expurgate all matter that the society considered to be obscene or immoral.

Soon enough, Osgood received a letter from Oliver Stevens, district attorney of Boston, announcing that his office had classified *Leaves of Grass* as an obscene work and threatening legal action. Osgood was not inclined to fight, and, despite his earlier statements, Whitman agreed to remove ten lines and half a dozen words and phrases, as he had done in earlier editions. "My proposition," Whitman wrote his publisher, "is that we make the revision here indicated & go on with the regular issue of the book. If then any further move is made by the District Attorney and his backer—as of course there is somebody behind it all—they will only burn their own fingers & very badly."

However, as the negotiations continued, it was clear that the district attorney—and his "backers" at the New England Society for the Suppression of Vice—were not giving in. They insisted upon the total elimination of two of the volume's poems, "To a Common Prostitute" ("Not till the sun excludes you do I exclude you / Not till the waters refuse to glisten for you and the leaves to rustle for you, do my words refuse to glisten and rustle for you") and the erotic "A Woman Waits for Me" ("I pour the stuff to start sons and daughters fit for these States, I press with slow rude muscle, / I brace myself effectually, I listen to no entreaties, / I dare not withdraw till I deposit what has so long accumulated within me."). Those demands were too much for Whitman. He terminated his contract with Osgood and took the book instead to Rees, Welsh, and Company, a Philadelphia publisher that changed its name to David McKay shortly afterward. The Philadelphia house published it in September 1882, selling out the first edition in a single day.

In Boston, the suppression of *Leaves of Grass* received condemnation from most of the press. The *Boston Globe*, noting that the book had "met with the approval of the clearest, purest intellects of the nineteenth century," assailed the "narrow-minded tyranny and bigoted self-righteousness" of those advocating censorship. The newspaper added, "If the sentiment and sense of Massachusetts uphold the law-officer of the State in striking this blow at intellectual liberty, let us relegate Shakespeare to the 'Inferno' of the Public Library, suppress the Bible and abolish the classics at one fell swoop, leaving only Mother Goose and Jo Cook's lectures as the legal literature of the Athens of America."

However, one newspaper defended the ban: the *Boston Evening Transcript*, the revered newspaper of the city's upper classes. "To tell the honest, shameful truth," editorialized the newspaper, "the very portions objected to are all that have made the book sell. We feel safe in asserting that no one person in a hundred who ever purchased a copy of 'Leaves of Grass' did so with the single and only purpose of literary enjoyment." The editorial then launched into some dubious literary criticism. "It would be an exaggeration to say that Whitman has written nothing of poetic merit," it continued, "but it would not be exaggeration to say that every line from his pen worthy of preservation could be crowded with the limits of half a dozen pages." In its later days, when the *Transcript* was the favored newspaper of New England intellectuals, featuring as many as two pages a day of book reviews, it undoubtedly rued those words.

The New England Society for the Suppression of Vice had kept itself out of the limelight throughout most of the controversy. It preferred to work behind the scenes, particularly on a matter like this that might alienate some of the upper-class constituency that it was trying to build. Still, in the society's April 1882 annual report, in an obvious reference to *Leaves of Grass*, Allen noted, "The District Attorney has at our instance notified a number of booksellers that a certain immoral book, which had hither been freely exposed for sale, comes within the prohibition of the law, and that any further sale will render the dealer liable for prosecution. A prominent publishing firm has, in consequence of a similar official notification, agreed to expurgate one of its books containing much indecent matter."

And, in a magazine article, society president Sprague wrote that "dirt eaters, each rolling before him his darling morsel of literary filth" were the ones "finding nutriment in *Leaves of Grass* but not in fig leaves." (A later *New York Times* account held Allen responsible for the suppression, claiming he considered the book "not insidious but gross.")

Meanwhile, in Philadelphia, the publisher there attempted surreptitiously and without success to get the local vice society to go after the book. "The Boston fools have already made me more than $2000," he is reported to have said. As early as 1882, the phrase "Banned in Boston" seemed a useful tool for selling books.

Neither the Watch and Ward Society nor the New England Society for the Suppression of Vice invented censorship in Boston. After all, the first book was burned in the city by the Puritans back in 1654, and the maypole dance was banned even earlier. All performances of plays were outlawed for half a century starting in 1750. A room in the Boston Public Library, called the "Inferno," was the repository for books whose circulation was restricted because of their "immoral" content. Among them were Balzac's ninety-plus-volume *Comedie Humaine*, Boccaccio's *Decameron*, and Sir Richard Burton's *Arabian Nights*. Such books could be read only for scholarly purposes and with special permission. One of the great controversies of the 1890s revolved around sculptor Frederick MacMonnies's statue of the nude Bacchante (a female devotee of Bacchus), which was removed from the courtyard of the Boston Public Library and shipped to the Metropolitan Museum in New York in 1897 after a huge public outcry. The Watch and Ward was not publicly involved in this affair, which was front-page news in the Boston papers for months.

Even during the height of the Watch and Ward's prominence, the organization kept its distance from some of the most outrageous cases of censorship that earned the sobriquet "Banned in Boston." Because the society usually chose to operate behind the scenes in many cases, it is sometimes hard to discern its exact censorship role. Its participation in the *Leaves of Grass* matter was revealed to the general public only in 1896, fourteen years after the fact.

The Watch and Ward insisted that the society was not a censor but was simply expressing the public will. "We are simply trying to represent you, the thoughtful, pure-minded men and women of this community, in seeing that our laws are executed," noted Allen in a March 18, 1900, speech to the society's annual public meeting.

But it was the Watch and Ward that had pushed for many of these very laws. And in a speech at the same meeting in 1900, the Reverend Endicott Peabody, headmaster of the elite Groton School and later a vice president of the society, summed up the Watch and Ward view with particular clarity: "Put bad books before young people, and they read them, the evil things they read stay in their minds and poison their character. I sometimes think that bad books are worse, far worse than bad companions. There is something in the personality of a bad person which repels those who are not already degraded, and the nature shrinks back from the person, while the book is a perfectly decent-looking thing and steals subtly into the imagination."

Although the first book that it attempted to censor was quintessentially American, the Watch and Ward Society and other Boston moralists long viewed anything European, particularly French, as intrinsically corrupting. Besides *Leaves of Grass*, the two other books that the society had originally contemplated suppressing were Boccaccio's *Decameron*, the medieval Italian collection of bawdy tales, and Balzac's *Droll Stories*, a series of racy stories written in the Boccaccio manner, both of them "foreign" works.

In his annual address, delivered at the January 20, 1901, meeting of the Watch and Ward at the Old South Church, Allen related how the famed preacher Phillips Brooks, on his first trip to Europe, had been impressed by "the provision for corruption and profligacy which seemed to mark all old civilizations." Allen echoed Brooks's words, noting that if you go to the old world, you would find "an absolute distrust in the possibility that men should be pure—an absolute skepticism of the fact that any men are continent and virtuous." To Allen, there were "two opposite types of beliefs as to purity of life"—the European and the American. And "the poorer one is very generally the continental standard."

In a speech to that 1901 Watch and Ward annual meeting, Rev. Endicott Peabody put it even more baldly. Referring to the many cases of objectionable plays that were adaptations and translations from the French, the Groton headmaster told the audience, "I do not see why these things should be foisted upon us. We do not live as the French live; we do not think as the French think: we have not the same ideals as they have. When we borrow their plays we are apt to borrow the very lowest and worst." (Peabody himself makes a cameo appearance in Louis Auchincloss's 1964 novel, *The Rector of Justin*, based on a Groton-like prep school, in which he is devastatingly summed up, by name, as "well equipped to train young men for the steam room of the Racquet Club.")

Not surprisingly, the first time the license of a prominent Boston theater was revoked since the ban on live theater was overturned in Massachusetts in 1806 involved a French play. The date was October 16, 1890, and the name of the play was *The Clemenceau Case* (*L'Affaire Clemenceau*), largely forgotten today. Written by Armand d'Artois and Alexandre Dumas *fils*, author of the popular *La Dame Aux Camelias*, the play tells the story of a countess who persuades her married daughter, Iza, to embark on an affair with a wealthy duke. When Iza's husband finds out and she refuses to break things off with the duke, the husband, a sculptor, kills him. What was shocking to Boston was not the plot but the scene in which Iza poses in her husband's studio for a piece of sculpture that he is working on. She appears on stage in tights.

The play had had successful runs in Paris and London, as well as New York—where Anthony Comstock made no attempt to close it down. In Boston, expectations were high. The Park Theatre, where the play was scheduled to open, had one of the greatest advance sales in its history, with the orchestra sold out for the play's two-week run. Word of the famous "posing" or "studio" scene had created great interest, particularly among Harvard students, who made up a large number of ticket holders. It also created great interest among Boston's city fathers and guardians of morality. The Watch and Ward's Henry Chase and Rev. Frederick Allen, the police board, the corporation counsel, and the mayor all agreed, in newspaper interviews, that the licensing committee of the city's Board of Aldermen had the legal authority to decide whether the play should go on.

So, on opening night, October 14, just before the curtain went up, a delegation from the Board of Aldermen took their seats in the left-hand lower proscenium box. When Iza appeared in Act III, posing in tights, it took all of about ten seconds before the character's husband draped a cloak around her, according to a *Boston Globe* reporter. After the play finished, members of the board were noncommittal. When the *Globe* reporter suggested to one alderman that it was "not very bad," the alderman smiled an embarrassed smile and replied, "Not particularly good either." Another said, "Why, I hardly know what to say." However, by noon the next day, the aldermen had made up their minds. They summoned the theater manager and the play's producer and immediately revoked the Park Theatre's license. By the end of the afternoon, notices for the play had been removed from bulletin boards and a sign at the box office announced it would refund all tickets the following day. For that evening's performance, three hundred Harvard students arrived at the theater only to return to Cambridge; the performance had been canceled.

While some newspapers such as the *Transcript* defended the closing, even as its critic pronounced the play relatively innocuous, the *Boston Globe* responded with a biting editorial headlined "PUBLIC MORALS SAFE." "The Aldermen, in their capacity as saviors of society, visited the

Park Theatre, took seats where they could have an uninterrupted view, adjusted their opera-glasses, and for two or three hours gazed upon the undraped model in the play as though their salaries and re-elections depended on their diligence," the newspaper wrote in its October 16 issue. "It is believed that they nearly wore their opera-glasses out, so conscientiously thorough were they in their search for something immoral. Of course they found it. People who give their whole minds to discovering immodesty are seldom unsuccessful." The editorial suggested that a major factor in the aldermanic decision was that the Park Theatre had been insufficiently generous with free passes for the aldermen. "Anyhow," continued the editorial writers, "the present board has nobly done its duty, beside conveying to the management of the theatre a proper intimation that a more liberal policy in the matter of aldermanic passes will be desirable hereafter. Thus society is saved; let us rejoice."

It is not clear what happened between the conclusion of the opening-night performance and the following noon, when the aldermen shut the theater down. Had pressure been brought to bear upon the aldermen during that twelve-hour period? If so, the events that followed might shed light on the origin of that pressure.

Forced out of Boston, the play's producer decided instead to take *The Clemenceau Case* to the nearby shoe-manufacturing city of Lynn for a three-day performance. The play was scheduled to open on Thanksgiving afternoon and, given all the hoopla in Boston, there was a rush for tickets by many people from outside the city. One of the visitors in town was Henry Chase, who had arrived two days earlier, spending three days in Lynn in an effort to persuade the city fathers to block the performance. But it was just before a city election, and he found it impossible to obtain a quorum of aldermen or to convince the mayor to call a special meeting of the board.

Still, it was a partial victory for the Watch and Ward. When the play opened—with a large crowd lining up and close to a thousand people in attendance at the performance—there may have been some disappointment. The *Boston Globe* reported that Sybil Johnstone, in the role of Iza, was "charming and not one move was made that would cause even the most modest to blush." In the famous posing scene, "Miss Johnstone's form was partially concealed by a pink tarlatan, and then only for an instant was she thus seen."

Chase stayed for the opening performance, prepared to serve a warrant to shut it down if there was any departure from propriety. But apparently, he found everything in order. Writing in its annual report, the Watch and Ward noted that the play was presented in Lynn, "but the company were compelled, by the moral pressure incited by us, to expurgate everything which by its eye or mind had made the play specially objectionable."

The Watch and Ward report told only part of the story, however. In fact, *The Clemenceau Case* reopened in Boston just a few weeks later—at the Park Theatre, no less, which had been handed back its license after only a five-day suspension. It boasted a different cast, and the ever-vigilant aldermen were there to view a special late-morning performance. A reporter for the *New York Times* said it was difficult to see the new version as any improvement on the score of morality. "It is in the main the same thing only worse," he noted. Iza's posing scene had been lengthened, and "instead of one posing and a short one, there are two exhibitions. There is a little drapery thrown in, which did not appear in the earlier production, but this serves rather to emphasize than to obscure the obvious purpose of the scene." This time, beyond demanding that the second posing scene be cut—which the producers agreed to do—the aldermen made no attempt to close the play. Within a week, the revamped *The Clemenceau Case* was being treated like any other play in Boston. In a pre-Christmas roundup of local theater, the *Globe* wrote, "There was a well-filled house at the Park last night, when the second week of the revised production of 'The Clemenceau Case' was opened. The play runs much more smoothly than during the opening performance and was well-received. Miss [May] Wilkes as the erring Iza has greatly improved in her work and Countess Demobronowska in the hands of Jeffreys Lewis is a clever piece of work. The three male characters are improving every day. . . ."

Throughout most of the 1890s, following the attempt at suppressing *The Clemenceau Case*, the Watch and Ward didn't bother itself much with theatrical censorship, perhaps because it feared its upper-middle-class constituency might not approve. The organization focused instead on indecent theatrical posters, obscene phonograph records, and burlesque and dime museums (carnival-like sideshows). The latter tended to attract working-class audiences, far from the core group of upper-class Watch and Ward supporters.

A city ordinance—enacted through the efforts of the society—required that all posters and placards that advertised public performances be approved by the committee on licenses. By the late 1890s, Watch and

Ward investigators were scouring theater billboards every Monday morning in search of any poster that had not been submitted to the licensing committee or possessed objectionable features that might have escaped notice. They wanted to make sure the city was doing its job. On Monday afternoons—when burlesque theaters premiered their shows—investigators from the society would head to Scollay Square theaters like the Old Howard, the Lyceum, and the Palace, as well as "dime museums" like Austin and Stone's, to examine the character of the entertainments. Frequently, burlesque companies would play for only a week in Boston. So it was essential for the Watch and Ward to move swiftly. If its investigators found anything of a suggestive or immoral character, they immediately confronted the proprietor of the theater and requested that it be cut. If an entire act or scene was specifically objectionable, they would bring it to the licensing committee of the Board of Aldermen.

"The directors of the Society have nothing to say against the theatre itself," explained the 1898–99 annual report. "They judge not by the name, but the character, and object no more to the dime museum or the nickel show, as such, than to the grand opera, as the past year's history will show. But they see no necessary connection between low prices and low morals, and seek to secure as pure an entertainment for the poor newsboy and bootblack as is provided for the wealthiest families."

In its quest to suppress low entertainment, the Watch and Ward met with mixed success. In February 1898, for example, the society took out a complaint against a couple of kouta kouta dancers named La Belle Freida and Phil Hamberg. The kouta kouta (aka hoochy-coochy or coochy-coochy) was a variation on the belly dance or "hip dance" that had been the sensation of the Chicago World's Fair of 1893 and was fast becoming a staple of burlesque shows. Anthony Comstock had seen these dancers in Chicago and been so outraged by them that he wrote, "I would sooner lay my two boys in their graves than they should look at the sights I saw yesterday." He told a newspaper reporter that the entire World's Fair should be razed to the ground if the shows did not stop. The reaction was milder in Boston, but the Watch and Ward followed Comstock's lead, as was often the case.

When the two kouta kouta dancers were arraigned before Judge Frederick D. Ely in municipal court, the judge realized that this was no ordinary case. "Let's adjourn to the lobby," he suggested. The counsel for the dancers had told the judge that defense testimony would involve the "correct" exhibition of the kouta kouta by the defendants. They needed a larger space than the judge's courtroom. Judge Ely agreed, and La Belle Freida retired to the privacy of an adjoining room to put on her tights.

The first witness was Albert Busteed, a Watch and Ward investigator. His evidence primarily consisted of a demonstration of the dance that he had seen the defendants perform. His was a pathetic performance—gyrating and moving his hips to simulate what he had viewed on stage. "He did the best he could," wrote a *Boston Globe* reporter in a wry account of the hearing, "but at his best his apparent object seemed to be to do some injury to his body." After he finished, he announced bravely, "That's a kouta kouta."

However, Judge Ely clearly needed some firsthand evidence to make his decision. At this point, Freida emerged, in costume, and began what could be described as a much more polished performance. The judge, more accustomed to the prosecution of petty thieves and Sunday "blue law" breakers, followed her movements closely from start to finish. When she was done and her male companion began to perform an apparently inferior version, the judge's attention was seen to wander.

In the end, Judge Ely discoursed enthusiastically on the subject of dancing in general and proclaimed that he didn't see anything criminally wrong with the kouta kouta. He ordered Freida and her companion to be released. As the *Globe* reporter noted, "This is the first time in the history of the court that a girl won her case by a dance in tights."

CHAPTER 3

Politics, Poker, and the "Social Evil," 1884–1897

IN THE 1880S AND EARLY 1890S, gambling of all sorts was wide-spread in Boston. Perhaps the most popular form—certainly the most fashionable—was a card game called faro, a favored game of Russian aristocrats and Old West legends like Doc Holliday and Wyatt Earp. Twenty or more "faro banks" were operating in the city. Some three hundred men were said to make their living as faro bank "cappers" and "ropers in," luring young men to what the Watch and Ward called "gambling hells where they lost both money and character." In addition, there were eight "pool rooms" (not to be confused with billiard establishments) where patrons placed bets on horse races and baseball games. Add to this at least one hundred "policy shops" where Bostonians gambled away some $800,000 a year in various forms of lotteries that the Watch and Ward described as requiring "no skill, judgment, or intelligence" and "played by the poorest and most ignorant." And then there was the Louisiana Lottery, dubbed "The Serpent," chartered by the state of Louisiana just after the Civil War and by far the most popular of these pastimes in the country.

Agent Chase evaluated the situation in the winter of 1884, when four of his investigators visited ten faro banks in the city on the same night. They found, on average, fifteen persons present in each place. Chase

noted that if you estimated the number of gaming-houses to be forty—
and that, in his view, was "a very low estimate, especially if we include
the prop games, roulette tables, *rouge et noir*, keno, and German hazard"
—you could find six hundred patrons at such establishments at any given
hour in the evening. That number didn't include the hundreds who visited policy shops, which had a greater number of patrons than even the
faro banks. "The knowing ones would probably laugh at the ignorance of
anyone who should declare the numbers of persons who visit the various
gambling places of Boston every 24 hours to be less than 1,500 or 2,000,"
Chase observed.

To the Watch and Ward, gambling was an obvious evil, corrupting
young men, encouraging them to pilfer money from their employers,
and often resulting in the destruction of families. As the Reverend Frederick Allen put it, "The gaming-houses have done more to break down
the integrity of young men than any other influence." In this, the society
echoed the arguments of Anthony Comstock in his campaigns against
gambling in New York City. Beyond that, opposition to gambling was an
attractive issue for the fledgling vice society as it strove to establish itself
in Boston in the 1880s and '90s. Unlike book or theater censorship, it was
an issue that could unite the Watch and Ward's upper-class constituency.
It also tapped into nativist feelings. In the public mind, gambling was
associated with alcohol, corrupt politicians, and the Irish, as sociologist
Nicola Beisel observes. "Tackling the issue of gambling gave the anti-vice
campaign direction and funding," she writes. Beisel notes that contributions to the society, only $617 in the year ending March 1882, rose to
$1,777 two years later, as its anti-gambling campaign gained steam. By
1890, they stood at $2,411.

What the Watch and Ward learned quickly was that the police generally tended to ignore such activity, both in Boston and nearby cities, and
some court officials were equally unsympathetic. The Boston police department, as we know it today, was founded only in 1854—some twenty-
four years before the Watch and Ward—and was not as well organized or
effective (or as free from corruption) as one might have desired. In 1883,
for instance, when the society obtained evidence against fourteen gambling houses with the intention of bringing about police raids, the police
commissioners declined to act until they had first given the gamblers notice to close up shop. The police's argument was that raids and arrests
would only drive gambling "underground." Some places did close, but

when the police finally got around to raiding those that remained open, the Watch and Ward dismissed these operations as "a sham and a pretense" that were "utterly discreditable to the force."

The society's relationship with the police—not just in Boston but in other cities as well—was frequently difficult. The Watch and Ward could investigate cases and accumulate evidence in the manner of private detectives or journalists—but it was unable to make arrests on its own. (In its annual reports, it frequently took full credit for arrests actually made by the police, however.) To compel the police to act, the society was able in many cases to obtain a search or arrest warrant from a judge and then deliver it to police officials. The police were then legally required to serve the warrant. Still, police officers had the ability to undermine the Watch and Ward by "tipping off" the parties in advance that they were about to be raided, in the 1883 cases, for example.

The Watch and Ward's frustration was mounting. "Without a radical and thorough reform of our police administration, nothing whatever will be done or even attempted against gambling," wrote Allen in the society's 1883–84 annual report. So the society turned to the state legislature. In large part through Watch and Ward's efforts, in 1885 the legislature enacted the Metropolitan Police law, changing the mechanism by which the three commissioners in charge of the Boston police were appointed. Under the new law, they would be chosen by the governor instead of by the city's mayor. The assumption was that the governor's appointees would be less corrupt and more likely to crack down on gambling. Temperance groups, who lobbied for the legislation as well, believed the change would force the city to get tougher on alcohol, too. However, this legislation—strongly opposed by newspapers like the *Globe* and the *Herald*—was widely viewed as an egregious violation of home rule as well as a crude effort by Republicans, dominant in state politics, to control the police in a city that was trending Democratic. It also was perceived as a Yankee attempt to take over the largely Irish Boston police force, and this only intensified the ethnic conflict and rivalry that was increasingly coming to define Boston.

Although arrests increased dramatically under the new setup, gamblers (not surprisingly) found ways of circumventing the law. Still another law, promoted by the Watch and Ward and enacted by the legislature in 1887, made it possible for an officer with a search warrant to arrest anyone in a place where gambling implements were found, even though no game was in progress. This law would make it far easier to gain convictions in gambling cases.

Using that law, in June 1894 the society obtained search warrants to authorize police raids on the two last remaining—and the most fashionable—faro banks in Boston, haunts of Harvard and MIT students. The establishments featured luxuriously furnished rooms, where dinners featuring wines and liquors were served every night. "How could this have happened?" lamented the proprietor of one of the faro banks as police officers armed with fire axes smashed through his bolted doors. (One Watch and Ward agent had already infiltrated the faro game inside.) The raiders seized and destroyed roulette wheels; $5,000 worth of fixtures and furniture were seized and later sold for the benefit of the county. The next morning, twenty-five men, including twelve Harvard students (under assumed names), pleaded guilty to being present at a place where gambling implements were found. "Worst of all," noted the Watch and Ward, "we found a little box containing blank checks upon a bank in Cambridge in which parents deposit funds for the education of their sons in the University." The proprietors of the faro banks were convicted and were fined $100 each; one was sentenced to four months in prison. The players were fined $10 each.

These raids came just a month after the Watch and Ward executive committee voted to give its agents the power to enter suspected places for the purpose of gathering evidence. In the past, the society's own strict rules had blocked its investigators from doing this. The restriction had been a problem in terms of repressing gambling but also in terms of cracking down on prostitution. Watch and Ward agents had patrolled the streets at night watching suspected houses of ill repute and reporting them to the police, but society rules prevented them from infiltrating such establishments and thus gathering more extensive—and perhaps conclusive—information. Now, in the spring of 1895, this was all changed, and the society's guidelines permitted agents to enter such places to gather whatever evidence was necessary to obtain search warrants.

With gamblers seemingly run out of town, and the new strategy in the place, the Watch and Ward was ready to move against "houses of ill fame" (prostitution), as well. "The society has now in its employ a number of intelligent young men of good reputation who are ready to set in the way of obtaining evidence and securing convictions," noted the Boston Globe in a June 12, 1894, article. "The chief difficulty has been in get-

ting men to do this work who will always be above bribery. Agent Chase
says that not a man has ever been employed by the society who has not
been offered money." The Globe headlined its article: "LOOK OUT FOR
RAIDS. Watch and Ward Society Mean Business. Agents are Employed to
Enter Suspected Places At Will."

To the Watch and Ward, prostitution (also known as the "social evil")
was "the foulest inheritance bequeathed by pagan institutions to Christian civilization," as it stated in its 1896 annual report. In an essay called
"How Should a Great City Deal with the Social Evil?" published both in
the society's annual report and later as a pamphlet, Allen deplored the fact
that men who patronized prostitutes escaped public disgrace while they
inflicted on women "an irreparable ruin." Prostitutes were not the only
victims, either, Allen insisted. A doctor had told him that at least a third
of the men brought to the outpatient department of one of the city's large
hospitals for treatment for ordinary accidents were also found to be in-
fected with venereal disease; other doctors put the numbers at 50 percent.
The result was "a secret history of sorrow" in hundreds of homes where
innocent wives suffered from their husbands' vices, he said. The culture
of public vice caused men to equate self-indulgence with manly vigor.
He called on men to "accept the appeal which the outraged womanhood
of our great cities makes to them; to take the side of honor, of purity, of
generous manliness, and to fight to the utmost this base code. . . ."

Perhaps encouraged by the Watch and Ward's growing aggressive-
ness, the police began to move against prostitution, closing some two
hundred houses of ill-repute by April 1895. "It is unquestionably true
that visiting places of immoral resort was never so dangerous, and the
Social Evil was never so fully repressed in Boston as today," stated
the Watch and Ward in its 1894–95 annual report. That year, the Watch
and Ward took credit for securing the convictions of twenty-one women
for keeping houses of ill-fame or working there, as well as two men. The
following year, it claimed fifteen convictions, and by 1897, convictions
had grown to fifty-seven, and an additional 159 notices had been served
on owners of houses occupied by persons had been convicted of keeping "disorderly houses," meaning those featuring prostitution, or places
where gambling had taken place. "Many such houses have been broken
up," the Watch and Ward reported.

By 1897, the Watch and Ward could boast that there wasn't a pool room
or a faro bank left in the city of Boston, with gaming and betting largely

pushed out of town to suburban racetracks. "There is not a great city in the country that can present so good a record as Boston in regard to gambling," said the Watch and Ward annual report of that year.

But although the Watch and Ward could take credit for freeing certain young women from the scourge of prostitution—or protecting parents of Harvard students from liens on their sons' allowances by faro bank "cappers"—there was often a pettiness and a sense of harassment of average citizens that characterized some Watch and Ward activities. One such example, reported in an article published September 18, 1897, in the *Boston Globe*, involved a raid on what the newspaper called "the great American game." A few days earlier, a Watch and Ward investigator was wandering down Summer Street, near where the new South Station was being built. He passed a large toolshed used by contractors and heard a series of exclamations from inside—"I'll raise you two," and "That pair is no good, I've three aces," and "Ante up or leave the table." Intrigued, the agent stopped and saw men grouped around improvised tables. He had stumbled upon a poker game.

The game had apparently been going on since the beginning of the excavation work on the new station. When the crew was small, the participants played on pieces of timber or granite or in partly demolished buildings. Once the toolshed was built, the number of players increased: all they needed was a quarter's worth of pennies to participate.

The investigator stopped by the next day and saw the same thing going on. After he told Henry Chase, other investigators went to see what was happening. Within a few days, they had sufficient evidence to go before a judge and ask for a search warrant. Chase, with the warrant in his pocket, went to police headquarters the next afternoon. The superintendent agreed to serve it. A police squad stationed themselves around the toolshed at exactly noon the following day. Through cracks in the building walls, they could hear the rattle of lunch pails. Then out came the poker tables.

Once three games were in progress, the police made their move. Captain Brown of the liquor squad entered the shed, along with a sergeant. "I'm sorry but I've a search warrant, boys," announced an almost apologetic Brown. Suddenly, there was a rush to escape through windows and doors; players threw their cards in all directions. Twenty-two men were brought to the LaGrange Street police station—"the most indignant crowd of men ever seen at the station," according to the *Globe* account. There they were detained until their employers could furnish $2 bail per person. They were arraigned and charged with being present at a place where gambling implements were found.

The Watch and Ward could add these convictions to "beef up" the statistics in its annual reports. Whether such activities contributed to the health and well-being of Boston's citizens was another matter, but on that subject, the society had no doubt. The battle against the card game, the roulette wheel, and the lottery ticket would go on for almost the entire life of the Watch and Ward.

CHAPTER 4

Mrs. Glyn and Sin, 1903–1909

ONE SATURDAY AFTERNOON IN NOVEMBER 1903, a respectable-looking gentleman who appeared to be in his late thirties or forties strode into the Old Corner Bookstore, at the corner of Washington and School streets in Boston. The Old Corner was the most venerable and distinguished bookstore in the city. For many years, it shared its building with one of the city's leading publishing firms, Ticknor and Fields. Boston's literati would visit their publishers and stop in to browse at the Old Corner. That day, the visitor asked, "Do you have anything by Rabelais?" referring to the French Renaissance author of *The Adventures of Gargantua and Pantagruel*, the fantastical and often scatological tales about a giant and his son. He was buying it for a friend who lived in the country, or so he told the clerk. The store rarely sold more than one or two copies of Rabelais's works a year—sometimes it obtained copies when buying old libraries or book collections—but there happened to be a set on hand, imported from England by a Philadelphia publishing house. The clerk, whose name was Walter H. Knight, sold it to the visitor for $3.75.

The purchaser was an agent of the New England Watch and Ward Society, and the following Monday, the same man, this time armed with a search warrant and accompanied by a police officer, reappeared at the store and announced that Knight was under arrest for selling obscene literature. The clerk was alone in the store and asked for five minutes to get someone to take over for him, especially since there were books sitting on shelves outside the shop. His request was refused. He was taken to the police station and grilled as if he were an ordinary criminal. The clerk had no idea there were any legal restrictions on selling Rabelais.

The proprietor of the Old Corner was later arrested, as were the proprietor and a clerk at two of the city's other leading bookshops—the Old South Bookstore and Colesworthy's. All were charged with the possession of obscene material that most educated individuals considered to be classics—albeit bawdy classics—either the works of Rabelais, the *Decameron*, or the *Heptameron*, a *Decameron*-influenced collection of 72 tales written by Margaret, Queen of Navarre. The penalties were fines ranging from $100 to $1,000.

The same thing had happened almost ten years before, in 1894, when Watch and Ward agents secured the arrest of another Boston bookstore clerk, Alexander McCance, who was charged with selling the *Decameron*. The defendant was found guilty by a lower court and appealed to the Superior Court. His dramatic trial featured a police inspector reading a number of racy tales from the *Decameron* and the defense attorney asking permission to read extracts from the Bible, presumably to show that Holy Writ wasn't exactly pure either. (The judge refused his request.) The defense attorney also claimed that a copy of the *Decameron* had come over on the *Mayflower* with the Pilgrims. "Why convict the old masters of literature?" the defense attorney demanded. "Is it not better for your sons to have something spicy to read of a winter's night than to play poker, resort to gambling houses, and the like?" The jury repaired to its quarters with a copy of the *Decameron* and determined the book to be legally obscene for the first time in its 550-year history. In the end, the defense appealed the case to the state supreme court, which threw it out because the indictment had failed to specify exactly which passages were obscene.

The Watch and Ward was particularly concerned about these classics because during the late nineteenth century, large numbers of them began to appear in the United States, sold not just in respectable bookshops like the Old Corner but also by purveyors of pornography in cheap editions with racy covers. Sometimes these classics were even expurgated to remove parts that had little or no erotic interest. Anthony Comstock had prosecuted a number of cases against publishers who sold the *Decameron*, at one point comparing the book to "a wild beast" that he was determined to prevent from "breaking loose and destroying the youth of the land."

In a *Boston Globe* article in the midst of the 1894 case, virtually all the booksellers in Boston condemned the arrest of the bookstore clerk—although almost none were willing to be quoted by name. One of the few who did, a Mr. Littlefield of the Cornhill Bookshop, said, "I think it is an outrage and I believe that the book dealers of the city ought to come to this young man's rescue. The idea of these fellows [Watch and Ward agents] hanging around a little store like that in order to trap an inexperienced boy, and for selling a book that has been on the market for 300 years and that will be sold when the members of this society are all in their graves."

One of the things that particularly infuriated booksellers was that the law awarded half the fines imposed in such cases to the complainants. With fines ranging up to $1,000, according to law, it offered the Watch and Ward and its agents a financial incentive to entrap booksellers and book dealers.

In the Rabelais case of 1903, however, after three of the booksellers, including the Old Corner Bookstore clerk Knight, were convicted and fined $100 each, Boston booksellers were determined to stand up to the Watch and Ward. They raised $400 for a defense fund and prepared to appeal the case to a higher court. Rumors circulated that the Watch and Ward was preparing to raid libraries in search of proscribed books; the society heatedly denied this. In the end, a compromise was reached. The parties settled out of court and the indicted booksellers agreed not to display any of the books openly. It would be many years before any Boston bookseller would try and challenge the Watch and Ward again.

Three years later, in 1907, it was a contemporary novel by an Englishwoman named Elinor Glyn that caught the Watch and Ward's eye. The novel, called Three Weeks, was a literary phenomenon that had sold the extraordinary number of 2 million copies worldwide. "Bishops and headmasters inveighed against it; schoolgirls and schoolboys read it under the bedclothes," wrote photographer Cecil Beaton in an introduction to a 1974 reissue of the novel. To Beaton, it was a vastly entertaining "tale of what we might now call high-camp." To the Watch and Ward Society (and to the government of Canada, which banned it), it was an immoral book that glorified adultery.

Three Weeks contained no obscene language and no description of physical intimacies beyond kissing. The author's lush and florid style made it the target of countless parodies. Glyn's way of describing sexual congress was: "And outside the black storm made the darkness fall early. And inside the half-burnt logs tumbled together causing a cloud of golden sparks, and then the flames leapt up again and crackled in the grate."

The book was high romance—highly improbable romance. Paul, a handsome young man of twenty-three—"a splendid young English animal of the best class," in the novel's words, who had attended Eton and Oxford and whose main interest is hunting—goes off to Switzerland accompanied by his valet. In Lucerne, in his first night at his hotel, he is seated near a mysterious woman, ten years his senior, dressed all in black, with a corsage of tuberoses. Her eyes seem to change color from moment to moment. She never tells him her name or nationality, but she appears to be a princess, probably from some country to the east, most likely a Slavic one. Brilliant and worldly, she teaches him to ignore the "puny conventions of the world." They conduct a torrid affair, related in overwrought prose. (" 'Remember, Paul,' she whispered when, passion maddening him, he clasped her violently in his arms, 'remember—whatever happens—whatever comes—for now, tonight, there is no other reason in all this but just—I love you—I love you, Paul!' 'My Queen, my Queen!' said Paul, his voice hoarse in his throat.") But this woman, who really is the queen of a Balkan country, is caught up in intrigue at home, where her husband plots to murder her. After the two lovers spend three weeks together in Lucerne and Venice, she disappears, leaving him distraught—and carrying his child. Needless to say, the book ends tragically.

One of the book's moments of "high camp" comes when Paul presents his "queen," as he constantly refers to her, with a glorious rug made out of tiger skin. That inspired the rhyme

> "Would you like to sin
> With Elinor Glyn
> On a tiger skin?
> Or would you prefer
> To err
> With her
> On some other fur?"

Many readers assumed that the book was a roman à clef of the Romanovs, the Russian royal family; in fact, it was based on the 1903 murder of Queen Draga of Serbia. Mrs. Glyn insisted that she was shocked at the book's notoriety and the tendency of some people to see it as evil. "For me 'The Lady' was a deep study, the analysis of a strange Slav nature, who from circumstance and education and her general view of life was beyond the ordinary laws of morality," Glyn wrote in the preface to the American edition of 1907. "If I were making the study of a tiger, I would not give it the attribute of a spaniel because the public, and I myself, might prefer a spaniel."

The highbrow critics laughed at it. The *New York Times* reviewer ridiculed the book as "erotic silliness," noting, "She [Mrs. Glyn] recites whole decalogues of trite, feeble, pompous phrases, and honestly believes that she is expounding a new and noble philosophy; she executes page after page of pinchbeck rhetoric, happily and pathetically unconscious that she is writing nonsense."

The *Times* may have dismissed *Three Weeks* as silly and trite, but the Watch and Ward Society clearly did not view it as so benign. In the society's view, it had a "degrading tendency," and, at a meeting on December 4, 1907, the board of directors decided to move against it. They sounded out a Boston Municipal Court judge, George L. Wentworth, and the judge's view was that the book would most likely be ruled obscene should it come to trial. With this assurance, the Watch and Ward sent a notice to Boston booksellers warning them that the sale of *Three Weeks* could subject them to legal action. The novel quickly became unavailable.

But the publisher, a New York firm called Duffield, had a raging best seller on its hands and would not give up so easily. It attempted to sell *Three Weeks* by mail, but Boston newspapers refused to accept advertisements for it; the Watch and Ward had already contacted postal authorities, who threatened the papers with loss of mailing privileges. The publisher contacted the Watch and Ward, offering to sell a copy of the book to the society and thus test the legality of the ban. When the Watch and Ward declined—fearing this was just a scheme to advertise the book—the publisher's representative, Joseph Buckley, sold a copy of the book to a Boston police officer instead. Buckley promptly found himself under arrest. A Superior Court jury found him guilty under the obscenity law and fined him.

The publisher appealed to the Massachusetts Supreme Court, arguing that the book was neither obscene nor indecent, nor did it tend to corrupt the morals of youth. "If the statute is to be construed to cover all language which conveys or suggests thoughts of sexual relations, or even illicit intercourse," claimed the defense, "it will certainly include a great part of what is considered good and decent literature."

However, in his January 6, 1909, decision, Judge John Wilkes Hammond was unconvinced. Perhaps many readers might find Mrs. Glyn's literary style attractive, noted the judge. Perhaps they might not heed the "thinly veiled allusions to an intense desire for sexual intercourse and to the arts of seduction." But the reading public as a whole couldn't be trusted to react that way. "Descriptions of seductive actions and of highly wrought sexual passion, even when sanctified by what the author has called 'love,' are very likely to be seen in another light tending towards the obscene and impure," the judge insisted.

Judge Hammond declared Three Weeks obscene. The Watch and Ward, referring to Three Weeks in its annual report only as "a certain fashionable novel," was delighted. "The effect of this trial has been to make it clear that Boston has well-defined literary standards, and its average citizen feels himself cultured enough to apply them in the interest of morals," it went on.

Mrs. Glyn turned the book into a play that opened in both New York and London, where she played the role of the doomed queen herself. Curiously, a little more than a year after the Massachusetts court decision, the theatrical version opened at the Grand Opera House in Boston. This time, however, it didn't feature Mrs. Glyn in the leading role. If the audience was expecting something sensational, wrote the Boston Globe critic, "it must have been disappointed, for no matter how it may have been played elsewhere, there was nothing in the version presented last night that might be censured upon the grounds of vulgarity." As far as is known, the Watch and Ward made no objection.

The author wrote a number of other novels, although none as successful as Three Weeks. She eventually wound up in Hollywood, writing screenplays for silent film stars Gloria Swanson and Clara Bow and coaching Rudolph Valentino in acting.

Eventually, the Watch and Ward Society and the booksellers of Boston decided that it was in their interest to create a situation that avoided a constant recourse to bookstore raids and court cases. So Watch and Ward secretary J. Frank Chase proposed a solution. The society would pass along to booksellers the names of any books whose sale, it believed, might lead to legal action on grounds of obscenity. The booksellers would then have one of two choices: They could withdraw the book from circulation or risk indictment.

Starting in 1915, Chase, who had ascended to the position of Watch and Ward secretary eight years before, and Richard F. Fuller, president of the Old Corner Bookstore (the same shop whose clerk had been entrapped by a Watch and Ward agent in the Rabelais case), established the Boston Booksellers Committee. It was an unofficial book jury, established to rule on any book whose moral purity was in question. The group was made up of Fuller, two booksellers named by him, and three Watch and Ward directors. If the committee members disagreed on a particular book, they agreed to submit it to the district attorney or a magistrate for a final decision.

The committee would read a current novel. If it was acceptable, Boston booksellers could sell it without fear of court action. If it was deemed "actionable" (unacceptable or obscene, in the eyes of the committee), all Massachusetts book dealers would be notified by postcard. Anyone selling such a book forty-eight hours after that notification was subject to Watch and Ward prosecution. At the same time, Boston's newspapers wouldn't advertise or review a condemned title, and the police stayed out of the matter, rarely, if ever, prosecuting a book on their own. If the police took it upon themselves to ban a book—which was rare during the system's heyday—both the Watch and Ward and the booksellers would be notified before any action was taken against any bookseller.

That was the case as late as 1925, when Suffolk County district attorney Thomas O'Brien, apparently new to his office, met J. Frank Chase on the street and said, "Chase, I have a case you ought to have."

"What's that?" Chase asked.

"Tomorrow we're going to indict the Old Corner Bookstore for a book called Flaming Youth [a 1923 pulp novel by Samuel Hopkins Adams, written under a pseudonym]."

"You can't do that," Chase replied.

And the district attorney didn't—instead he worked through the committee, as his predecessors had done.

Boston's way of censorship was called the "gentlemen's agreement," and it essentially remained in force from 1915 to 1927, when it fell apart. The Old Corner Bookstore's Fuller viewed the system as flawless. "If the bookseller won't sell and the reviewer won't review, the book might as well never have been written," said Fuller. The sway of the Watch and

Ward's power extended beyond Boston; bookshops in Boston suburbs and Massachusetts cities like Worcester and Springfield tended to follow Boston's lead. It is difficult to know exactly how many books were banned under the "gentlemen's agreement," but in his book, Purity in Print, Paul S. Boyer estimates that the committee quietly suppressed fifty to seventy-five books from 1918 to 1926. Among them were works by major American and British writers, including John Dos Passos's Streets of Night, Sherwood Anderson's Many Marriages, and Aldous Huxley's Antic Hay.

There were a few books that defied the system. One was Simon Called Peter, written by Robert Keable, a novel about the loves of a Baptist preacher. It turned out that the book had been the favorites of Mrs. James Mills and her lover, a minister, who were the victims of a sensational double murder in New Brunswick, New Jersey, in September 1922. Everyone wanted to read the book for this reason, even though the committee had found it "actionable." (The book was so well known that it even received a disparaging mention in F. Scott Fitzgerald's The Great Gatsby.) Although most bookstores unhappily went along with the ban, Secretary Chase filed a complaint against the owner of a circulating library and periodical store in the Boston suburb of Arlington, accusing her of circulating the book to students at Arlington High School. In court, the owner admitted loaning the book—she had a long list of customers waiting for it—but insisted she hadn't loaned it to high school students and furthermore didn't consider it obscene or improper. The judge determined the book to be obscene and fined the defendant $100, suspending the fine for a year.

Mostly, the "gentlemen's agreement" satisfied all parties. Bookstore owners were happy because they avoided messy court cases and the arrest and entrapment of their employees. The Watch and Ward was pleased because it was essentially able to keep morally questionable books out of Boston and nearby towns in a genteel, behind-the-scenes, Brahmin fashion. The general public knew almost nothing of what was going on. The names of banned books were never announced, and such books were never reviewed or advertised; Watch and Ward annual reports never mentioned them, either. It was as if they never existed. Boston newspapers rarely, if ever, wrote about the system until it crumbled. All this was in contrast to what was going on in New York City, where there were several noisy censorship cases and court actions, particularly in the early 1920s, including the suppression of magazine extracts from James Joyce's Ulysses, among others.

However, critics like H. L. Mencken particularly hated the idea that J. Frank Chase and a compliant bookseller—the Old Corner's Richard Fuller—essentially controlled what Bostonians could read. It was a literary dictatorship of six people, operating in secrecy and behind closed doors, with two of them—Chase and Fuller—possessing inordinate power. In a speech before the American Booksellers Convention in 1923, Fuller admitted that occasionally a bootlegger would "slip through the lines.

"There is where you have got to have a strong organization that will hold them in line," he told his fellow booksellers. "If the Watch and Ward catches them, it means going to court, and . . . the courts are backing us up in this move." Massachusetts, he added proudly, "stands today as the cleanest state in the Union."

CHAPTER 5

Tough Guys and "Blue Bloods," 1907–1925

W̲HEN BOOK REVIEWER A.L.S. Wood first laid eyes on the Reverend J. Frank Chase, secretary of the Watch and Ward, in 1925, Chase was sitting with his feet on the desk of his office in Boston's Park Square, dictating a letter and smoking a little cigar. The vice crusader sported a "not luxuriant crop of tousled white hair," his walrus mustache masked a "virtuous mouth," and his eyes hid behind the "glaze of glasses." He was dictating furiously. Someone had been caught selling a book called *The Memories of a Young Girl*—an apparently pornographic work—as well as indecent pictures to "the high school literati of Fitchburg," a small city west of Boston. The same thing had occurred in nearby Worcester. So here was Chase, dictating a letter using quasi-legal language, cocking a knowing eye at his waiting visitor, "as doom was made to settle on the Fitchburg miscreant in a multitude of 'in the cases' and 'in the matters.'"

Wood was writing his article for H. L. Mencken's magazine, the *American Mercury*, and, of course, the "wowser"-hating editor was determined to portray Chase in the worst possible light. Chase had called Wood "brother" on the phone, clearly a misjudgment on the secretary's part, for the resulting profile mocked him throughout, refusing to spare even his brand of cigar—called Between the Acts. As Wood noted, "the pallid cigar of truthful rice paper still carries an implication of evil in reforming circles." Between the Acts was different, however: "Tan its complexion to a wholesome brown and it becomes fit for the lips of righteous men."

The only thing that the Watch and Ward secretary would not have objected to, in all probabilities, was the article's title, "Keeping the Puritans Pure."

Jason Franklin Chase was a formidable character. The word frequently applied to him was "pugnacious." He had become the day-to-day head of the Watch and Ward almost twenty years earlier, when its agent, Henry Chase, retired at the age of eighty-three after twenty-five years of service. J. Frank took the elder Chase's position, now given the more elevated title of "secretary" instead of "agent." He was not yet thirty-five years old and his salary was $2,000 a year.

The Watch and Ward had been languishing during Henry Chase's last years. But a year after J. Frank Chase took over, the society's successful prosecutions for gambling increased almost fourfold over the previous year (from twenty-one to seventy-nine) and those for obscene pictures were up a similar amount (from ten to thirty-eight). These were all-time highs for the Watch and Ward. One of the targets of the first year of his secretaryship was Elinor Glyn's novel *Three Weeks*. The 1907–08 annual report boasted of "a forward movement" that built "on the splendid foundation laid by Henry Chase in his twenty-five years of faithful and wise work." The new secretary beefed up the staff as well. In fact, there had barely been a staff before the second Chase arrived. Expenses for special agents climbed from $197.42 to $1,739.25 in a year. Donations, which had totaled $3,113.50 in 1906–07—Henry Chase's last year—almost doubled to $6,223.50 in 1907–08, when J. Frank Chase took over. By 1909–10, they had jumped to $7,855.73, an impressive amount in those days.

At the annual public meeting at Trinity Church on March 15, 1908, the Watch and Ward president, the Reverend Frederick Baylies Allen, evaluated the new secretary's first year: "[W]e have this past year done as vigorous and as useful work as ever in our history . . . and the zeal and fidelity of our Secretary gives a promise of great usefulness and a larger measure of success in the future." By 1910, Allen was claiming "the most successful year in our history." This was largely due, he maintained, to the "courage, intelligence and devotion of our Secretary [Chase] . . . who deserves the greatest credit for his valiant fight against evil."

Under J. Frank Chase, the Watch and Ward's conviction rate was somewhere between 95 and 100 percent.

Chase fancied himself a true soldier of the Lord. Some of the most stirring moments of his career as Watch and Ward secretary involved World War I raids against gambling and prostitution in various cities surrounding Boston, sometimes accomplished by Watch and Ward agents going over the heads of corrupt or complacent local police forces. John W. Hawkins, a writer for the *New Bedford Sunday Standard*, penned an admiring profile of Chase following a huge 1916 Watch and Ward vice raid in that city. He remarked favorably upon Chase's "bulldog jaw" and "wellknit body which somehow conveys the impression of strength and swiftness of action." Wrote Hawkins, "At practically every period of his life, he has had a fight on his hands and he says he likes it. In every battle so far in his career, he has left the field with colors flying. He is a hard man to down." Chase's tough-guy persona was very much part of a cultural transformation in the late nineteenth and early twentieth centuries. During this period, men turned to "martial ideals and images as a way to focus their vision of a manly life," as E. Anthony Rotundo points out in his book *American Manhood*. That was particularly true of reformers who attempted to "masculinize" the idea of reform in an effort to dispel the Victorian-era image of progressives as effeminate and overly moralistic. Anthony Comstock was a notable example. Theodore Roosevelt, that great exponent of the "strenuous life," was another. When he ran for mayor of Boston in 1910 on a reform ticket, John F. "Honey Fitz" Fitzgerald used the slogan "Manhood Against Money."

Hawkins observed that when "on the field of battle," Chase was "rather careless with his personal appearance," but he was so engaged in the work at hand that "he has no time to spare for unnecessary details." The *Sunday Standard* reporter also described him as a fluent talker who spoke so rapidly that "he would baffle a stenographer."

Unlike his blue-blooded employers at the Watch and Ward, Chase was a self-made man. He grew up on the mean streets of Chelsea, an industrial city just outside Boston. As a boy, he was constantly getting involved in fights. "There was a time when I had licked every red-headed man in Chelsea," he told reporter Hawkins. "I've got plenty of red blood and I like to fight. . . . Nowadays when I go into a raid, I always take my glasses off and fight with my fists first."

Chase learned to fend for himself early. By eleven, he was working during school vacations. At age fourteen, he quit school and got a job at a Boston toy store, becoming assistant manager while still a teenager. At eighteen, he decided to dedicate his life to the ministry, making up two years of grammar school and entering high school, where he was elected president of his class. When he matriculated at Wesleyan University in Middletown, Connecticut, he had $17 in his pocket, earning his way through school by canvassing during the summer. (He was also helped by a loan of $100 a year from his church.) At Wesleyan, he played on the football team until he broke two ribs and his collarbone. There he also won the debate prize. After Wesleyan, Chase received a theology degree from Boston University, where he also studied law, something that would serve him in good stead when he ascended to the position of Watch and Ward secretary.

Chase served for five years as the minister of a Methodist Episcopal church in West Roxbury, an inner suburb of Boston. When he left—Methodist ministers were allowed to remain at a single parish for no more than five years—his congregation gave him a trip to Italy as a going-away present. One morning, in Florence, he was standing around the Campanile of Giotto when a vendor of indecent pictures tried to interest him in his wares. An offended Chase approached a police officer, asking him, in French, about laws in Italy regarding such pictures. But the police officer, believing that the American had been cheated by the vendor and was trying to lodge a complaint, walked away in disgust. When Chase compared the moral conditions in Italy with those in Massachusetts, he decided that conditions in Italy were worse. Still, "Massachusetts was far from spotless and there was a task awaiting someone to clean it up," he later told the Sunday Standard reporter. At that point, he didn't realize that that "someone" would turn out to be himself.

He came home to a new parish, this time in nearby Allston. A wealthy Harvard graduate and social worker of his acquaintance, Delcevare King, who was a member of the Watch and Ward board of directors, approached him about taking Henry Chase's job because the aging agent was ill and preparing to retire. Chase was reluctant at first, but that incident in Italy stuck in his mind. "I had had some business experience in my life and I had knocked around a great deal," he recalled, "and after I thought the situation over very carefully, it struck me that the Watch and Ward society offered a great field for a man who was rough and ready."

As secretary, one of J. Frank Chase's major crusades involved drugs—"the dope vice," as he preferred to call it—something that the society began to move against during the early years of his tenure. Watch and Ward agents participated in a series of crackdowns, raiding opium dens and arresting dealers of morphine and cocaine; at the same time, the organi-

zation successfully pushed the Massachusetts legislature to pass tougher
laws to control the drug trade and worked hard to educate the public on
the subject, which was relatively unknown at the time. (Chase himself
wrote a book entitled The Dope Evil.) In his speech to the February 25, 1912,
annual meeting, held at the Old South Church, Chase bragged that since
July 1909, the society had taken to court and convicted 178 people for the
illegal sale and distribution of opium, cocaine, morphine, heroin, and
hashish. The previous year, in one day, Watch and Ward officers swore
out warrants against 17 people for illegal sales of cocaine and morphine;
14 were arrested and 13 found guilty and sentenced to prison. Previously,
little had been done to crack down on drugs in Massachusetts. "There is
no vice in the whole category [of vices] which is so insidious, so tenacious
and so deadly, as that of the dope habit," Chase said.

He ended his talk at the annual meeting that night with a reference
to the overrunning of the Roman Empire by Goths and Vandals. "The
dopes [drugs] are the Goths and Vandals of modern life pillaging the
souls of men," he told his audience. "The soul is dismantled by them, and
like a dismantled ship—a derelict—it is blown about upon tempestuous
seas only to find its last resting place on some strange shore half buried
in the sands, a shipwreck. This is the Vice, the mercenary promoters of
which we are fighting." (In another address that evening, William DeWitt
Hyde, president of Bowdoin College, described liquor and hypnotic drugs
as "reducing man to a brute, the woman to a beast, making the one the
reckless agent, the other the pliant instrument of all the vices that infest
society.")

Chase's self-described "rough and ready" quality sometimes caused
him trouble. Over the years, he made many enemies—gamblers, drug
dealers, and also some law enforcement officials who resented his tactics
and the vigilante-like methods of the Watch and Ward.

The public got a glimpse of the unattractive side of his pugnacity in
the spring of 1915, when Chase was accused of slugging a Boston attorney, John J. Cronin, in the corridor of Boston Municipal Court. Cronin
had appeared in court as an attorney for a defendant whom the Watch
and Ward had accused of illegal drug trafficking. (Cronin lost the case.)
As Cronin walked out of the courtroom, Watch and Ward agent Jefferson
Parker accused him of trying to bribe witnesses in a previous case. "If you
repeat that comment, I'll have you indicted," Cronin warned Parker. Chase
apparently overheard him. "I'll have you indicted," Chase said loudly to
Cronin, and then he hauled off and struck him. The shaken Cronin's de-

fense was purely verbal: "They almost got you the other night. You've just served a term in jail. I saw you coming out of a house the other night." At that, Chase gave Cronin a vigorous push in the face. The attorney wound up with a swollen jaw, a lacerated lip, and a loose front tooth.

Cronin promptly brought an assault and battery charge against Chase, and the Watch and Ward secretary then charged Cronin with slander over the remark "You've just served a term in jail." At the slander hearing, the testimony took a sharp turn that caused Chase to appear in an even more unfavorable light. It turned out that a rumor was circulating among lawyers that an affidavit against Chase had been filed in the district attorney's office concerning an incident that had taken place the previous year. At the slander hearing, Cronin's lawyer, John P. Feeney, asked Chase, "Mr. Chase, do you, a minister of the gospel, admit that with a woman not your wife, you went to a Boston hotel after midnight, registered as a man and wife under a fictitious name, were assigned to a bedroom, and spent some time there?"

"Yes, I did," Chase replied.

In his testimony, Chase said that the two were at the hotel for twenty minutes on Watch and Ward business, just "watching the corridors." The woman's name was Miss Sterritt. Cronin's attorney got Chase to admit that he had taken a drink that night, although Miss Sterritt had not.

"You're trying to blast my reputation," the Watch and Ward secretary said.

"Impossible, Mr. Chase," replied Cronin's lawyer.

The reason they were at the hotel—and under false pretenses—Chase insisted, was as part of a campaign by the Watch and Ward to clean up certain cafés and hotels, where it was believed prostitution was going on. "A member of my board of directors asked me to ascertain the character of certain business of the hotel," he said in court. "I took an agent and attempted to secure evidence concerning which chambermaids had made affidavits." There was nothing done that night between him and Miss Sterritt to show "moral turpitude," he added.

So it went in court. Afterwards, Chase was forced to issue a long defense of his conduct, blaming "various wrongdoers, particularly those in the drug traffic" for an attempt to besmirch his character through "baseless insinuations." After all, he had just concluded a series of prosecutions against drug dealers—forty-one of them, in fact—"a splendid campaign," in his words. The result was animosity against him personally. He said that "investigating work where one has to simulate what he is not is dangerous at best to a man's reputation since his acts can be distorted and made to mean what was not intended. In the particular case on which the insinuations of today were based, there were believed to be large results of distinct value to the community to be gained. This led to what now is obvious was an unwise course." The Watch and Ward's board of directors backed him up. A month later, Chase pled guilty to assault and battery and was fined $25.

It was all a nasty business, but it was the way Chase did things at the Watch and Ward—the only effective way to gain evidence, he argued. When you were fighting vice and evil, you sometimes had to stoop to the level of your opponents. That could open Watch and Ward agents—even the secretary himself—to false charges of wrongdoing and accusations of hypocrisy. As he told John Hawkins, the friendly *New Bedford Sunday Standard* reporter, "There is only one way to get evidence against gambling houses and red light resorts, and that is to go into them and mingle with the people who frequent them."

But with the Watch and Ward always the target of gamblers and vice interests, Chase's decision to register at a hotel with a woman who was not his wife, under false names, provided dangerous fodder for his enemies. And his guilty plea and fine in the dustup with Cronin gave his opponents the ability to claim that he had a criminal record.

In an anonymous 1916 pamphlet called "Rob Roy's Pellets," which attacked Chase in highly personal terms for everything from allegedly betting on horses to usurping the powers of the police, this episode evoked the following comment: "Well, all you sons of Adam, with your full faculties and physical health, just recall what [the evangelist] Billy Sunday said in his first sermon in Boston. He declared that he never allowed himself to be alone in a room with any woman but Ma Sunday, and for which he got many 'God bless him's.' Billy Sunday made no claim to being stronger minded than Father Adam, and dear old Adam could not be trusted in a fruit garden."

Chase had a major ally, though: one of the most powerful men in Boston —the ultimate Brahmin, Godfrey Lowell Cabot. Godfrey L. Cabot was a Cabot and a Lowell, too, and in Boston, a city obsessed with genealogy (the *Boston Evening Transcript* even featured a weekly genealogy column), that meant a great deal. The Cabot family took up two whole pages in the *Boston Social Register*, more than any other Boston family. As the ditty went,

"And this is good old Boston / The home of the bean and the cod / Where the Lowells talk only to the Cabots / And the Cabots talk only to God."

Godfrey L. Cabot was born in Boston's Park Square in 1861 and died on Beacon Street in 1962. His life stretched from the Civil War to the Cuban missile crisis. As his biographer, Leon Harris, put it, "A product of America's closest approximation to aristocracy, Godfrey Lowell Cabot had to an exaggerated degree its particular combination of arrogance and naiveté and the social security which enabled him to be both consciously and unconsciously eccentric. He was afire with the 'Yankee passion for self-improvement' and a terrible compulsion to cleanse the Augean stables of life, a man of the sort who often, in Chesterton's phrase, 'pours righteous indignation into the wrong things.'"

Much of that righteous indignation went into the Watch and Ward Society. He started contributing to the society as early as 1891, became an official member in 1900, joined the board of directors in 1908, and served as treasurer from 1915 to 1940. After stepping down as treasurer, he became honorary president, serving well into the 1950s.

Cabot made a fortune in the manufacture of carbon black—a powder made from natural gas that was first used in printer's ink and later as a reinforcing agent in tires. Trained as a chemist, he inherited $80,000 from his father, a sum that helped him establish his business. By 1892, Godfrey L. Cabot, Inc., located primarily in Pennsylvania and West Virginia, was the third- or fourth-leading manufacturer of carbon black in the United States; in 1912, Cabot made a deal with Standard Oil to sell them millions of cubic feet of gas, giving him a vast income and enabling him to expand his business significantly after the war.

By the time he died, he was said to be Boston's wealthiest man, his worth somewhere between $75 and $100 million. He was also a generous man. Cabot himself once estimated that by the time he died, he would have given away $3 million to charity, and a good chunk of that to the Watch and Ward.

As Watch and Ward treasurer, however, Cabot was a stern taskmaster, keeping a tight rein on the society even during relatively flush years. (In 1915 and 1916, Cabot's first two years as treasurer, donations approached $10,000 each year; in 1916, Cabot himself contributed $1,025, by far the largest individual gift.) Observes biographer Harris, "[J. Frank] Chase soon learned that no complaint was too small, no expense item too insignificant, to merit Cabot's attention." Cabot insisted on signing every

check himself. He put pressure on Chase to keep employee wages low and
to reduce the payroll of the society—hiring as few detectives and as few
lawyers as possible. As a result, the society had a staff of only three by
January 1919, including Chase (but not Cabot). That month, while Cabot
was in the military, Chase wrote him, "I assure you, Mr. Cabot, that I
shall bring the expenditures for the rest of the year down to a bare existence." As Harris wryly observed, "Cabot's war against wickedness was
one of the most minutely audited attacks in history."

Cabot shrewdly insisted that the society rent office space and never
own real estate to avoid punitive tax valuations. The threat of such valuations made owners of large properties in Boston reluctant to complain
about official corruption; if they did, they ran the risk that their taxes
could be raised. Cabot was concerned that the Watch and Ward's integrity and financial situation could be jeopardized if it gave the authorities
a weapon to use against it. (Nonetheless, in 1946, after Cabot stepped
down as treasurer, the Watch and Ward bought the building at 41 Mt.
Vernon Street on Beacon Hill, where it had had offices since 1933.)

Even in the late 1940s and 1950s, when the Watch and Ward was in decline, Cabot was contributing large sums of money—$1,000 each year for
1949, 1951, 1952, and 1954. But probably more important than anything,
he lent the prestige of Boston's first family to the Watch and Ward.

Cabot was a larger-than-life personality and a man of great determination and self-reliance. Fascinated by the Wright brothers, he was an
early proponent of aviation and tried to get the U.S. government interested in the possibilities of flight long before almost anyone else. During
World War I, he was so appalled by the German invasion of Belgium and
France that he asked the Secretary of the Navy for permission to apply for
the Naval Air Service. The secretary said no, largely because Cabot was
fifty-four years old at the time. But Cabot would not be deterred so easily. If the government didn't think it required his services, he decided he
would protect the country himself. So Cabot purchased a personal sea-
plane, built a hangar on one of the Misery Islands, off Salem Harbor, and
learned to fly. Then he patrolled the coast on his own, looking for German submarines. Finally, in March 1917, he was appointed a lieutenant
in the U.S. Naval Reserve Flying Corps by the new secretary of the Navy,
Franklin D. Roosevelt.

In 1923, Cabot ran for mayor of Cambridge as an Independent (that
is, a Republican), a quixotic venture. He faced an uphill battle: the in-
cumbent Democratic mayor, Edward H. Quinn, was popular, serving his

fourth term, and the city was overwhelmingly Democratic. Cabot promised a variety of "good government" reforms: competitive bidding for city contracts; appointments based on qualifications, not political debts; and an end to corruption. In the end, Cabot was easily defeated by a vote of 16,897 to 9,861, and Quinn's vote total was the highest ever received in a Cambridge mayoralty race. That campaign was both the beginning and the end of Cabot's political career.

In later life, he became almost a caricature of himself. He arose every morning at seven o'clock, took a cold bath, and walked to and from his downtown office. He did this until he was ninety-three. His employees could set their watches by his arrivals and departures. It was said that, at seventy-two, he could beat opponents half his age at tennis and played a "savage" game of chess until he was eighty-five. When he was ninety, he took the subway to Cambridge, received an honorary doctor of law degree from Harvard, put it under his arm, and took the subway back to his home on Beacon Street.

Cabot was very much a puritan. He neither smoked nor drank, and he refused to allow coffee or tea in his home. "With father, there was no middle ground between good and bad," wrote his son, Thomas D. Cabot. In their household, the son recalled, "duty always overshadowed fun. We were governed by an ascetic father who lived by puritanical tenets. Hard work, self-denial, and self-improvement were his paramount concerns. Art, literature, and nature were to be studied rather than enjoyed."

From his youth, Cabot was a prodigious reader and an avid theatergoer and operagoer, but he was "always keeping a Pecksniffian eye for any obscenity or naughtiness," according to Harris. And Harris notes, "From his youth on, Godfrey was much happier when he found something to condemn." To a young Cabot, almost anything French was of questionable morality, a view that the Watch and Ward echoed. In his view, The Three Musketeers was "coarse and immoral," and Les Misérables was "by no means free from coarseness and voluptuousness." Censorship begins at home, and Cabot tried to restrict his wife's reading. "I question whether George Eliot is good reading for you, especially when I am away," he wrote his wife. He also questioned whether Leo Tolstoy's books were "wholesome reading" for her. The Russian novelist was "a moral pervert," in his view, "oscillating between bestial licentiousness on the one hand and a gloomy and morbid asceticism on the other."

Interestingly, he approved of Boccaccio's Decameron—that perennial Watch and Ward target. It was "a most versatile and amusing collection,"

in his view. "In spite of its immorality, I think it a book worth reading, at
any rate for me, and I regret that I did not read it years ago, for it shows a
very important side of human nature and one with which my life does not
bring me into contact and God willing never shall, but yet which it is well
to appreciate not wholly without sympathy."

When Leon Harris was rummaging through the Cabot papers to write his
biography, he discovered letters composed by Cabot to his wife, Minna,
that show a side of the great man totally at odds with his public image.
Written from West Virginia, where Cabot had gone on business trips,
they display erotic fantasies that were more intense, more perverse even,
than those contained in any book the Watch and Ward ever sought to ban.
In one letter, composed at 4:12 a.m. on May 8, 1904, from the Chancel-
lor Hotel in Parkersburg, West Virginia, Cabot, writing in German, tells
Minna that he just woke up from a dream in which she urinated into his
mouth and he "greedily" swallowed it. His desire for her, he writes, made
it impossible to fall back to sleep. Then he switches into English, going on about the weather and his daily activities. A second letter, dated
May, 17, 1905, from the Waldo Hotel in Clarksburg, is even more passionate, this time (again in German) combining fantasies of urination with
imaginings of his Proper Bostonian wife as "an utterly starved giantess"
who would devour him alive, an act he describes in explicit, highly erotic,
almost ecstatic detail. Switching back to English, he suggests that Minna
destroy "this silly letter." If she couldn't understand it, however, even with
the assistance of a German dictionary, he promises to translate it when he
returns home. Both letters are addressed "Dear Wife," and signed, "Your
Lover, Godfrey L. Cabot."

It is difficult to imagine how Cabot's family, who gave Harris access to un-
published papers and personal effects, reacted to these letters when Harris
included them in their entirety in his unauthorized biography published in
1967, five years after Cabot's death. Here was a man, after all, whom his
son described as "ascetic" and "puritanical." Here was a man who clung
to moral absolutes throughout his 101 years and who made a major part
of his life's work the support of an organization devoted to stamping out
even the mildest sexual references and innuendos in books and on the
stage. But perhaps fear of his own vivid sexual imagination prompted his
intense involvement with the Watch and Ward in the first place. What he
could not repress in himself, he wished to repress in others. Perhaps these

letters indicate a lack of integration of the various aspects of his personality. While it is probably not useful to attempt to psychoanalyze Cabot on the basis of these letters, it does call into question the motivations of Cabot and others in their involvement with the Watch and Ward Society and indicates that their involvement might, in some cases, represent some public way of attempting to resolve inner conflicts. Perhaps there was no inner conflict at all in Cabot's case, but at the very least, one can say that the outwardly rigid and judgmental Godfrey Lowell Cabot—the heart and soul of the Watch and Ward—had an uncommon fantasy life.

But the greatest financial benefactor of the New England Watch and Ward Society was not Godfrey Cabot, but a little-known Somerville woman named Martha R. Hunt. Miss Hunt, who died at age eighty-eight in the spring of 1910, had lived in a relatively modest house on Thurston Street, in the Winter Hill neighborhood of Somerville, since just after the Civil War. Unmarried, living alone, and with no close relatives, she suffered from an incurable spinal condition for forty years. For the last thirteen years of her life, she never stepped off the verandah of her house. Miss Hunt's father had been a leather manufacturer who died when she was eleven, leaving her the sum of $200,000. Thanks to some shrewd investments, and working without anyone's advice, she parlayed that inheritance into $920,000—an astonishing sum at the time—by investing in stocks, bonds, and gold.

In an article headlined "INVALID, ALONE, MADE FORTUNE OF $1,000,000. REMARKABLE STORY OF MISS MARTHA R. HUNT, AGED SOMERVILLE WOMAN," the *Boston Globe* described her last years in her Thurston Street home: "Lying on her back, with her feet propped up to secure bodily ease, she knitted hundreds of articles which were given by her to church fairs to be sold. . . . Her tastes were simple. She kept but two servants and an attendant. She had her house equipped with an elevator 15 years ago and used it to descend to the first floor until her ailment made such inroads as to make it impossible for her to leave her room."

Over the years, she had donated money to various community organizations, including $10,000 to help establish Somerville Hospital. She hated attention of any kind: that donation was given under the name of "A friend." But no one who knew her imagined that upon her death she would be worth such a fabulous amount of money.

When her will was filed, it was revealed that she gave $100,000 to relatives and friends and $281,000 to various public institutions, mostly in

$5,000 and $10,000 amounts. The remaining money was divided equally among five organizations: the Massachusetts Society for the Prevention of Cruelty to Children, the Massachusetts Society for the Prevention of Cruelty to Animals, the Humane Society of Massachusetts, the Hampton Normal and Agricultural Institute in Hampton, Virginia [a school to train African American teachers, attended by Booker T. Washington], and the New England Watch and Ward Society.

Suddenly the Watch and Ward was rich. Within three years—once the will was finally processed—the society possessed an endowment of $101,849, courtesy of Martha R. Hunt. Add to this some smaller bequests and special gifts that it had received over the years, and by 1913 the Watch and Ward endowment reached $112,874.09, all of it invested in reliable utility and railroad stocks and bonds. That was an extraordinary boon for an organization that had primarily survived on $5 memberships and $10 and $20 donations. Thanks in large part to income from the endowment, the yearly expenditures of the Watch and Ward were able to increase almost twofold, from $8,836 in 1911 to $15,883 in 1915. With the Hunt bequest, the Watch and Ward now had a substantial income to keep it going through lean years, or years when it ran afoul of public sentiment.

The society reported the gift in a footnote in its 1910–11 annual report. "Miss Martha R. Hunt had been a life member since 1887 and on her decease left the Society as residuary legatee a generous share of her large estate," it read. "This will give us an opportunity to do a still larger work." That modest announcement was probably how the reclusive Miss Hunt would have preferred it.

PART II

The Watch and Ward
Goes to War

CHAPTER 6

New Bedford, 1916

In HIS NOVEL *Moby Dick*, published in 1851, Herman Melville gives New Bedford, the old whaling port on the south coast of Massachusetts, a distinctly romantic flavor. To Melville, it was a city of patrician-like houses and opulent parks and gardens, a place where "fathers gave whales as dowers for their daughters" and "portioned off their nieces with a few porpoises apiece." In summertime, he wrote, "the town is sweet to see; full of fine maples—long avenues of green and gold." As for the women of New Bedford, "they bloom like their own red roses," and while roses bloomed only in summer, "the fine carnation of their cheeks is perennial as sunlight in the seventh heavens."

By the first two decades of the twentieth century, the glories of the city's whaling days were over, and Melville's vision of New Bedford—and New Bedford's women—was tarnished. The city's population continued to grow, thanks to a textile boom that employed some 30,000 people in thirty-two cotton manufacturing firms. But New Bedford had another side. In 1916, the Watch and Ward saw New Bedford as a "vice-ridden" place where immorality and gambling were flourishing on a scale greater than anywhere else in New England. "This is a beautiful city, but the conditions here with respect to the social evil [prostitution] are worse than in any city of this size in the state," said J. Frank Chase. "Our investigation here has showed that there are more open houses of prostitution in New Bedford than there are in Boston."

The Watch and Ward had tried to work with police officials there to stamp out gambling and prostitution, but to no avail. While the rank and file of the New Bedford police department were "as good as any in the state," in Chase's view, their hands were tied by law enforcement officials connected to vice interests. One crusading lieutenant in the department, he said, made frequent visits to houses of prostitution to admonish proprietors "as far as he dare[d]" and had rescued young girls who had fallen into their clutches. "That man's case is pathetic to me," Chase said. "He is a good officer and a conscientious one. He wants to do his duty but his hands are tied by the men higher up." The society decided to take matters into its own hands.

It was during this period that the Watch and Ward, flush with Martha Hunt's money and under J. Frank Chase's aggressive leadership, transformed itself into what was essentially a private police force, a vice squad of its very own. The society didn't have the ability to make arrests—it depended on either the local or state police to do that—but it could persuade a judge to grant a warrant. Armed with such warrants, it was often able to go over the heads of corrupt or complacent local authorities to crack down on gambling and prostitution, following up its detective work by leading state police or sheriff's deputies on raids. And once the United States entered World War I, it even had the authority and assistance of the federal government to do this in some cases. Its June 8, 1916, vice raid in New Bedford, a year before the United States entered the war, represented one of the most spectacular accomplishments in the society's history up to that point and provided a glimpse of what was to come over the next two years.

On a busy Saturday night, six Watch and Ward agents, led by Secretary J. Frank Chase and Assistant Secretary Jefferson Parker and accompanied by a squad of deputy sheriffs, moved with stunning force and speed against gambling joints and houses of prostitution in New Bedford. They did so without the cooperation or even the knowledge of the heads of the city's police department. The targets ranged from pool rooms, lunch carts, and variety stores, where gambling machines and baseball pool tickets were seized, to a number of "disorderly houses" where prostitution was taking place. Some fifty people were arrested that first night. "Never in the history of the city has a greater anti-vice crusade been conducted than that which stirred the center and west end last night," reported the *New Bedford Sunday Standard*. The newspaper greeted the raids with a banner headline: "50 PRISONERS IN SATURDAY NIGHT

RAIDS—BIG CLEAN UP MADE BY WATCH AND WARD—MEN AS
WELL AS WOMEN CAUGHT IN ALLEGED DISORDERLY HOUSES—
21 FOUND AT CRAP GAME—'ONLY THE BEGINNING' SAYS WATCH
AND WARD SECRETARY."

The *Sunday Standard* presented a vivid picture of the first raid of the
evening, involving a gambling parlor on the second floor of a three-story
frame structure on 7 North Second Street. Two Watch and Ward agents, as
well as operatives from the Woods Detective Agency, had been frequenting the place for a number of weeks, becoming regular patrons. That evening, shortly after nine o'clock, the raiders surrounded the building. A
Woods detective gave a secret knock on the door, and the agents pushed
inside. There, "[t]hey found themselves in an anteroom which was dark,"
the newspaper reported. "There was a pile of broken furniture in the place
and a dilapidated piano. . . . [The raiders] then burst into another room,
lighted by two incandescents. Immediately there was a wild scramble.
There were about twenty-four men in the room and as soon as they realized what was taking place, they made frantic efforts to get away." Four
of the men jumped out of the second-floor windows and fled. Others who
remained inside exchanged blows with the raiders until they were sub-
dued. All in all, twenty-one people were arrested. "The room was fitted
with a big crap table covered with green baize [felt-like covering]," wrote
the *Standard*. "The baize was worn away in spots, indicating that the outfit
had had hard usage. Several sets of dice were taken as evidence and the
crap table was also removed during the night."

A deputy sheriff who was part of the raiding party went to the central
police station to ask that a patrol wagon be sent for the prisoners. Only at
that moment did police officials learn that a major raid had taken place
in their city.

This was only the beginning. A large crowd had gathered outside the
gambling place, almost making it impossible for the raiders to move on
to their next target—a "disorderly house" kept by a woman named Sadie
Johnson, one of four such houses to be raided that night. Finally, they
were able to shake off the crowd, and within a few minutes, they were
rushing up the stairs of Johnson's establishment.

In both raids, a local man named Bernard C. Dupuis played a leading role. Dupuis had resigned as a reserve police office in New Bedford
because "he was unable to do his duty," according to the *Standard*. While
he was an officer, and through his own personal investigations after that,
Dupuis had learned a lot about both gambling and prostitution in New

Bedford. (He was most likely the crusading lieutenant that Chase had referred to.) He led four Watch and Ward raiders inside Johnson's house, where they found three men with three women in upstairs rooms. Downstairs, Johnson, only partially dressed, was apprehended in a parlor bedroom while entertaining four men—apparently most, if not all of them, "foreigners," according to the *Standard*. When the police wagon arrived, one of the patrons, Edward F. Souza, a twenty-three-year-old prizefighter of some local renown, attempted to block Dupuis's way and otherwise interfere with the arrests. Dupuis picked him up bodily and threw him into the patrol wagon.

In that raid, Mrs. Johnson was charged with illegal sale of intoxicating liquors (seventy-two bottles of beer were found on the premises); three women were arrested on charges of being idle and disorderly; four men with fornication; and three other men with being lewd, wanton, and lascivious persons. Souza, the prizefighter, was charged with interfering with a police officer.

The lack of high-level police involvement in—or even knowledge of—the raids was striking. Several months earlier, in February, a joint Watch and Ward action with the local police on the same gambling establishment had been a total failure. Someone had tipped off the gamblers: By the time the Watch and Ward agents and the police arrived, the patrons had fled and the place had been entirely cleaned out. On the night of the June raid, therefore, not a word was said to the New Bedford police higher-ups. That night, police chief Timothy C. Allen had been in his upstairs office in the police station until midnight as prisoners were being brought in. However, as the *Standard* wrote, "As far as any active participation or interest in the big raid was concerned, the chief might just as well have been at his home as at his office." When a *Standard* reporter found the police chief at midnight, alone in the dark hallway that led to his office, preparing to go home, he couldn't get New Bedford's top law enforcement official to comment at all.

"Well, chief, what do you think of the raids tonight?" the newspaperman asked him, assuming a casual tone.

"Who are you?" asked Chief Allen.

"I represent the *Sunday Standard*."

"I have nothing to say," said the chief.

When the reporter persisted, asking the chief if he was aware that such places existed in New Bedford, the chief became testy, saying, "I told you, young man, that I have nothing to say." Then he pushed his way out.

The Watch and Ward's Chase reported that he never had any contact with Chief Allen or talked to him before the raid. "To my knowledge, I have never even seen the gentleman," he said. (Chief Allen was replaced before the year was out.)

Arrests continued in the next few days. One of twelve licensed liquor dealers arrested on Watch and Ward complaints in the week following the raid was Thomas H. Kearns, proprietor of the Mansion House. He was charged with "maintaining a liquor nuisance." Kearns probably knew he was in trouble as he watched the prisoners being unloaded at the police station on the night of the raids. On that night, Kearns was mortified when he recognized two of the men who were wearing badges. They had stopped at his hotel often during the previous two months, claiming to be coffee salesmen. In reality, they were the detectives who had been inside the gambling parlor at 7 North Second Street and opened the door to let the raiding party inside.

Altogether, in the arrests of that night and in the days that followed, seventy-nine individuals were charged with various offenses, and all but two were found guilty. The Watch and Ward was very pleased with the verdicts in New Bedford Municipal Court, particularly in contrast with other courts around the state. As it noted in its 1916–17 annual report, "One leaves the court of that city with the feeling akin to having worshipped—in a 'temple of justice.'"

CHAPTER 7

The Battle of Diamond Hill, 1917–1918

In the summer of 1917, the War Department's Commission on Training Camp Activities (CTCA) appointed the Watch and Ward as its agent to keep the commission apprised of vice conditions in the vicinity of military training camps in New England. The United States had entered World War I in April of that year, and Section 13 of the Draft Act gave the Secretary of War special powers. One of them was to do everything necessary to suppress the establishment and keeping of "houses of ill fame, brothels, or bawdy houses" within "such distance as he may deem needful" of all training camps. In response, the Secretary of War established ten-mile "moral zones" around training camps throughout the country; within those zones, prostitution and alcohol were strictly prohibited.

The primary goal was to establish a military that was "fit to fight," as a CTCA training film was titled, and the enemy was not just the Germans, but venereal disease. (Penicillin, the first real cure for venereal disease, was not discovered until ten years after the war.) The Watch and Ward president, the Reverend Frederick B. Allen, explained this in an August 2, 1917, letter to Godfrey Cabot. "Their [the War Department's] desire is to eliminate all vice conditions which would render less efficient the soldiers and sailors who are to take part in the war," Allen wrote. "These vices are named as immorality, gambling, and the use of habit-forming drugs and intoxicating liquor by soldiers and sailors." All but one—liquor—had been Watch and Ward concerns over the previous ten years. "We regard our selection as an honor, and as an opportunity to do our 'bit' to assist our country in its crisis," he added.

In fact, the society had already begun to do its bit. As the United States was preparing to enter the war, newspaper reports in western Massachusetts began speculating that the area near Springfield might be used for a large military camp. The CTCA had barely been established yet, but the Watch and Ward knew where its patriotic duty lay.

On April 21, 1917, just two weeks after President Woodrow Wilson declared war on Germany, the society assembled its forces—fifteen Watch and Ward agents, two State Police officers, and four Hampden County deputy sheriffs. The staging ground was Springfield's North Congregational Church, and the targets were two houses of prostitution situated between Holyoke and West Springfield. As in the New Bedford raid the year before, local police were kept in the dark. At eleven o'clock that night, four seven-seated touring cars brought the men to the two houses, known collectively as "The Farms" and individually as "Prudy's" and "Carrie's." The raiders had the advantage of total surprise and entered the houses without opposition, revolvers drawn. There they found liquor spread out for the customers, the rooms occupied, and, in one house, two men "in flagrante delicto," in J. Frank Chase's words. One raid was led by Jefferson Parker, the other by Eben Sears, both Watch and Ward veterans. Thirty five people were arrested—including nineteen women, one of whom was the infamous "Prudy" herself. (Several were found hiding in the cellars.) All were found guilty—the women received $20 fines; two couples found having "incriminating" relations were fined an additional $25. The harshest sentences were left for the keepers of the houses, who were given two years in the House of Correction.

The Watch and Ward then brought an injunction against the owners, resulting in an agreement that the property could be used only for moral purposes in the future. "It was a clean-cut victory for decency," noted the Watch and Ward's 1917–18 annual report, "and when a few weeks later thousands of our soldiers were camped in the proximity of that property, we could rejoice at what our work had accomplished for the soldiers as well as the citizens of the three large manufacturing cities of the vicinity."

The Springfield raid was only the opening shot of the Watch and Ward's war. Three months after being anointed by the CTCA, the society had already investigated conditions in the vicinity of military and naval camps in every New England state except Vermont, giving special attention to port cities like Portland, Maine; Newport, Rhode Island; Portsmouth, New Hampshire; and New London, Connecticut. It took the moniker "The First Corps of Moral Engineers."

The largest training camp in New England was Camp Devens, a wooden barracks city of 1,100 buildings constructed on sandy hillsides and scrub-covered fields near Ayer, west of Boston. It opened in September 1917, hosting 40,000 soldiers. As the war continued, its numbers swelled to 50,000. The Watch and Ward immediately began a survey of the towns for ten miles around Devens, discovering six houses of ill repute that had been left alone by town authorities for years. Society agents raided two, and local police forces shut down the other four. The Watch and Ward announced, "We are glad to say that for a wide zone the vicinity of Camp Devens is now clean."

All this was part of a national effort. In the past, the military had resigned itself to the idea that soldiers and vice went together. But concern about venereal disease was growing, partly in the wake of the U.S. punitive expedition in which 10,000 men were sent to fight against Mexican general "Pancho" Villa in 1916. An investigation had revealed that camps of U.S. soldiers along the Mexican border were surrounded by brothels and saloons. As Allan Brandt points out in his book, No Magic Bullet, social hygienists and Progressive-era reformers were determined that U.S. participation in World War I would not be a repeat of the Villa experience. The result was the establishment of the CTCA, charged with eliminating prostitution from areas close to concentrations of soldiers and sailors.

Starting just a few weeks after the United States entered the war, the CTCA's law enforcement division sent investigators to examine conditions near training camps. Existing "purity" and anti-prostitution organizations such as the Watch and Ward were enlisted in the cause. The CTCA set up various recreational and educational programs for soldiers. Its investigators also met with various civic and political leaders and pressured judges to give prostitutes the maximum sentences. Local officials began campaigns against prostitution, particularly in cities where there were well-known—and sometimes officially recognized—"red-light districts." San Antonio and El Paso were among the first to eliminate their districts of prostitution, and in early October 1917, Charleston, South Carolina, did the same. In St. Louis, police arrested more than 1,000 women, and in California, officials closed down 300 houses of prostitution. Finally, in late 1917, New Orleans's Storyville—described by one CTCA commission investigator as the "Gibraltar of commercialized vice . . . twenty-four blocks given over to human degradation and lust" —was shut down, even though the mayor of New Orleans travelled to Washington to plead its case. (He insisted no soldiers or sailors were ever admitted.) All in all, the CTCA claimed 110 red-light districts were destroyed during the war.

For the Watch and Ward, it was an ideal situation. Always eager to shut down houses of prostitution but often lacking the resources and the cooperation of local officials, the society now had the sanction of the federal government to do so. Its anti-vice work had acquired an officially patriotic rationale. "It is generally recognized that a bad and diseased woman can do more harm than any German fleet of airplanes that has yet passed over London," wrote J. Frank Chase. "One woman of such character as effectually destroys a solider as a German gun would, and more so." As for liquor, now a focus for the society, "It is recognized today that it is the artificial stimulants that promote the Social Evil," Chase continued. "Drink must be kept away from the solider because it weakens self-control and leads to debauch and disease."

The long-sought opportunity to finally rid New England of the "social evil" had arrived. Chase, the exponent of "muscular Christianity," was determined to prove his mettle. And he was prepared, if not eager, to act beyond the restricted ten-mile limit of the training camps, when necessary. In May 1918, a year after the war began, the Watch and Ward campaign moved into a new phase.

The red-light district of Gloucester, the fishing port on Cape Ann, was the first target. On May 4, 1918, on a Saturday night when it was known that houses of prostitution would be busy (most likely with sailors and soldiers), a contingent composed of four deputy sheriffs, four Watch and Ward agents, including Chase, and several young men in the employ of the Watch and Ward arrived in the city. With the assistance of the local police, they descended on seven different houses, arresting a total of thirty people. The surprise raids caused "the wildest excitement," according to the *Gloucester Daily Times*, with two streets completely blocked and a large crowd gathering. Watch and Ward agents had been in town for some time gathering evidence. "It is also said that the society agents came here as a result of complaints that sailors and soldiers had been frequenting the houses," the newspaper reported. The newspaper noted that besides the prisoners, the officers seized "four gallons lager beer at 32 Rogers Street, one fourth gallon lager beer at 33 Rogers Street, a half pint whiskey, and half gallon lager beer at 6 Porter Street."

Two weeks later, it was New Bedford's turn again. On another Saturday night, May 18, the Watch and Ward repeated its raid of two years before. As in its previous New Bedford raid—and unlike in Gloucester—the local police were not informed and did not participate. J. Frank Chase still had little faith in their loyalty and reliability in any campaign against vice. There were nineteen Watch and Ward agents involved, led by assistant secretary Jefferson Parker, plus four deputy sheriffs. This time, unlike the raid two years before, the focus was entirely on prostitution. The agents, who had been in the city for a solid month gathering evidence, raided four different houses of ill repute, booking fourteen prisoners and "filling the wine cellar of the new police station with enough liquor to stock a fair sized barroom," according to the *New Bedford Times*.

As Chase told the newspaper a few days after the raid, "Conditions two or three weeks ago were even worse than they were when this society was here two years ago. Women of the underworld were not only allowed but encouraged to sit around in cafés and have men buy them liquor. They were also allowed to ply their trade and secure rooms in hotels. That sort of thing is going to be stopped if this society can stop it and I believe it can."

The campaign continued through the summer. Taunton, another southeastern Massachusetts city, followed, on Saturday, August 26, when Watch and Ward agents (including Chase), led by a deputy sheriff, raided a "disorderly house" in that city. The raiding party not only took five women into custody but also seized a number of letters that showed that the place had been patronized by soldiers and sailors. "Some of the men in the service have been rather indiscreet in their use of correspondence," the *Taunton Gazette* reported. At the trial two days later in district court, the prosecutor declared that at least one letter from a soldier at Camp Devens to one of the women was too filthy for him to read aloud; the judge allowed it to be admitted into evidence anyway because it showed the character of the place. One Watch and Ward investigator told the court that he had seen one of the women dressed in a "pink creation for the conservation of cloth." In summing up the case, the judge noted that the federal government was eager to close the house because of the large number of soldiers and sailors who patronized it. The day before, he said, an army major in charge of suppression of vice near camps had called him and urged him to give the women substantial sentences. This he did. The two women who ran the establishment were sentenced to three months in the House of Correction and fined $175 and $225, respectively.

The culmination of the Watch and Ward's wartime activities—and one of the most dramatic episodes in its history—came two months later, in a raid of a "house of shame" on Diamond Hill Road in Cumberland, Rhode Island, just over the Massachusetts border. The war was nearing its end, with the Providence Journal proclaiming, "ACCEPTANCE OF ALLIES ARMISTICE CONDITIONS BELIEVED CLOSE." For some time, the Watch and Ward had been aware of the goings-on at two houses of prostitution outside Woonsocket, Rhode Island (a city characterized in the society's annual report of 1918 as "a largely foreign mill town," an apparent reference to its large French-Canadian population). The Rhode Island establishments, easily accessible from the army base at Camp Devens and from a rest camp at Framingham, where some 3,500 Navy personnel were in residence, were a popular destination for servicemen.

Three Watch and Ward agents, plus Secretary Chase, had visited the houses on a Saturday night in October and found them to be of "a most vicious character," as Chase wrote in his account of the incident. On that exploratory visit, they found forty-seven men lined up at the entrance to one of the houses; seven young women were inside, offering sexual favors to the men. In talking to the men in line, the agents learned that some were solders from Camp Devens and sailors from Framingham. At the second house, two agents went inside, where they witnessed the sale of liquor and men heading upstairs with women.

After that initial visit, Chase met with Department of Justice authorities in Providence and persuaded them to act, even though the houses were beyond the ten-mile "moral zone" around military bases. The Department of Justice agreed to inspect the two houses officially on the next Saturday night. They would not be alone.

On that night, October 26, 1918, the Watch and Ward Society and the Provost Guard of Camp Devens were on high alert. The leader of the raids was Lieutenant Hannibal Hamlin, a direct descendent and namesake of Abraham Lincoln's first vice president and the commander of a special squad of the military police. On the night of the raids, Hamlin and his troops went to the first of the two houses, in East Woonsocket, but left after finding that there were no soldiers or sailors present. But at the old Staples roadhouse on Diamond Hill Road in Cumberland, it was a different story.

When Hamlin arrived at Diamond Hill that evening, he found that his Provost Guard, six Department of Justice agents, four U.S. marshals, and ten agents of the Watch and Ward Society had taken cover behind automobiles and trees. The situation had gotten out of hand already. "Lieutenant, the people in the house have fired upon us," his sergeant informed him gravely. "Already a Watch and Ward man has been shot!" Indeed, Watch and Ward agent C. F. Caswell of Lynn was nursing a wound in his leg. Some Department of Justice agents were inside the building, from which more shots had been heard. Immediately Hamlin ordered his men, revolvers drawn, to surround the building. "Surrender in the name of the President of the United States or I will burn the house down!" he bellowed. Those words were followed by a volley of gunfire from inside.

Once Hamlin issued his surrender order, customers of the house began jumping out the windows, pursued by soldiers and government officials. Hamlin, with another group, moved along the side of the house until he came to a rear window. He lifted the blinds from their hinges with the butt of his pistol, tore a curtain, and thrust his pistol through the window, shouting, "All hands up!" The occupants of the room pleaded for mercy. "Send that man down with the shotgun or I will burn the house," Hamlin insisted. When nothing happened, Hamlin pulled a torch from his coat pocket and tossed it at one of his officers. The soldier ignited the torch, which lit up the yard as if it were midday.

Soon enough, the lieutenant and his men broke open the front door and rushed into the house. They went through the rooms, training their revolvers on everyone. Hamlin seized a man who was holding a shotgun and turned him over to the deputy marshal. Then fifty customers were marched outside, with their hands over their heads, into the glare of automobile lights. The raiding party headed back inside and found "seven girls still dressed in the garb of their profession, some hysterical, some defiant," in Chase's words. A woman was found in one of the rooms, gasping for breath, apparently suffering from pneumonia. The gallant Hamlin telephoned for an ambulance to transport her to the hospital.

To Chase, it was all "a pitiable sight," with women crying and male patrons looking dejected. The front room of the first floor was filled with gambling implements, and the pantry was well stocked with cases of liquor, empty bottles, and glasses.

Shortly afterwards, several touring cars and a police ambulance arrived to take the prisoners to the Woonsocket police station. The Watch and Ward agents had not notified the police in Woonsocket, Cumberland, or the surrounding towns in advance of what was happening out of fear that they might compromise the raid; as in New Bedford, the police were just not deemed sufficiently trustworthy. It was only when Hamlin telephoned for an ambulance that the local police realized what had occurred.

Forty men were taken to the Woonsocket police station, but some were released after showing their draft cards. Twenty-five were kept overnight for further questioning. But despite all the concern about military personnel frequenting the establishment, only one soldier was apprehended; he was sent back to Camp Devens under guard. (Others may have escaped during the melee, and the Providence and Boston newspapers claimed that 150 persons were actually in the building when the raid began.) The next morning, six women and two men were arraigned in Providence. The men, including Lester Staples, the owner of the house, were charged with resisting government officers, and the women were charged with violating the Mann Act, which banned the transport of women across state lines for "immoral" purposes.

The Watch and Ward was pleased at the outcome. "More deadly enemies than Huns [Germans] were in that House, the spreaders of diseases which maim as effectively as German machine guns," wrote J. Frank Chase. Two weeks later, the armistice was declared.

CHAPTER 8

Café Society, 1917–1919

In BOSTON ITSELF, the crusade against the "social evil" took a different tack, before and during the war. Unlike in cities like Gloucester and New Bedford, in Boston proper the traditional house of prostitution had largely vanished, replaced by cafés where women solicited men for sex. This development occurred largely because of Watch and Ward pressure. The Boston Licensing Commission had enacted a regulation in May 1915 that prohibited male patrons from entering a public room where liquor was sold and where women were allowed, unless the man was accompanied by a woman. The purpose was to reduce solicitation. But the law wasn't being enforced, and Watch and Ward president Frederick B. Allen called for partitions in such cafés to separate men and women. "There must not be places where men and women are openly and defiantly induced to lead lives of shame," Allen said. (This idea was later instituted.)

One way or another, the Watch and Ward was determined to put a stop to this activity. In the spring of 1916, the society hired a number of Harvard and Tufts medical students—at $3 a day and $5 a week—to enter these cafés in the guise of regular patrons and secure evidence of solicitation. As a result, some forty-one women were arrested and charged.

These were the kind of tactics that J. Frank Chase thrived on. But in this situation, they caused a major backlash. As the arrests were going on, in late March of that year, a group of several hundred people—"all apparent sympathizers of the women whom the society is prosecuting," in the words of the *Boston Globe*—chased agent Jefferson Parker and ten Harvard students working for him from Bowdoin Square through Tremont Row and Scollay Square. The pursuers shouted obscenities and threats and hurled objects at them. The noise of the mob attracted the attention of police officers, who spirited the Watch and Ward men to safety at the District 2 police headquarters. A week later, at the Pemberton Square courthouse where some of the women were on trial, angry spectators set upon a plainclothes police officer, whom they mistook for a Watch and Ward "spotter." The officer wound up with a black eye.

But anger against the Watch and Ward came not just from "sympathizers" of arrested women. Judge Thomas H. Dowd, who presided over the trials of a number of the women, denounced the use of college and medical students as informers. "I do not consider it proper practice to put men through college and later expose them to immoral cesspools," he said.

At the trial of one of the alleged prostitutes, her attorney, former assistant district attorney Thomas Lavelle, told Judge Dowd that when he was a prosecutor, he had found some Watch and Ward agents to be "vicious little rats." After the judge ordered that comment stricken from the record, Lavelle went on: "The Watch and Ward Society agents are in the business of making crime in order to justify their narrow-minded efforts to suppress crime." He also got Watch and Ward agent Parker on the stand to admit a "secret"—that the Watch and Ward used fictitious names on all forty-one warrants, matching the first letter of each girl's pseudonym with the first letter of a café where such activity was going on ("Fanny" for the Florence Hotel Café, etc.). Lavelle argued that no court should issue a warrant unless the identity of the arrested person could be accurately established. If not, he demanded to know, what would prevent any girl from being arrested by these agents? The Watch and Ward could just adjust the warrant to arrest anyone it wanted.

The Watch and Ward was not accustomed to this kind of criticism. At the very least, it represented a public relations blunder, especially coming on the heels of J. Frank Chase's guilty plea after slugging attorney John J. Cronin the year before. As a result, the board of directors was forced to issue an unusual statement defending the society's tactics. Not only were the cafés "openly allied" with immorality and "white slavery," according to the statement, but a system of "cadets" ("pimps," in today's terminology) "who live personally upon the shame of these poor women" had been created, and "some of this class of men were in the gangs who

recently attacked our witnesses and later, by mistake, a police officer."
The society also defended the use of students as informers in prostitution
cases, noting that none of them were younger than twenty-four years of
age, while state police recruits needed only to be twenty-one.

At the society's annual public meeting, held on March 29, 1916, just a
day after the mob set upon agent Parker and the Harvard students, Professor William T. Sedgwick of MIT lavished praise on these young men. "In
a time of war," he said, "spies and informers are heroes to those whom
they are protecting and to whom they are bringing information, and the
work that this society is doing is a kind of war: It is a war upon evil."

Once the United States entered World War I the following year, the Watch
and Ward, in its official capacity as an agent of the CTCA, took it upon
itself to investigate Boston cafés again, this time sending reports of immoral activity to Washington. As a result, the federal government ordered
that twenty-five Boston cafés be segregated by sex. But this had only a limited effect, as demonstrated by a Watch and Ward report of February 4,
1918. In the report, an agent, referred to only as #1, relates that he entered
the Florence Hotel Café in the North End, a café with two sections and
two entrances, about 9:35 p.m. On his way to the toilet, located on the
women's side of the café, he was beckoned by two women. Even when
the agent was seated, he could see three other women through the lattice
dividing the two sections. One of them signaled persistently to him and
twice went to the women's toilet to solicit the agent in plain sight. Each
time she invited him to go "upstairs."

At 10:00 p.m., the bar was closed, the lights were shut off, and young
women lined up along the walls and stairs, soliciting men to go upstairs
and grabbing at their hands, arms, and coats. The very persistent one
shook her fist in the agent's face, saying laughingly, "I could kill you; now
let's go upstairs. Come on."

Referring to himself in the third person, Agent #1's report contin-
ues, "Agent tried to talk with her and draw her on but there was so much
pulling, shoving, bickering, and confusion that it was impossible, with
the result that after a number of the girls pulling and soliciting agent,
he reached Fleet Street, with the persistent one still pulling at his arm.
Several couples were going upstairs and this girl said to agent, 'Come on
now, he's shutting the doors.' Then she said to the janitor, 'Here let that
man in. He's going upstairs with me.'"

The report, signed by J. Frank Chase, never indicated whether Agent #1 actually went upstairs with the "persistent" young woman.

Within a few months, however, there was little need for these kinds of tactics. For after a conference of civil and military authorities, mass arrests to eradicate prostitution began to take place on the streets of Boston. On June 11, 1918, thirty-four women were arrested and taken into custody for being idle and disorderly. The following day, sixty-one more were arrested, with the police promising to arrest what the Boston Globe called "streetcorner loafers, many of whom are secretly allied with the women."

The following night, June 13, saw the arrest of thirty-three women and eleven men in just half an hour. The Globe reported that the reduction in the number of women arrested was due to the realization on the part of the "undesirables" that the streets of Boston were too dangerous. "It is understood that several women of the underworld have fled to other cities and towns, where they will remain until the Boston crusade dies out," the newspaper noted. Some of the men arrested were believed to live off the earnings of these women. In other cases, arrests included presumably homosexual men, perhaps male prostitutes or men just caught up in the sweep. Six of them, the Globe reported, "were found acting in a decidedly effeminate manner. When brought into the station house, such things were found as powder puffs and vanity cases and an intense aroma of perfumery was noticeable."

Clearly something larger than the usual vice raids was occurring. Military police were stopping soldiers and sailors in the company of prostitutes and sometimes in the company of "charity girls," as they were called—young women who were not hardened prostitutes but instead were swept off their feet at the "charm and glamour" of a uniform, in the words of CTCA social worker. Anyone—female or male—in the company of military personnel risked arrest or worse. "Courts, prosecuting attorneys, Army and Navy officials, and local Boards of Health are severally active in efforts to rid the city of immoral women and questionable men, who are endangering the lives, health, and morals of soldiers and sailors," the Globe reported. Meanwhile, District Attorney Joseph Pelletier was promising that women on the street would be dealt with "severely" and that he would recommend prison sentences.

In the next several days, another fifty-four people were arrested, although the numbers dwindled each night, indicating that the dragnet had been effective at least in driving women off the street. In courtrooms, with naval and military authorities present, sentences varied: Some women who had previous arrest records were sentenced to the House of Correction at Sherborn; others were detained pending investigation (and perhaps quarantined for venereal disease) or released. One woman, known for soliciting men in uniform from the window of her house, was sentenced to an indefinite term at the State Farm at Bridgewater.

In early fall, some 500 members of the Boston, Cambridge, and Park police forces were brought to the Boston City Club to view the War Department's anti-VD film, Fit to Fight. Various military and health officials made speeches encouraging the officers to assist the crusade against venereal disease among the civilian population. Major R. W. Pullman of the Washington, D.C., police told the officers that cleaning up a city was like polishing a brass rod. "When you have got the rod nice and bright, you must polish it every day to keep it shining," he said.

Perhaps the most highly publicized Watch and Ward action in the city of Boston during the war was its campaign against the Revere House. Located in Bowdoin Square at the bottom of the north side of Beacon Hill, this hotel with imposing Corinthian columns was one of Boston's most famous. When it first opened in 1847, it represented what the Boston Globe called "the last word in elegance in its day," featuring marble floors, velvet upholstery, and accommodation for 250 guests. Over the years, guests had ranged from President Ulysses S. Grant to the Prince of Wales to the emperor of Brazil; Daniel Webster had lived there during the last five years of his life, supposedly bellowing constitutional principles from the balcony above the hotel portico. By 1917 and 1918, its proprietors included a number of men prominent in Boston business and financial circles, including its treasurer, George U. Crocker, a former city treasurer of Boston.

To the Watch and Ward Society, however, the hotel was anything but respectable. In late 1917, under a relatively new and untested state law dubbed the "Red Light Law," the society instituted a lawsuit for an injunction against the Revere House on the grounds that the hotel was used for purposes of "prostitution, assignation, and lewdness." The suit sought an end to such activity and to have the building closed for one year.

Crocker quickly denounced the suit, claiming it was simply the result of vindictiveness. "The whole business is this man [J. Frank] Chase's attempt to repay a personal grudge against me," he asserted. "I had to show him up a few years ago and I suppose he has never forgotten it. The attack on the Revere House is a means of reaching me."

But the Watch and Ward had substantial evidence, and much of it emerged in the hearing before a judge in the equity session of Superior Court that began on January 8, 1918. In his testimony, Watch and Ward agent Nicholas Cockinos testified to solicitation taking place in the hotel café, of hotel rooms being occupied three, four, and five times a night by various couples, and of fifteen-year-old girls going to different rooms. Cockinos knew all this because he had taken a room at the Revere House for an entire month, along with another agent and a stenographer. Cockinos had placed a dictagraph—an early eavesdropping device that was a precursor to the tape recorder—in adjoining rooms. He also stood on the radiator in the hallway and looked over the transom at what was going on in various rooms and bored holes through the doors of two others. In the downstairs café, the agent claimed he was solicited by nine women and that intoxicated soldiers and sailors fraternized with women there. A chambermaid who had worked in the hotel for ten years backed up his testimony, as did a white-haired widow who had worked at the hotel for seven months. The day after his testimony, Cockinos created a bit of a stir when he was banned from the courtroom for carrying a revolver.

When the defense made its case, one of the witnesses was Morris Rosenberg, aged twenty-three, who said he had been offered a position with the Watch and Ward to "frame up" the Revere House. Another former Watch and Ward agent claimed that Chase told him it was his life's ambition to close down the hotel. Chase had asked him to steal the registry of the Revere House and to photograph it, he claimed, an allegation that Chase denied on the witness stand.

In the end, because of challenges by the defendants to the constitutionality of the new law, it took almost a year for the judge to announce his decision. On March 22, 1919, he issued a decree contending that the Revere House derived a considerable portion of its revenue from immoral activities. The downstairs café, he stated, was used for "immoral bargaining," and the rooms on the third floor of the hotel were used almost continuously for immoral purposes.

This decree sealed the fate of the Revere House. By June of that year, the famous hotel was turned over to an auctioneer and stripped of its valuables. Oil paintings, furnishings, and gold-plate and silver-plate items were sold; secondhand dealers and lodging housekeepers squabbled over the price of mattresses. The *Boston Globe* noted that among the contents sold were the rosewood bed on which the Prince of Wales had slept, the mirrors before which opera singer Jenny Lind had made her toilet, and "the cabinet with the secret drawer in which perhaps Duke Alexis [of Russia] or King Kalakaua [of Hawaii] had their valuables." In the August 31 classified pages of the newspaper, the American Building Wrecking Company advertised a number of remnants from the Revere House for sale: a revolving door "in good condition," a passenger elevator, a beautiful garden fountain, and fifty enameled lavatories, among other valuables. So the Revere House passed into history.

CHAPTER 9

Corruption Fighters, 1913–1924

As with so much in which the Watch and Ward involved itself, the story started with sex or, more accurately in this case, sexual abuse. Sometime in 1913, an unmarried woman of twenty-nine went to see a Boston physician complaining of a variety of nervous ailments, including insomnia, depression, and anxiety. The physician had a reputation of curing women who suffered from similar complaints. His "treatment" began with neck rubs and massages and developed into sexual relations. If she remained a virgin, he warned her, there was a strong chance her condition could progress to full-blown insanity. There were also the inevitable declarations of love. The doctor, a white-haired man with a close-cropped mustache, claimed that he was a Harvard graduate and a former Texas cowboy.

One day, in the doctor's waiting room, the woman in question started talking with another female patient—apparently, the doctor's office had made the mistake of scheduling the two at the same time, and the doctor happened to be late that day. In utter disbelief, she learned that both had received the identical "treatment."

The woman was devastated and fled the waiting room. She related her story to one of the most well known medical practitioners in Boston, Dr. Richard Cabot. Dr. Cabot realized that this was more than just a medical problem. "I want you to go and talk to my cousin Godfrey," he told her, referring to Godfrey Cabot, the treasurer of the Watch and Ward Society. And so she did.

Godfrey Cabot was so outraged by her story that he went to see Joseph Pelletier. Pelletier, who had been elected district attorney of Suffolk County in 1909, was a popular figure with both Democrats and Republicans in the state legislature, an ally of Mayor James Michael Curley and a leading figure in the Knights of Columbus, the national Catholic fraternal organization. The meeting did not go as Cabot had hoped. According to Cabot, Pelletier treated the entire matter as a joke, even expressing admiration for the physician's wiles. Shortly after his conversation with Cabot, the district attorney called the doctor into his office, and the man disappeared from Boston, presumably forever.

Now Pelletier became the object of Cabot's rage. Perhaps his own sexually conflicted nature had made Cabot particularly rabid on the subject, but the Watch and Ward stalwart was absolutely convinced that, by refusing to take the woman's complaints seriously and prosecute the doctor, Pelletier had demonstrated his unfitness to hold office. Cabot was determined to oust him as district attorney—no matter how long it took, no matter what the cost. That would not be easy. Pelletier was a powerful person, in an extremely powerful position, with a sharp tongue and influential allies.

Suddenly, Cabot and the Watch and Ward found themselves in a new role—as fighters against political corruption. It was the heyday of James Michael Curley, the colorful mayor of Boston, first elected in 1914. Curley was the "mayor of the poor" who enriched himself at the public's expense and was loved by many and hated by more than a few. During this time, tension and division between the city's Protestant elites and Irish working class reached its height—tension and division largely stoked by Curley. And in the Watch and Ward's descent into the rough-and-tumble world of Boston politics, the organization found itself in the middle of ethnic conflict.

As Cabot soon discovered, Pelletier's inaction in the woman's case was only the proverbial tip of the iceberg. Pelletier and his Cambridge counterpart, Middlesex County district attorney Nathan A. Tufts (as well as Tufts's predecessor, William A. Corcoran), were engaged in an extortion ring that involved the blackmail of well-heeled Bostonians, among others. In this, they worked in league with a Boston lawyer named Daniel Coakley. If Pelletier was a French-Irish Democrat, devoted to the Catholic Church and the Knights of Columbus, Tufts was his sociological opposite—a *Mayflower*-descended Republican and former Brown University football player who had a "second career" officiating at college football games. As for Coakley, he was a self-made man: a former teamster, Boston Elevated Railway Company conductor, and newspaper reporter who started out as a personal-injury lawyer and quickly became the ultimate "fixer" and sometime lawyer for Curley himself. "When Coakley waved his wand over the two district attorneys' offices, indictments vanished, prosecutions were stopped in their tracks," wrote Francis Russell in *The Knave of Boston*, his profile of Coakley. "A call from Coakley's office, a quick conference and charges of larceny, fraud, theft, practicing medicine without a license, abortions, adultery, assault, receiving stolen goods, running a disorderly house, vanished from the files like snow in April."

In what was known as the "badger game," Coakley employed various women who would lure a gentleman of means into a hotel bedroom. Shortly thereafter, there would be a knock on the door and the arrival of either detectives or the supposed husband (or father) of the woman. Soon enough, someone would refer the gentleman (and, in most cases, his attorney) to Dan Coakley. "Dapper Dan," as he was known, would inform them that, for a substantial fee, he would contact either the Suffolk or Middlesex district attorney—depending in whose jurisdiction the offense had occurred—and get the charges dropped.

Probably the most notorious example of this kind of blackmail was the Mishawum Manor case. On the evening of March 6, 1917, Paramount Pictures gave a dinner for silent film comedian Roscoe "Fatty" Arbuckle at Boston's Copley Plaza Hotel. Paramount executives Adolf Zukor, Hiram Abrams, and Jesse Lasky attended, as did Paramount theater owners from all over New England. Arbuckle and his wife retired to their room shortly after the dinner. At that point, a group of some fifteen or so of the guests decamped for the Boston suburb of Woburn, where Abrams had arranged a chicken-and-champagne party at a roadhouse called the Mishawum Manor. The establishment was essentially a "house of ill fame" whose proprietor was a woman known at various times as Brownie Kennedy, Lillian Kingston, Stella Webber, Helen Morse, Lillian Dale, and Stella Kennedy.

Soon after the guests arrived, a huge silver tray found its way to the center of the room. Its cover was removed, and out jumped a voluptuous young woman, wearing only "a few small pieces of parsley and a sprinkling of salad dressing," as David Yallop described it in his book about

Arbuckle called *The Day the Laughter Stopped*. A few moments later, fourteen other young women, "wearing only inviting smiles," sauntered into the room. The party—or, more accurately, the orgy—ended at 4:00 a.m.

Two months later, on a visit to his hometown of Portland, Maine, Abrams received a telephone call from Mayor Curley, advising him to come to a meeting. There, Curley and Coakley warned him that the Mishawum Manor affair was being investigated by Nathan Tufts, the newly elected Middlesex County district attorney. They informed Abrams that some of the women in attendance were under the age of consent, while in the case of others, their "husbands" were threatening to bring an alienation-of-affection suit against the Paramount executives. Brownie Kennedy had already been arrested after a raid a few days later. (After this conversation, Curley seems to have had no further role in the matter.) Coakley arranged a meeting with Tufts, who lambasted Abrams and his cronies as "licentious Jews" who had besmirched the reputation of an upright Boston suburban town (one that, four years before, had banned all movies as corrupting). In the end, $100,000 made its way from the Hollywood magnates to Coakley, supposedly to silence those outraged husbands. On the day the money was paid, Tufts cancelled a grand jury summons issued to the counsel for the motion picture executives. The case vanished.

Not all these "shakedowns"—and there were many of them—involved sexual indiscretions. For instance, in 1916, Coakley informed a lawyer for the Emerson Motors Corporation that Pelletier had begun investigating the company's advertising of its stock. There was reason to investigate: Emerson advertised ownership of a four-story brick factory in Long Island City, New York, and promised to produce 500 cars the following year; in reality, however, its headquarters was a tiny office in that building, littered with auto chassis and spare parts and with just a single car assembled. The lawyer gave Coakley a $500 retainer with the understanding that another $20,000 would be paid when the investigation stopped. Thirty-six hours after Coakley received his money, Pelletier's investigation of Emerson Motors came to an abrupt halt. No prosecution ever took place, and before too long, $5,000 suspiciously moved from Coakley's to Pelletier's account.

Into this world of greed and intrigue, enter the incorruptible moralist, Godfrey Cabot. Cabot was a highly successful businessman, he came from one of Boston's most distinguished families, and he helped keep the Watch and Ward afloat, but in the treacherous world of Boston politics, he was a relative novice. Nonetheless, after that fateful meeting with

Pelletier about the lascivious doctor, Cabot began a relentless—some might say, obsessive—pursuit of Pelletier and Coakley, spending as much as $100,000 of his own money over a period of several years. Although his investigation was not officially a Watch and Ward operation, he used Watch and Ward resources, including some of the organization's agents. He hired detectives who shadowed Pelletier, standing guard outside the district attorney's home and following him to New York and Chicago.

In the winter of 1916, Cabot and the Reverend Frederick B. Allen, the Watch and Ward president, persuaded two legislators to introduce a bill in the Massachusetts Senate, demanding an investigation of the Suffolk district attorney's office. Pelletier pushed back, charging that one of the legislators had defended the Birth Control League in court. "The same man introduced legislation for the inspection of convents," he asserted. After a single hearing, the investigation died. In December 1917, Cabot and Allen filed a petition for the impeachment of Pelletier with the Supreme Judicial Court, charging the district attorney with negligence in prosecution. But the chief justice rejected it out of hand.

Cabot subsequently persuaded the Boston Bar Association, an elite group of mostly Yankee lawyers, to initiate what became a three-year investigation of Pelletier, Coakley, Tufts, and Tufts's predecessor, William Corcoran.

In the meantime, Pelletier and Coakley tried to trap Cabot with a prostitute. She telephoned him, saying that she would give him the "goods" on Pelletier if he would pay her a visit; but the upright Cabot did not fall for this ploy.

Cabot became convinced that by taking on such influential people, he was putting his own life in danger. After the Supreme Judicial Court rejected his petition to oust Pelletier, Cabot instructed the executors of his will, in the event of his death, to use $30,000 from his estate to continue the investigation.

Then Cabot made his most daring move. In November 1917, perhaps anticipating that the Supreme Judicial Court decision might go against him, he had a dictagraph installed in a closet in Pelletier's office at Barrister's Hall, where some of Boston's best-known law firms were located. Cabot's agent, disguised as an electrician, concealed it behind a pile of papers at the top of Pelletier's clothes closet and connected it by a thin silk wire through various conduits to nearby rooms, where two stenographers wrote down in longhand what they heard.

The dictagraph remained in Pelletier's closet for nineteen months until the outraged district attorney discovered it, had it removed, and made the knowledge public. In a statement, Pelletier denounced "spies of the Watch and Ward Society" who, he said, were responsible for "one of the most dastardly attempts to subvert the course of law and violate all sense of decency that has ever come to light in Massachusetts." Since the winter of 1916, he fumed, he had been "the object of the most active and virulent attack and opposition of the Rev. Frederick B. Allen and Godfrey Cabot, president and treasurer respectively of the Watch and Ward Society." Pelletier claimed that the origin of this persecution lay in his refusal to prosecute complaints that Watch and Ward had made in "sting operations" for which the society had hired Harvard and Tufts students to solicit prostitutes. "I have consistently refused to exploit the innocent or the unfortunate derelict to bolster up Watch and Ward cases," he stated. "Because of this attitude on my part, these men were determined to put their own man in the office of district attorney."

Pelletier's emphasis on the Watch and Ward's role indicates that the organization was becoming a convenient whipping boy for certain politicians, particularly in the wake of public disapproval of some of J. Frank Chase's more audacious operations. The society was viewed by many as the symbol of Brahmin arrogance as ethnic tensions between the Irish majority and the Yankee elite grew, in large part exacerbated by Mayor Curley's battles with the reformist, Yankee-dominated Good Government Association (or "Goo-Goos," as Curley disparagingly referred to them). Pelletier and Curley shared an identical political base—the Irish Catholic voters of Boston—and blaming the Watch and Ward played well with their supporters, stoking fears and perceptions that the Irish were under siege from moneyed old-line Protestant interests. (Despite his French surname, Pelletier, who had an Irish mother, was thoroughly part of the world of Irish Catholic Boston.)

Pelletier was determined to counterattack and he did so, when it was revealed that Cabot had planted a detective as an employee in the office of attorney Dan Coakley. The detective—paid $70 a week by Cabot and $30 a week by Coakley—had stolen various incriminating documents from Coakley's office that linked Coakley and Pelletier to the shakedown of Hollis Hunnewell, the scion of a wealthy Wellesley family, who had kept a mistress. The papers turned up at a hearing before the Bar Association, investigating Pelletier and Coakley.

Soon enough, Cabot, along with two of his attorneys, found themselves charged with larceny in a sensational trial that riveted Boston through the fall of 1920. During the trial, one Cabot employee was revealed to be a double agent for Coakley and testified for the prosecution. Midway through the trial, Coakley paid for a front-page display advertisement in several Boston newspapers headlined "HUNNEWELL MYTH EXPLODED."

In the advertisement, Coakley lauded Pelletier as "the leading Catholic layman in Massachusetts," adding, "Despite this (or should one say because of it), Mr. Godfrey L. Cabot of the Watch and Ward Society boasts that he has spent $100,000 in his campaign and has arranged by will after his death to perpetuate the pursuit of the District Attorney." Coakley claimed that he, himself, was the victim of "the bigoted pack now yelping at my heels." This was a misstep on Coakley's part. As a result of the ad, with its allegations of anti-Catholic prejudice, the judge declared a mistrial. In January 1921, Cabot and the other defendants were acquitted on a technicality.

It was a narrow escape for Cabot, but in fact the noose was tightening around Pelletier and Coakley, not Cabot. The Boston Bar Association was continuing its investigation, and several months after Cabot's acquittal, Massachusetts Attorney General J. Weston Allen filed petitions to have Tufts and Pelletier removed from office and Coakley and former Middlesex district attorney Corcoran disbarred. As indication of the momentous nature of these cases, the attorney general announced that the trials of Tufts and Pelletier would take place before the five justices of the Massachusetts Supreme Judicial Court. The justices would serve as judge and jury, and there could be no appeal, except to the U.S. Supreme Court. (Although these were to be conducted like criminal trials, the defendants would not face prison sentences, only removal from office. Any harsher penalties could be decided in a later trial.) It was the first time in sixty years that the Supreme Judicial Court had ever presided over a trial. Allen would be the prosecutor. The spectacle of two major district attorneys facing ouster and probable disbarment was unprecedented, and the national media rushed to cover it. "Altogether the situation is providing a thriller the like of which has not been unreeled for Boston's benefit since the police strike of 1919," wrote Arthur Warner in the Nation magazine.

Tufts's trial took place first, perhaps because he was the only non-Catholic of the four, and the Yankee Attorney General Allen, who was prosecuting the case, was concerned that religious tensions might taint the cases. Allen was also a Republican, as was Tufts, lending more cre-

dence to the attorney general's objectivity. The evidence was damn-
ing—the Mishawum Manor case was just one of many charges against
the Middlesex district attorney. Still, Tufts received some sympathy. As
Warner noted, "There are a good many who think he was rather a victim
of the hold-up trust than a leader or a beneficiary of it; but even the charitable admit, as one of them put it, that he was 'a little more than careless.'" After a five-week trial, he was convicted of "willful misconduct"
in office and ousted as district attorney.

Tufts received the news stoically. On the day he learned of his removal from office, October 1, the district attorney was officiating at a
football game between Princeton and Swarthmore in Princeton, New
Jersey. "Mr. Tufts had been carrying out his duties as referee with the
utmost strictness, imposing heavy penalties on both teams," reported
the Boston Globe, "and was just leaving the field at the end of the first half
when he was handed the telegram. At the beginning of the next half, he
returned to the field and carried out his official duties as strictly as in the
first period." Refusing to answer any questions, he got into his car and
returned to Boston.

Pelletier had his own singular strategy for dealing with the threat of
removal from office. In a move that stunned the public and the prosecu-
tors, he announced that he would run for mayor of Boston in the upcom-
ing election slated for December 13, 1921, just a week before his trial was
to take place. The idea was for him to be elected mayor and then resign as
district attorney, therefore avoiding the legal scrutiny and public humili-
ation of his trial, which in his view would be moot since he was already
leaving office. In the campaign, he played the ethnic populist card to
the hilt, declaring the election a battle between "new bloods" and "blue
bloods" to decide "whether the classes or the masses will rule." In his
speech announcing his candidacy, Pelletier blamed all his troubles on the
city's elites and reformers, singling out the Watch and Ward Society, the
Boston Bar Association, and the Good Government Association.

But Pelletier's candidacy faced problems. One was that his erstwhile
ally, former mayor James M. Curley, was also running, and the two of
them threatened to split the ethnic populist vote and elect the candidate
of the reform faction. The other was the spate of negative publicity in
advance of Pelletier's trial. As Curley biographer Jack Beatty notes, Godfrey Cabot and the investigation he sponsored turned out to be Curley's
"secret weapon" in the campaign. In the end, Pelletier took himself out

of the race, dramatically throwing his support to Curley, on December 2, just minutes before the deadline for a candidate to remove himself from the ballot.

Pelletier's trial, described by the Boston Globe as "the most sensational trial in the recent annals of the history of the Massachusetts judiciary" began a little more than three weeks later. The twenty-one counts included the Emerson Motors case. His defense attorney was Senator James A. Reed of Missouri, who was known for his oratorical brilliance. Pelletier did not take the stand in his own defense, despite promises that he would do so. Toward the end of the trial, former Middlesex district attorney William J. Corcoran turned state's evidence and confessed to three of the counts on which he was listed as a co-conspirator with Pelletier.

In his final summing up, Attorney General Allen compared Pelletier to Macbeth and the biblical Esau. "The sword of justice was placed in his hands and he has made of it a highwayman's club," Allen told the court. "He has used the scales of justice to weigh the price of corrupt favors." In his four-hour defense summation, the silver-haired (and silver-tongued) Senator Reed suggested that anti-Catholic prejudice and a Watch and Ward vendetta were to blame for the entire business. He cited Pelletier's exemplary role as a national leader of the Knights of Columbus and noted that Pope Benedict XV had named him a knight of the Order of Saint Gregory, a major honor. "Does this diabolic prosecution spring from religious prejudice? Is that the thing that inspires Cabot and his crew, that makes them gather witnesses from the four quarters of the earth?" he demanded. "But this I boldly say, that I have never seen in all my life such digging in the catacombs of the past, such raking of the dust of time, such malicious ingenuity, such fixed determination; and as I have witnessed the scene, I have thought of a story I once read of a gallant steed, high-headed, flashing-eyed, proud of soul, and a lizard fastened his crooked teeth into his flank and there hung on until, at last, the glorious steed, whose feet had spurned the desert sands, whose nostrils had drunk in the breath of morning, was dragged down to death. I thank the Court."

Reed's fondness for metaphor could not save Pelletier. The district attorney was found guilty of ten of the twenty-one counts and removed from his post. The court concluded that he used the processes of law "as instruments of oppression in an attempt to wrest money from the blameless and the aged." In May of that year, he was disbarred—as were Tufts,

Coakley, and Corcoran, as well—and in June 1922, Pelletier resigned as the Supreme Advocate of his beloved Knights of Columbus.

But Pelletier refused to give up. That fall, he ran for district attorney again, even though he had been disbarred. After sweeping the Democratic primary by a two-to-one vote, he lost in the general election. The drama continued when rumors flew that he was dying of diabetes and traveling to Europe for treatment. He still faced possible jail time, however, as reports circulated of the likelihood of a Middlesex County grand jury indictment. In March 1924, newspapers reported that Pelletier was ill with pneumonia; a week later he was dead. Many believed that he actually had committed suicide rather than face going to prison.

The disbarred Coakley, for his part, lived to fight another day, serving in the 1930s as the most influential member of the powerful governor's council, which had control over many appointments and pardons. He was eventually impeached, after persuading the governor to sign a petition for the release of future New England Mafia boss Raymond Patriarca from prison. In his petition for a pardon for him, Coakley had described the notorious Patriarca as "a virtuous young man eager to be released from prison so that he might go home to his mother."

As for Tufts, he entered the hotel business in 1932 and managed three New York City hotels until his death twenty years later. His obituary in the *New York Times* noted that he had been well known as a football referee but never mentioned that he had been the district attorney of Middlesex County.

Godfrey Cabot was prouder of the ouster of Pelletier and Tufts and the disbarment of Coakley than of any of his other accomplishments, according to his biographer, Leon Harris. On his return from a trip around the world that he took with his wife shortly after the trials, Cabot told reporters that his connection with Pelletier began with the doctor who "had been guilty of wrongs to young women patients for which they hang men in some States . . . Mr. Pelletier's remark to me indicated he had more sympathy with the methods of the doctor who shortly thereafter disappeared from Boston than he had for the doctor's innocent victims . . . I have no personal feeling against Mr. Pelletier. I pity him."

PART III

Decline and Fall

CHAPTER 10

Mencken versus Chase, Round 2, 1926

H. L. MENCKEN WAS HOT IN PURSUIT OF J. Frank Chase. If Chase was at the height of his power in the mid-1920s, the same could certainly be said of Mencken. The editor of the *American Mercury* was one of the country's leading social critics and cultural figures. Columnist Walter Lippmann called him "the most powerful influence on this whole generation of educated people." Ernest Hemingway put it more simply in his novel *The Sun Also Rises:* "So many young men get their likes and dislikes from Mencken." High on that list of dislikes were Puritanism, censorship, and Comstockery. In one of his most famous phrases, Mencken referred to Puritanism as "the haunting fear that someone, somewhere, may be happy."

Mencken wrote that the contemporary Puritan of the J. Frank Chase mold was sometimes "a hireling of the Anti-Saloon League, sworn to Law Enforcement. Sometimes, he is a strict Sabbatarian, bawling for the police whenever he detects his neighbor washing bottles or varnishing the Ford on Sunday morning. Again, he is a vice crusader, chasing the scarlet lady with fierce Christian shouts. Yet again he is a Comstock, wearing out his eyes in the quest for smut."

By the 1920s, America was changing. It was the Jazz Age, the age of "flappers and philosophers" (as F. Scott Fitzgerald titled his first collection of stories) and of silent-film stars whose fabulous faces became the icons of the period. Prohibition created a nation of lawbreakers and rebels. Small-town verities were under siege. Author Sinclair Lewis laid bare the narrowness of small-town life in *Main Street* and poked fun at Middle-American boosterism in *Babbitt*. The 1925 Scopes "monkey" trial, in which a Tennessee high school teacher was accused of teaching evolution, pitted fundamentalist Christianity against science and former presidential candidate William Jennings Bryan against legendary trial lawyer Clarence Darrow. Scopes was found guilty, but organized religion seemed the loser, too. Anthony Comstock was dead. To increasing number of Americans, neo-Victorians like Chase and Cabot were remnants of the age of the dinosaurs. And H. L. Mencken, who covered the Scopes trial, coined terms like "booboisie," and, in the view of one critic, "wrote like a bat out of hell and picked his words like weapons," was at the center of it all.

What particularly irritated Mencken about J. Frank Chase and the Watch and Ward Society was that, in matters of censorship, they tended to operate in secret, ruling, in his view, through "threat and intimidation." He was determined to "smoke out" Chase and the Watch and Ward from their cozy confines of power. So he began doing everything he could to annoy, if not infuriate, Chase. When he and his friend, drama critic George Jean Nathan, founded the *American Mercury* in 1924 with Alfred A. Knopf's money, Mencken had the perfect vehicle to do so.

Despite Mencken's and the *Mercury*'s prestige and influence, he was unable to enlist any Boston reporters to take on Chase. Finally, he found A. L. S. Wood, a book reviewer for the *Springfield Union*, the local daily halfway across the state, who was willing to take up the cudgels. Wood's profile of Chase, called "Keeping the Puritans Pure," appeared in the September 1925 issue of the *Mercury*. Dripping with ridicule, the profile portrayed Chase as a petty autocrat, presiding over a compliant "court of preventative criticism" (a reference to Chase's euphemism for censorship), whose "interdict runs from Boston Bay through the Berkshires." The resulting article was "no great shakes as reporting," in Mencken's view, but it enraged Chase, which was exactly the editor's intention. Mencken received word from his Boston sources that Chase was threatening to ban the *American Mercury* in Massachusetts.

Mencken's next move was to get his assistant, Charles Angoff, a young man fresh out of Harvard, to pen an article called "Boston Twilight," an examination of the supposedly low state of Boston's culture. The article, published three months later in the *Mercury*, began, "Once the Athens of America, Boston now plunges downward toward the cultural level of

Port-au-Prince [Haiti] and Knoxville, Tenn." The city where the "intellectual aristocracy of the Republic" once reigned was now taken over by
"louts and fakes and rogues," and was a place where "an idea would feel
as much at home there as the Pope at a Ku Klux Konclave." Mencken and
Angoff didn't have to bother to say that the Watch and Ward moral policemen in general, and J. Frank Chase in particular, were at least partly
to blame.

Then, just in case anyone, especially Chase, missed the point, an article that Angoff wrote under the pseudonym of James D. Bernard in the
April 1926 issue, entitled "The Methodists," included some virulent words
about the denomination of which Chase was an ordained minister. Every
"witch-hunt" in the North was run by Methodists, the article claimed,
"whether it be directed against race-track gamblers, bootleggers, college
neckers, or street-walkers." In the article, Chase is mentioned by name as
"a Methodist vice-hunter of long practice and great native talent."

That same issue included the fateful "Hatrack." Written by Herbert
Asbury, a reporter for the New York Herald Tribune, it was the story of a
Farmington, Missouri, prostitute known as "Hatrack"—for her angu-
lar shape—who was driven deeper into misery and vice by the hypocrisy
of the local churchgoing folk. The story was tame by today's standards.
There were no descriptions of sex, and the language was mild: The word
"damned" appeared once, but nothing stronger than that. If it was offensive at all, it was offensive to small-town values and organized religion.
Its implication, that revivalist preachers actually encouraged vice, was totally inimical to Chase and the Watch and Ward. "For Hatrack there was
no forgiveness," wrote Asbury. "Mary Magdalene was a Saint in heaven,
but Hatrack remained a harlot in Farmington."

The controversial subject matter of "Hatrack" gave Chase a chance
to make his move. He took no formal action; he didn't have to. He simply informed John J. Tracey, a magazine wholesaler and chairman of the
Massachusetts Magazine Committee (a group set up partly by the Watch
and Ward for the purpose of determining which publications were suit-
able to be sold in the commonwealth), that the issue contained material
that violated the law. Tracey passed the word to the other wholesalers,
who informed the news dealers, who in turn removed the offending issue
of the American Mercury from their shelves. Word was then passed to their
counterparts in nearby cities like Worcester, Springfield, Fall River, and
New Bedford. This was the way the Watch and Ward operated—quietly
and efficiently, with little or no public notice. Finally, on March 30, once

the magazine was off the shelves, Chase issued a statement to the press, denouncing "Hatrack" as "immoral and unfit" to read.

Mencken's first impulse was to ignore the matter. The *Mercury* (national circulation 80,000) had few readers in Boston beyond Harvard Square newsstands and bookstores, and the April issue had already been on sale for a week before the ban took effect. But then he changed his mind. "As I reflected upon the matter," he wrote, "it became evident that something would have to be done, for if Chase were permitted to get away with this minor assault, he would be encouraged to plan worse ones, and, what is more, other wowsers elsewhere would imitate him." (*Wowser*, an Australian term defined by one Australian writer as "an ineffably pious person who mistakes this world for a penitentiary and himself as a warder," was a favorite expression of Mencken's.) After consulting with his lawyers and *Mercury* publisher Alfred A. Knopf, Mencken decided to challenge Chase directly. It was Arthur Garfield Hays, a lawyer for the American Civil Liberties Union with a great deal of experience in censorship cases, who suggested that Mencken go up to Boston, sell a copy of the issue of the *Mercury* containing the "Hatrack" article publicly, and force Chase to order his arrest. Perhaps Mencken's and Hays's attendance at the Scopes trial the previous summer had convinced them of the public-relations value of turning their enemies into caricatures.

But confrontation carried a danger. Mencken could be arrested, and he would face two years in prison if convicted. He was well aware that Chase and the Watch and Ward had great influence over the legal apparatus of Boston. But Mencken was ready to take the risk. His mother, to whom he was devoted, had died the previous December, "and I was now free to take chances, and in fact, somewhat eager for adventure," he wrote.

Chase, for his part, was wary of getting involved. When it came to issues of censorship, he preferred to work behind the scenes, and he also suspected a trick. But the appeal of facing Mencken down in public after all his insults, ridicule, and attacks on the Methodist church was simply too great. He reluctantly agreed to meet Mencken on Brimstone Corner at 2:00 p.m. on April 5, 1926.

The next day, at 10:45 a.m., Mencken went before Judge James P. Parmenter in Boston Municipal Court on charges of peddling obscenity. The hearing had much of the circus-like atmosphere of the faceoff at Brimstone Corner the day before. The *New York Times* noted that so many Bostonians lined up for admission to the courtroom that court employees "thought a second Scopes trial had been thrust upon them." Mencken's appearance at Brimstone Corner had drawn "an open air audience of thousands," wrote the newspaper, "and today half of them tried to squeeze into a courtroom that holds 200 with difficulty." Mencken testified, as did Chase and Herbert Asbury, the author of "Hatrack." In his summation for the defense, Arthur Garfield Hays warned that if a minority "which gets a certain reaction from the reading of certain articles because of its state of mind" could impose its will upon what the majority could read, the Bible and Shakespeare could be censored next. "I was in the Scopes case," Hays noted. "There Tennessee people were just as intent . . . that their children's souls should be saved [by banning the teaching of evolution] as Mr. Chase here is that the point of view of this society shall be forced upon the public."

The idea that a Boston court in 1926 would rule against the Watch and Ward Society was unimaginable, and Mencken himself was convinced that he would be found guilty. At the posh St. Botolph Club, where he dined with members of Boston's literary elite the evening following the court hearing, the mood was glum. The St. Botolph was "one of the holy places of the Boston Brahmins," as Mencken put it, and that evening the air was thick was cigar smoke and gallows humor. Boston Booksellers Committee head Richard Fuller was said to be offering bets at huge odds that Mencken would be convicted. Someone at the dinner told Mencken that the sixty-seven-year-old Judge Parmenter was a Unitarian, the most liberal of denominations, and Mencken's spirits lifted for a moment. But then someone else pointed out that large numbers of Unitarians were members of the Watch and Ward.

The following morning, the unimaginable happened. Judge Parmenter stunned the courtroom, absolving the *American Mercury* and finding Mencken not guilty of corrupting the morals of youth. "'Hatrack,'" he stated in his ruling, was a "rather frank expression but at the same time an intellectual description of prostitution," and he could find nothing in it that "would arouse sexual impulses or lascivious thoughts, as prohibited by statute."

Mencken was free; he had beaten the Watch and Ward in its own bailiwick. It was a stunning verdict, not to mention a huge blemish on J. Frank Chase's enviable string of convictions. After the verdict was announced, the triumphant Mencken crossed the river to Cambridge to go to lunch at the Harvard Union. When the judge's decision reached the students of Harvard, many of whom had been at the Common two days before, "the campus took on the electric glory that thrills it on days when the Harvard football eleven has won a match," in the words of *Time* magazine. But most of the students at the luncheon itself were totally unaware that Mencken had been acquitted; the intended purpose of the gathering had been to protest the anticipated guilty verdict. In any event, the large hall, called the Living Room of the Union, was packed, with 600 students sitting and another 1,400 standing among tables or peering in through windows to get a glimpse of their hero. "We had assembled to condole with a martyr," Harvard Law School professor (and later U.S. Supreme Court justice) Felix Frankfurter said, introducing Mencken. "We did not hope to greet the martyr vindicated. Mr. Mencken has done a dreadful and brave thing."

The guest presented Harvard University with a large silk flag of his native Maryland, and the students and professors rose to their feet, giving him a Harvard cheer three times. "From now on, we are going to make these fellows bring their charges into the open," Mencken told his audience. "And they're easy to beat. When you go after them, ninety-nine percent will run, and other one percent is easy picking."

It was a victorious day for Mencken, but something was amiss. J. Frank Chase hadn't been present in the courtroom for the verdict. Did he know he was going to lose and simply chose not to appear? Or did he have something else in mind?

Both suppositions were probably correct. Perhaps more aware of Judge Parmenter's judicial inclinations than Mencken and his attorneys had been, Chase had taken the train to New York. There he went to see the postmaster, John J. Kiely—"a notorious ignoramus and very friendly to wowsers," in Mencken's view—and persuaded Kiely to prevail on postal officials in Washington to act against Mencken and the *American Mercury*. When Mencken returned to New York, he found a three-line item in the late edition of the *New York Graphic*, announcing that the *Mercury's* April issue had been barred from the mails.

The news got worse when Felix Caragianes, the Harvard Square news dealer who was the first casualty of the *American Mercury* ban—he had sold a copy of the April issue to a Watch and Ward agent—was found guilty. Caragianes admitted that he had sold thirty-five copies to Harvard students and professors but insisted the magazine contained nothing indecent. Judge Arthur P. Stone fined him $100 in Cambridge District Court, the first of a string of cases in which Stone would rule in favor of censorship. Caragianes chose not to appeal, and Alfred A. Knopf, the magazine's owner, paid his fine.

Then Mencken's forces struck back. On April 14, his lawyers prevailed upon a federal judge to issue an injunction restraining the Watch and Ward Society from interfering with the distribution of the Mercury. The Watch and Ward had "no right to impose their opinions on the book and magazine trade by threats of prosecution, if their views are not accepted," agreed Judge James M. Morton Jr. Meanwhile, in U.S. District Court, Mencken's lawyers filed a suit for $50,000 against Chase, the Watch and Ward Society, and some news agencies, charging them with interfering with Mencken's magazine. These were serious blows.

Initially, Chase showed only bravado. Venturing into the "lion's den" of Harvard University on the day before Judge Morton issued his injunction, he was at his pugnacious—and quotable—best in a speech he titled "The New Puritanism." "As I read officially the product of the New York publishers of novels, I have to recognize that the writers have 57 varieties of creeping things and abominable beasts in their heart," he told a Harvard Liberal Club luncheon. "A whole high school class of unwedded mothers may be the result of a lascivious book. An author who shocks the sense of public decency differs little from a lewd and lascivious person, a common night walker, both male and female." Chase added, "Boston is a 'state of mind.' Some may believe that state of mind is conceited, even ridiculous, but it nevertheless is properly self-respecting in its opinions."

But despite his brave public face, Chase felt pressured. The Boston media was turning against him. The usually friendly Boston Herald—a newspaper that Mencken disparaged as "a stupid and vulgar sheet that printed very little serious news but was devoted mainly to reports of birthday parties, church raffles, and other such puerile events in the meaner Boston suburbs"—had first been editorially sympathetic to Chase, but it soon changed its tune. There was "much verbal castigation of Mr. Chase and the Watch and Ward Society in Boston," the newspaper admitted in an April 8 editorial, adding "the moral in this instance obviously is that a censor should be sure he has a case." For a newspaper that had fired a reporter just a few years before for saying an unkind word about the Watch and Ward, this was a significant turnabout.

Chase's position was not helped when, on April 21, just a couple of weeks after the Brimstone Corner episode, Police Commissioner Herbert A. Wilson issued an order regarding arrests in cases in which the complainants were the Watch and Ward Society or similar organizations. Now, when civic organizations made complaints or wanted to make arrests requiring the aid of the police, a captain at an individual station house would have to go before the commissioner personally before any action was taken. This had not been the case before. "The arrest of Mencken, it has been said in police circles, might have been made without so much 'fuss' and such a tremendous crowd witnessing it," noted the *Boston Globe* in its article on the new policy. "There was also intimation that a large amount of free advertising often is occasioned by such arrests." The *Boston Herald* headlined its article on the same subject "WILSON PUTS BAN ON STUNT ARRESTS." All this could hardly have heartened Chase.

That same week, the *Boston Telegram*, a brash daily that catered to the Irish working class and had a penchant for sensation, published a multipart series of articles condemning Chase and "exposing" the Watch and Ward. One headline screamed, "WATCH AND WARD HEAD EXPOSED; DUPES REFUSE TO GIVE MORE CASH"; another said, "PRETTY COLLEGE GIRLS USED AS LURES"; while still another proclaimed, "WATCH AND WARD THUGS COVER UP BACK BAY 'LOVE NESTS' OF RICH MEN." A *Telegram* article announced that "a discredited and shunned" Chase was about to leave Boston. And in an April 27 editorial, the newspaper wrote, "The Watch and Ward is but a name. . . . Chase stands discredited in Boston and Massachusetts. He has shamed all sincere, honest, and upright crusaders against vice. . . . Chase's sun has set. He is through as a fake reformer." Most of the articles contained nothing new, with little in the way of facts to back up the clamor of the headlines. They simply coughed up every accusation of Watch and Ward overreaching—and of the misdeeds of its agents—that had been made over the years to present the society in the worst possible light. The Watch and Ward policy of using students to entrap prostitutes was brought up anew; the incident in which Chase registered at a South End hotel with a woman not his wife was rehashed.

The fact that a major Boston newspaper, no matter how low its standards, would publish such a stream of invective against the Watch and Ward and Chase himself demonstrated how much the society had been wounded. It was the first time a daily newspaper had attacked it so forcefully and so viciously. The *Telegram* series also highlighted the enmity between the Watch and Ward and Boston's increasingly self-assertive Irish Catholic majority, an enmity that had intensified during the Pelletier affair. Their views on censorship might be similar to those of the Watch and Ward, but the Irish were not going to come to the aid of Chase and the despised, ruling-class Brahmins, even on an issue where they were in agreement.

Just a few weeks after his encounter with Mencken, Chase was faltering. There was some evidence that the Watch and Ward directors were trying to make him a scapegoat for the entire matter. The death the previous year of the Reverend Frederick B. Allen, longtime president of the Watch and Ward, had robbed him of a major ally, one whose prestige could not be matched by any successor.

Meanwhile, Fuller, the Boston Booksellers Committee's president, was extending feelers to Mencken's lawyers that Chase might be willing to apologize in exchange for dropping the lawsuit. Whether Chase had been consulted about this is unclear. Mencken's lawyers turned down Fuller's offer of a meeting. They didn't trust the bookseller and were convinced they had the Watch and Ward secretary on the run.

The "greatest chance" a man took in his line of work was to risk his reputation, Chase had told the New Bedford Sunday Standard ten years previously, just after the first sensational raid in that city. "For while you can recover from a black eye or a broken head—if you lose your reputation you can never get it back," he said. The latter was exactly what was happening.

At a meeting reported to Mencken's lawyers in a letter dated October 18, the Watch and Ward, with a threat of a $50,000 lawsuit hanging over its head, seemed prepared to concede a number of points. One of these was to end the "gentlemen's agreement" banning books and magazines. The Watch and Ward lawyers suggested that such matters be dealt with only in open court from now on. That would undercut, if not destroy, Chase's whole approach to his work. Significantly, the Watch and Ward secretary was not present at the meeting.

A week later, in the midst of these negotiations and continued legal maneuverings, J. Frank Chase fell ill with pneumonia. On November 3, he was dead. Chase was fifty-four. It was only seven months since he had dueled with Mencken on Brimstone Corner. His wife, overcome with anxiety at her husband's illness, suffered a shock and was confined to her bed; she wasn't even aware that her husband had died. The funeral was held four days later at the same West Roxbury church where Chase had served as pastor in his early days. The Reverend Raymond Calkins, the current president of the Watch and Ward, delivered the eulogy. A friend of the Chase family sang "Fight the Good Fight" and "Nearer My God to Thee."

Mencken suspected that Chase's illness and death might have been directly related to the October meeting, from which Chase had been excluded and in which Watch and Ward lawyers appeared to be distancing themselves from him and his way of conducting business. The Associated Press noted that he had been ill for a week with pneumonia and then suffered a shock that caused a relapse. "The nature of that shock was not disclosed, but we could at least indulge in surmise," wrote Mencken. The surmise was that Chase believed he was being betrayed.

In a letter to the *Boston Herald* published five days after Chase's death, Delcevare King—his friend and a pallbearer at his funeral, and who had originally persuaded him to take the Watch and Ward position—noted that Chase had broken down a year before from continuous overwork. When he was able to return to his job, "the great pressure of things to be done and his eagerness to do them" brought upon his fatal illness. To King, Chase was a "hero," underfunded and unappreciated, whose life had been sacrificed "for the common weal." He added, "His was the most difficult and disagreeable position of any man in New England. . . . Any mistakes he made—and there were very few—were blazoned forth, while his constant and successful fight against the devastating forces of evil was little noticed."

King noted that of the 3,937 cases that Chase brought in his almost twenty years as Watch and Ward secretary, he obtained convictions in 98 percent of them. It was one of the few that got away that spelled the doom of Jason Franklin Chase.

CHAPTER 11

Censorship Goes Wild, 1927–1928

J. FRANK CHASE WAS DEAD, and the Mencken affair had dealt the Watch and Ward a rare and well-publicized defeat, damaging its reputation and effectiveness. The Reverend Frederick B. Allen, longtime Watch and Ward president and "the most beloved man in Boston," was dead, too. The Watch and Ward Society was in disarray. In many respects, this couldn't have come at a worse time. The mid- to late-1920s was a troubled period for Boston. It was a period of great prosperity nationwide, but Boston shared in it to a lesser degree than other cities. Its key industries, like textiles and shoes, were in decline; its unemployment rate was among the highest in the country; its political leadership was famously corrupt. The executions of the anarchists Nicola Sacco and Bartolomeo Vanzetti, in the summer of 1927 after a controversial criminal trial, did little to enhance the city's reputation for justice and morality.

The enactment of Prohibition in 1919 had helped exacerbate the sense of decline. By the late 1920s, there were some 4,000 speakeasies in Boston, and fifty gangland killings in just a few years. Huntington Avenue was "lined with speakeasies cum bordellos," and streetwalkers in other parts of the city were "a common sight," writes Jack Beatty in *The Rascal King,* his biography of Mayor James Michael Curley. Speakeasies were forced to pay protection to corrupt policemen; to raise that money, many let rooms to prostitutes. Oliver Garrett, the dashing young officer who headed the city's liquor squad during the late 1920s—and who also played a role in Mencken's arrest at Brimstone Corner—became infamous for demanding payoffs from bootleggers and speakeasy proprietors, reportedly banking $120,000 over a six-year period on a salary of $40.36 a week. He was later convicted of extortion and served two years on Deer Island; it was said that he had Red Sox season tickets and free use of a motorboat whenever he wanted to leave the island prison to go to a baseball game.

It might have been a perfect moment for the kind of anti-vice and anti-corruption campaign that the Watch and Ward had led in the past, a moment for a new J. Frank Chase to arise and smite the city's iniquities. But Boston's attempt to cleanse itself during the late 1920s ignored liquor, prostitution, and political corruption. Instead, it turned towards censorship, in a wild orgy of book-banning the likes of which the city had never known.

Within six months of Chase's death, the "gentlemen's agreement"— that cozy, behind-the-scenes arrangement by which the Watch and Ward and the Boston Booksellers Committee determined what books could be sold in the city's bookstores—died, and a new kind of censorship emerged in Boston. Where there had been order, for better or worse, there was now near-anarchy, with the Suffolk County district attorney, the Boston police commissioner, and the Watch and Ward all playing a role in the suppression of books, with the Roman Catholic Church cheering from the sidelines.

The "gentlemen's agreement," brokered in 1915, was largely J. Frank Chase's brainchild. In January 1924, the Watch and Ward secretary told the Massachusetts Library Club that the organization had banned twenty-three books in the previous two years; five prosecutions had been made, with convictions in each case. If Chase hadn't made that revelation, the public would never have found out about these actions. But until the arrangement collapsed, no one realized how much it had depended on one man. When it all fell apart, even opponents of censorship were wishing—some of them publicly—that J. Frank Chase were still alive and making decisions as to what Bostonians could and could not read.

The revisionist history was expressed by the New England correspondent for the *New York Times*, F. Lauriston Bullard, in a kind of elegy for Chase that appeared in the newspaper in July 1927, at the height of the book-banning frenzy: "He was a fighter, yet he strove to be reasonable, as all the booksellers will testify. In life, he was lampooned, and lambasted; occasionally he was in personal peril. Today there are many who pronounce him a hero and some who traduce him still."

The death of Chase was not the only factor that facilitated the city's fall into "Wild West"–style censorship. For one thing, the publishing industry was changing, putting out books that were franker, more experimental, and more critical of conventional American mores than ever before. This reflected the societal changes of the "Roaring Twenties," with its loosening of sexual restrictions. A new, emerging breed of publishers and publishing houses, with names like Alfred A. Knopf and Boni & Liveright, was challenging their staid elders, who had, more often than not, published books more in line with the tastes of Watch and Ward censors. Boni & Liveright, which published some of the most adventuresome books of the era, had by 1924 signed up such groundbreaking writers as playwright Eugene O'Neill and novelists Theodore Dreiser and Sherwood Anderson; later, the company brought out the first works of Ernest Hemingway and William Faulkner.

Knowing that conflict and controversy helped sell books, these publishers reveled in battling the censors, particularly Boston censors, even though Boston had the highest per capita rate of book-buying of any city in the country. Some authors reveled in it, too. Muckraker-turned-novelist Upton Sinclair joked to a friend who had written a book banned in Boston that he wished his friend could use his "connections" with the censors there to get Sinclair's 1927 novel Oil! suppressed as well, to boost its disappointing sales. Sinclair's wish was soon granted.

Another factor was the growing role of the Roman Catholic Church in matters of censorship, both in Boston and elsewhere. In the spring of 1927, through Cardinal Merry del Val, secretary of the Supreme Sacred Congregation of the Holy Office, Pope Pius XI issued an official statement, urging Catholic bishops throughout the world to keep an eye out for immoral books and exert their powers to have such books removed from circulation. Books that "appeal to the sensuous passions, and to a kind of lascivious mysticism" were among "the worst evils which totally corrupt Christian morals," stated the pontiff. "POPE DECLARES WAR ON IMMORAL BOOKS" was how the New York Times headlined its article on the Vatican's pronouncement.

In Boston, William Henry Cardinal O'Connell, who had headed the Boston archdiocese since 1906, was known for his anti-modernist views and close ties to the Vatican. He had been a protégé of the powerful Cardinal Merry and had ascended to the top of the Boston hierarchy largely because of his close relationship with Merry and others at the Vatican, a relationship which he had developed during a stint as rector of the American College in Rome and solidified as Vatican "emissary" to Japan.

Not surprisingly, the Boston archdiocese, through its official newspaper The Pilot, strongly endorsed the Vatican's campaign. "Most readers suspected that there was something wrong with the fiction of the day, but few realized the extent of its corrupting influence until the Holy Father spoke," wrote The Pilot. The archdiocese may not have initiated the censorship campaign in Boston, but, at the very least, it leant enthusiastic support. Previously, the suppression of books had been mostly a Protestant affair.

A related factor in the explosion of censorship in Boston in the 1920s may have been the events taking place in Ireland—then called the Irish Free State—a country to which many Boston Catholics had close ties and contact. In February 1926, the country's minister of justice, Kevin O'Higgins, established a "Committee on Evil Literature." Its recommendations led in 1929 to the enactment of the draconian Censorship of Publications Act. A total of 1,048 books had been banned by 1938, including works by authors ranging from Sean O'Faolain to Hermann Hesse to Colette. That country's Roman Catholic bishops, clerics, and religious organizations played a major role in pressing for this legislation. As Boyer points out, it would be surprising if Boston's Catholic officials were not aware of—or influenced by—the goings-on in the Free State.

The spasm of censorship had begun in late 1926, with the arrest of two drugstore clerks in Dorchester for selling Percy Marks's The Plastic Age, a novel about college life that the New York Times had praised for its "photographic realism." The book had been published more than two years before, in 1924, and the Watch and Ward under J. Frank Chase had approved it for sale in Boston. But now the police appeared to be acting on their own—a clear warning to booksellers that something had changed.

A few months later, on February 12, 1927, bookstores received a notice from the Booksellers Committee informing them that the Boston Police Department objected to passages from two new novels, The Rebel Bird by Diana Patrick and The Hard-Boiled Virgin by Frances Newman. (New York Times reviewers dismissed the first as "tedious, silly, and devoid of real life," while comparing The Hard-Boiled Virgin to Jane Austen and Charlotte Brontë.) Significantly, the source of the warning was the Boston police, not the Watch and Ward. Ten days later, admonitions were received about two more books—this time the source of the information was given as the Watch and Ward. After that, two more notices were sent, this time originating from the Suffolk County district attorney's office. Altogether, nine books were banned in little more than a month.

In a March 12 article, the *Boston Herald* pointed to the police department and the district attorney's office as responsible for the book suppressions. Boston Police Superintendent Michael H. Crowley told the newspaper, "I do not pretend to be a literary censor, but one of my duties is to enforce the statutes of the Commonwealth. I have read these books and I think they are bad. . . . I do not believe that the police are depriving the book readers of Boston of anything they should legitimately have." Meanwhile, the newly elected district attorney, William J. Foley, announced that he had handed off two of the books submitted to him to an aide, who had found them objectionable. Foley said he hoped the books would be withdrawn to avoid the need for prosecution. Richard Fuller, head of the Boston Booksellers Committee, announced that his organization would accept the decisions of the police and the district attorney. The Watch and Ward was conspicuously silent. In the absence of Chase—a new Watch and Ward head had yet to be named—there was a vacuum. The district attorney and the Boston police superintendent, both good, churchgoing Catholics who read the *Pilot* and listened to Cardinal O'Connell's sermons, had stepped in to fill it.

This was small stuff, however, compared to what was to come. On Tuesday, April 12, the district attorney's office informed Fuller that it was banning Sinclair Lewis's novel *Elmer Gantry*, published the month before. Lewis was one of America's most celebrated authors, much admired by critics as a satirist; he would win the Nobel Prize for literature three years later. *Elmer Gantry*, his scathing, sometimes uproarious portrait of a philandering religious evangelist, was already a huge national best seller and had sold some 3,000 to 5,000 copies in Boston alone. The book was dedicated to H. L. Mencken, "with profound admiration." It wasn't precisely clear why the book was being banned. Most likely, the problem was that it satirized organized religion, and it did so with great effectiveness. The evangelist Billy Sunday lambasted Lewis as the "devil's cohort." (The author had mocked him as "The Reverend Mr. Monday" in his earlier novel *Babbitt*.) A publicity stunt that Lewis engaged in while addressing a Kansas City church meeting the year before outraged religious leaders and may also have contributed to the ban. At that meeting, Lewis gave God fifteen minutes to strike him dead as an infidel and thus prove his existence. God chose not to do so.

Every Boston newspaper featured the ban on its front pages. "FOLEY

SUPPRESSES 'ELMER GANTRY;' BIG BOOK CRUSADE ON" was the banner headline in the *Herald*. Fuller immediately notified all book dealers in Greater Boston of the district attorney's decision. The many copies of *Elmer Gantry* in the window of Fuller's Old Corner Bookstore—the best-known such establishment in Boston—were immediately removed. However, a clerk apparently neglected to remove a photo of Lewis. That same evening, whether by accident or by design, the window of the Old Corner featured the lonely visage of Lewis, surrounded by empty shelves once crowded with copies of his novel.

The next day, in a direct challenge to the district attorney, Fuller sent Foley a package of forty-nine books, including works by Ernest Hemingway, Theodore Dreiser, and H. G. Wells, all of which Fuller believed to be as frank and in danger of being banned as *Elmer Gantry*. Foley sent them back to the bookseller, unopened. The package was accompanied by a letter: "I am writing you to state that any arrangement now existing between you and this office, under which you have been enabled to procure the opinion of this office in advance as to any given book, is at an end. I feel that you gentlemen can determine just as well as, and probably better than, this office, whether or not a book is an improper book for you to sell."

In this manner, he formally announced the demise of the "gentlemen's agreement." Booksellers now had no protection, no structure of advance warning that a book might be banned and that they might be subject to prosecution. Along with Foley's letter came another from Boston Police Superintendent Crowley, broadly hinting that Theodore Dreiser's best-selling novel *An American Tragedy*, published in December 1925, should come off the shelves the following day.

The collapse of the "gentlemen's agreement" stunned booksellers and the book-buying public alike. "BOSTON 'BOOK WAR' OPENS; FOLEY ENDS PACT WITH SELLERS," trumpeted the *Herald* in a three-column headline. In the accompanying article, the newspaper wrote, "Apparently Boston's greatest need today is a successor to the Rev. J. Frank Chase," characterizing the often-vilified censor as "a pretty level-headed and reasonable sort of fellow after all." The *Herald* editorial writers took an even harsher tone, offering "just one bit of advice" to "the estimable gentlemen who are now endeavoring to tell us what we can and cannot read. . . . Our advice is simply this: Do not make us ridiculous. . . . Do not broadcast the idea that we are children. Do not conclude that somebody must tell us what we may see and read and hear and think. Do not revise our dictionaries by leaving out all the bad words, and all that might be proved to have unsavory connotations. Leave our dictionaries as they are and trust the human race to work out its own destiny, under free play of individual freedom." With this editorial, the Herald completed its transformation from an acolyte of the Watch and Ward to an ardent foe of censorship.

One of the "estimable gentlemen" referred to by the Herald was Michael H. "Mike" Crowley, Boston's superintendent of police. Sixty-one at the time, Crowley had joined the Boston police force in 1888. After Commissioner Stephen O'Meara had plucked him from the streets of Roxbury where he was a "cop on the beat," the popular Crowley quickly rose through the ranks. When he was made a captain in Dorchester in 1913, the Boston Globe wrote, "It is doubtful if Commissioner O'Meara ever made a promotion more pleasing to the rank and file." Two years later, when Crowley became the "dark horse" choice for superintendent, the newspaper reported "general rejoicing" among his peers and noted, "He believes in fair play. Even those whom he arrested knew that they were dealing with a fair man who would not take any advantages of them." At one point, he served as the president of the International Police Chiefs' Association. In an article in Harper's Monthly, journalist Elmer Davis suggested that Crowley's attitude towards the issue of sex in fiction was similar to "that held by almost all intelligent persons" twenty-five years earlier. "If a large number of people, generally regarded as decent and intelligent, have changed their ideas since then," he wrote, "their opinion does not disturb Mr. Crowley, just and tenacious of his purpose."

The day after the collapse of the "gentlemen's agreement," Donald S. Friede, vice president of the publishing firm of Boni & Liveright, journeyed to Boston to pay a call on Crowley. Boni & Liveright was the publisher of Dreiser's An American Tragedy, the riveting story of a young man whose search for wealth and status results in his drowning his pregnant girlfriend in a lake. (The novel was based on a real-life 1906 murder case in upstate New York, extensively researched by Dreiser.) Because the book was Boni & Liveright's biggest seller, having sold more than 50,000 copies by the end of 1926, the firm wanted to know exactly where things stood in terms of Boston—and at the same time perhaps take advantage of the publicity generated by the "Banned in Boston" label. The novel had been among the forty-nine books that Fuller had sent in his package to District Attorney Foley.

Friede was a colorful character in his own right. An international playboy whose father had become rich as the Ford Motor Company's agent for czarist Russia, Friede was expelled from Harvard, Yale, and Princeton and had entered the publishing business on the advice of his psychoanalyst, starting as a stock clerk at Alfred A. Knopf at a salary of $10 a week. He bought a half-interest in Boni & Liveright in 1925 at the age of twenty-four and was immediately made vice president. If there was one thing that Friede particularly loved about the publishing business, it was publicity. Arthur Garfield Hays, who had been H. L. Mencken's lawyer in the Brimstone Corner showdown with J. Frank Chase, arranged a similar "test case" for Friede.

At Crowley's office, the young publisher, accompanied by Hays, sold a copy of *An American Tragedy* for $5 to Lieutenant Daniel J. Hines of the Liquor, Narcotic, and Vice squad. All this had been prearranged. Friede was immediately arrested—although with far less fanfare than in the Mencken case the year before—and his case was set to go before a magistrate the following week. At police headquarters, attorney Hays also asked Superintendent Crowley to let him sell him a copy of Hawthorne's *The Scarlet Letter* and the complete works of Shakespeare. Crowley declined.

On April 22, Friede was convicted of selling literature "manifestly tending to corrupt the morals of youth" and fined $100. He appealed the case. In the meantime, copies of *An American Tragedy* had disappeared from Boston bookstores.

Bostonians were of various minds as to what was occurring. In a joint statement, the publishers of the *Atlantic Monthly* and Little, Brown, and Company—two of the leading Boston publishing companies—criticized the suppression of twelve popular novels as "high-handed, erratic, and ill-advised," concluding that "it is difficult for men of self respect to keep silent in the face of this violation of the historic tradition of Boston and New England."

A month later, at a meeting at the Ford Hall Forum attended by 1,000 people, the new wave of censorship was criticized by Alfred Harcourt, of the publishing firm of Harcourt Brace and Company, and Hiller Wellman, a Springfield librarian who was soon to become an anti-censorship leader. The Reverend Raymond Calkins, president of the Watch and Ward, deplored the current situation, defended the "old way" of doing things, and was greeted with applause. Publisher Harcourt paid tribute to the late J. Frank Chase. Watch and Ward nostalgia was in the air.

However, the new censorship had its defenders. The president of Boston University, Daniel L. Marsh, attacked *Elmer Gantry* as "pretty flabby." He suspected that most readers would "plow through it," as he had, in order "to be able to tell their friends what they thought of it." That, of course, did not justify its being banned, but it seemed to argue that the book's absence from Boston bookstores was no great loss to the public. *The Pilot* took a stronger position. In an editorial entitled "Commercialized Bunk," it backed up Foley, denouncing *Elmer Gantry* as "a piece of propaganda against organized Christianity." "Mr. Lewis may claim that his work is a satire and should be judged as such," said the newspaper. "But what do thousands of readers know of satire, and how can they differentiate between the exaggerations of satirical caricatures and the reportorial accuracy of Mr. Lewis's most famous characterizations!" It was a shame, wrote the *Pilot* editorial writers, that writers of "the Sinclair Lewis and Mencken type" should "prostitute their pens in the unholy cause of religious skepticism and agnosticism."

A few weeks later, the Vatican issued its statement "declaring war on immoral books."

And in a speech before the Catholic Total Abstinence League, District Attorney Foley warned that "as long as I am District Attorney, the standards of decency, purity, and morality set up by past generations in this country will be maintained by me." He added darkly, "The people who believe that the standard of our fathers and mothers is not the standard for us are also the people who believe in teaching birth control and sex education in our public schools."

Then, on May 31, came the suppression of Upton Sinclair's novel *Oil!*, a panoramic look at the corruption of the California oil boom of the 1920s. The police had objected to nine pages of the text in which the book's protagonist, a young and naive heir to an oil fortune, is seduced by a young woman, attends a "petting party," and is educated about a "new ethical code" that includes information about contraception. The result was a circus that summed up what had become of Boston censorship. First, in late May, Richard Fuller announced that he was forbidding the sale of *Oil!* in his Old Corner Bookstore, fearing police prosecution; other bookstores quickly followed suit. That prosecution happened four days later, on

June 4, when John Gritz, a twenty-year-old clerk in the bookstore Smith & McCance, sold a copy of *Oil!* to two police detectives. Gritz—in Sinclair's words, "the nearest approach to a cherub that you can find wearing trousers"—was arrested, found guilty, and fined $100 bail. The judge ruled the book to be immoral.

The circus really began in earnest when Sinclair arrived in Boston by train from California. He brought along his twenty-five-year-old son David, who, he announced, had actually witnessed some of the scenes in the book, especially those descriptive of high school and college life. For his part, Sinclair suggested that the accusations of immorality might be a ruse, and that Boston authorities really objected to what he called "my Socialist novel" on political grounds. After all, insisted Sinclair, he had long had a reputation as "the prize prude of the radical movement." He noted that the police objected to 9 pages out of a total of 527, while there were 26 pages about how to lease a tract of ground for a drilling site.

Sinclair was determined to get arrested in the Mencken manner—all the more to gain publicity for his book—but the authorities were not as obliging as he had hoped. They had learned from the antics of the past. Even before arriving in Boston, Sinclair had tried to get his name substituted for the cherubic bookseller Gritz on the indictment, but the judge wouldn't hear of it. Then, at a June 12 rally on the Boston Common, where Sinclair defended his book before a crowd that grew from 25 to 2,000, the muckraker practically begged the police to take him into custody.

"Are you going to arrest me?" he asked a police officer who broke up the rally, demanding various permits.

"We will if you start any funny business," replied the officer.

"I wish you would," retorted Sinclair. "I would consider it the greatest privilege ever accorded me. And if it wasn't for the fact that I might be charged with bribery, I would gladly offer you $1,000 to place me under arrest."

The officer would not oblige. Still, Sinclair left the rally with a big smile on his face.

The author then went to visit Police Superintendent Crowley. The superintendent had previously told Sinclair's lawyer that his book was "the worst of the lot" and that if he sold a copy in Boston, he would personally appear to prosecute him. Sinclair engaged in a colloquy with Crowley that, according to Sinclair, went like this:

"Surely, Mr. Crowley, you can't be very familiar with standard literature. Shakespeare, for example—"

"You don't find any of these bedroom scenes in Shakespeare."

"Have you ever happened to read *Cymbeline*, Mr. Crowley?"

"Oh now, of course, you can put it over me in an argument about books. But there's terrible things in that book of yours, Mr. Sinclair."

"What, for example?"

"Ain't that the book in which the girl says that she can have a lover, because her mother has one, and she knows it?"

"Yes, that's in here."

"Well now, is that the kind of thing to be putting into a book?"

"It happens to be a real case, Mr. Crowley. I knew the people."

"Well, there might be such people, I don't deny, but that's no reason for spreading the story. Such things destroy the reverence that young girls ought to feel for their mothers, and such things ought to be hushed up, and not put into books for girls to read."

The following day, at another rally, Sinclair convinced a police officer to buy a copy of *Oil!*, but it turned out to be a copy of the Bible with the *Oil!* dust jacket on it. At one public meeting, Sinclair read Act III, Scene II of *Hamlet*, which contained what he called "indubitably obscene language," and invited the police to buy the book; they refused. He also read them passages from Genesis featuring the story of Lot and his daughters; the police wouldn't take that bait, either. "The only way to fight the Massachusetts law is to make a monkey of it," said Sinclair. Clearly, that was what he was trying to do.

Next, he paraded on the Boston Common, carrying a sandwich board in the shape of a fig leaf promoting "*Oil!* Fig Leaf Edition. Warranted 100% Pure Under Boston Law." He had persuaded his publisher to print up 150 copies in which a black-leaf silhouette was substituted for the nine offending pages. A photo of Sinclair selling a copy to a Boston matron found its way onto the front pages of newspapers across the United States and Europe.

Finally, on June 21, he got his wish. Lieutenant Daniel J. Hines, who had bought the copy of *An American Tragedy* from Donald Friede two months earlier, purchased a copy of the "real" *Oil!* from Sinclair, this time without fig leaves. Sinclair was arrested, but a judge refused a warrant and the case was dropped. "We think, Mr. Sinclair, you've had your share of book advertising," the judge told him. That was that. But Sinclair had achieved his objectives, making a joke of Boston censorship and gaining a raft of free publicity for his book. He headed back home to California.

When Sinclair stopped in New York City after his Boston sojourn, the first thing that caught his eye was a four-foot-high stack of his books at a newsstand at Grand Central Station. That particular stack would be gone in a day, the clerk assured him. The books were selling like hotcakes, mostly to visitors from Boston, who purchased copies before boarding the train for home.

In the United States, sales of Oil! jumped from a little over 2,000 during the first three months of 1927 to more than 6,000 a month during that summer, ultimately reaching 75,000. "We authors are using America as our sales territory, and Boston is our advertising department," said Sinclair proudly.

At this point, the Watch and Ward got back in the game. The same month that Upton Sinclair was making fools of Boston censors, the Reverend Charles Sherman Bodwell was named the society's new secretary. It was eight months since the death of J. Frank Chase. A Congregational minister turned Unitarian, the fifty-year-old Bodwell had been active with the Anti-Saloon League and had spent ten years doing "Americanization" work among immigrants in Lawrence, a textile manufacturing city north of Boston. The New York Times noted that there was "much curiosity" as to what the policies of the Watch and Ward would be under Bodwell's leadership. "Presumably the directors will strive for the renewal of the 'gentlemen's agreement,'" wrote the newspaper, "but the success of the censorship . . . depended until last November on the influence of one man, and now that Mr. Chase is gone, it may require time for the new regime to establish itself in a comparable position of influence."

Clearly, there were various forces at work now—other players in what had once been the Watch and Ward's exclusive province. Superintendent Crowley was certainly not going to withdraw from the field. And various "freelancers" began to emerge as well in the vacuum of Chase's death. Most notable was the Reverend Paul Sterling, an Episcopal minister and chairman of the Trustees of the Public Library in the Boston suburb of Melrose. Many of the complaints that Crowley received that led to book suppressions apparently came from him. There are hints that Sterling may have been responsible for the original complaint about Oil!

When the Watch and Ward determined that British author Rosamond Lehman's novel Dusty Answer, whose lesbian content had been the subject of complaints, was "not actionable," the ever-vigilant Sterling asked Superintendent Crowley to overrule the decision. "It may be that I shall not be able to remain in the harness with Mr. Sterling very long," a frustrated

Bodwell wrote in his November 1927 secretary's report. "I believe his intentions are of the highest, but in the case of *Dusty Answer*, he seemed unable to use his imagination sufficiently to realize how the book would appear to the average person, since the objectionable features appeared so clear to him." The book was not banned, however.

By October of that year, three months into his tenure, Bodwell was taking an energetic role in terms of censorship. In that month, he conferred with Fuller, Crowley, Sterling, and with various Watch and Ward vice presidents who were responsible for reading books. He sat in on the Book Review Club of Librarians while the club was discussing which books would be recommended for librarians and which put on the restricted list.

But Superintendent Crowley was still in the dominant position, as is evident from the outcome of a meeting that included Crowley, Sterling, and Watch and Ward officials. As a result of that meeting, Sterling agreed to make his complaints about books to the Watch and Ward, not to Crowley. But if there was a disagreement between the two, Crowley would make the ultimate decision. In addition, Crowley would send any book on which there had been a complaint to the Watch and Ward, and the Watch and Ward would have forty-eight hours to read the book and return it to him. That certainly didn't give the Watch and Ward much chance to make a thoughtful decision, especially if there was disagreement among Watch and Ward "readers," as was sometimes the case. And there was no promise on Crowley's part to defer to the Watch and Ward's opinion.

The first book Crowley sent to the Watch and Ward was *Zelda Marsh* by Charles Gilman Norris, a Dreiser-like novelist who was the brother of the more famous writer Frank Norris. The Watch and Ward told Crowley that it was "not actionable." But after Crowley referred the book to Wilfred Bolster, chief justice of the Municipal Court in Boston, who thought it should be banned, Crowley overruled the Watch and Ward. He informed Booksellers Committee head Fuller that he would attempt to buy a copy and take legal action. A similar thing happened with a novel called *The Mob*, a series of portraits of Madrid's poor by the Spanish novelist Vicente Blasco Ibáñez. Crowley sent a copy of the book to Bodwell, and the Watch and Ward ruled it not actionable. However, Crowley told the Watch and Ward that his view was unchanged. "I do not believe he intended to buy copies of that book for the purpose of making arrests," wrote Bodwell.

Crowley also overruled the Watch and Ward in the matter of Sherwood Anderson's best-selling novel *Dark Laughter*, banned in January

1928. The book tells the story of a big-city intellectual who leaves his wife and changes his identity, lives as a factory worker and small-town gardener, and eventually runs off with another man's wife. Crowley and the Watch and Ward, which had stopped the sale of Anderson's *Many Marriages* earlier in the decade, both agreed that this novel should be banned. (Anderson's earlier and most famous book, *Winesburg, Ohio*, seems to have escaped the censor's ax.) But the Watch and Ward argued that since it was more than two years old at this point, there was no sense proceeding against it. Crowley was determined to go his own way, however, and another work by a major American author disappeared from the shelves of Boston's bookstores.

Crowley seemed to have the last word, but, at the same time, the Watch and Ward continued censorship activities on its own, as if nothing had changed and the "gentlemen's agreement" was still in effect. Meanwhile, Fuller and the other booksellers acquiesced to whoever was doing the censoring. So in November 1927, the Watch and Ward, without any help from Crowley, deemed "actionable" the first issue of *American Caravan*, an annual anthology of American literature, which contained a story by Ernest Hemingway and the first act of Eugene O'Neill's play *Lazarus Laughed*. The booksellers were informed, and the book vanished. Just to make sure, however, Watch and Ward investigators made several attempts to purchase the book at local bookstores. "Our investigator was met with the response that the book had been suppressed by the W&W Society, and that they were not allowed to sell it," wrote Bodwell. "Mr. Fuller and I concluded that this was a very successful outcome."

Since, unlike Superintendent Crowley, the Watch and Ward had influence beyond the borders of Boston proper, it could exercise censorship powers in areas where Boston law enforcement officials had no legal authority. Thus, *Elmer Gantry*, originally suppressed by the Boston district attorney, became a Watch and Ward target in March 1928. When the society learned that the novel was being circulated by a lending library in the Boston suburb of Arlington, the Watch and Ward informed the local police chief, who got it removed. The chief wrote Bodwell, "I now have the book and it will be destroyed."

By January 1928, some seventy books had been banned in Boston within less than a year's time, mostly, although not entirely, works of fiction. The list was unofficial, mostly compiled by newspapers. Many on the list today are considered major works, if not classics, of American literature: *An American Tragedy, Elmer Gantry, Oil!,* Ernest Hemingway's

The Sun Also Rises, John Dos Passos's *Manhattan Transfer*, and William Faulkner's *Mosquitoes*. Carl Van Vechten's *Nigger Heaven* and H. G. Wells's *The World of William Clissold* were also banned. So was Bertrand Russell's *What I Believe*, a critique of organized religion that is today considered the best introduction to the philosopher's thought.

This was in marked contrast to the situation prevailing in New York, where a "clean-books law" toughening book censorship there had been defeated in the state legislature earlier in the decade. The law limited censorship to books that appealed to a "prurient interest" and made rampant book-banning on the scale of Boston's to be difficult, if not impossible. Attempts by John Sumner, successor to Anthony Comstock at the New York Society for the Suppression of Vice, to ban books ranging from D. H. Lawrence's *Women in Love* to Radclyffe Hall's *The Well of Loneliness* eventually ended in dismal failure.

The murkiness and often downright confusion of the Boston situation in the wake of the Watch and Ward's decline created "a veritable bugaboo," as the *New York Times* described it in a January 22, 1928, article. Its reporter, Mary Lee, made the Boston situation sound like something out of a Kafka story. "No one is sure who the censor is," she wrote. "Nobody understands the reasons for his decisions. Nobody knows whether or not the violation of the taboo against certain books would actually mean prosecution or, if it did, whether it would be upheld in a court of law. Nevertheless, the mysterious 'censor' is obeyed, and obeyed through what might almost be termed a panic of fear."

Go into a Boston bookshop, the *Times* reporter suggested, and ask about a well-known and much-discussed book like Julia Peterkin's *Black April* (a novel about blacks on a remote South Carolina plantation by an H. L. Mencken protégé and later the first Southern author to win a Pulitzer Prize), or Olive Schreiner's *Man to Man* (a posthumous novel by the well-regarded South African novelist), or Sherwood Anderson's *Dark Laughter*. You would be told they were banned, and when you asked why, you would be told that it was "by the censor, that they were on the list." To the question of who makes up the list, you would get no answer. "The names come on slips of paper, the bookshop people tell you, and they write them down," Lee continued. "What do the slips of paper say? Nothing. Just the name of the book written down, with no recommendation whatever. But they understand."

Lee noted that only two books of the seventy on the unofficial list had been held to be obscene by an actual court—*An American Tragedy* and

Oil! The other sixty-eight were there because of "someone's private opinion." How these private opinions were arrived at or communicated, she
said, was "a matter of mystery." Sometimes decisions were the result of
guesses on the part of the booksellers themselves that isolated passages
might be obscene. Other times they resulted from tips from the police
department. In still other cases, the "belief" of the Watch and Ward Society that the passages might be held to be illegal was enough to get a book
banned. The city, an anonymous official at the Boston Public Library told
her, was "in a perfectly nonsensical position."

Meanwhile, the Times noted, you could not find a copy of An American
Tragedy in a Boston bookshop or at the Boston Public Library. But in Cambridge, ten minutes away by subway (and in a county where the Boston
district attorney had no authority), not only could you buy it, but three
copies were catalogued at Harvard's Widener Library, all of them circulating and in the hands of presumably eager readers.

CHAPTER 12

Boston, 1929

AND THEN PEACE BROKE OUT. For more than a year, through the middle of 1929, few "book massacres" or censorship issues riled the city of Boston. The Watch and Ward tried to distance itself from the madness of the previous year. "It will doubtless be a surprise to many persons to learn that of the approximately sixty-five books that have been suppressed during the past year, only six were acted upon because of our complaints," Secretary Charles Sherman Bodwell wrote in the annual report, dated March 1, 1928. The major event touted in the report took place far from the scene of any literary crimes: a raid in Waterbury, Connecticut, in which state police arrested sixty-eight people at five gambling establishments based on Watch and Ward evidence.

By March 1929, Bodwell could write that over the past year, only three books had been withdrawn from sale at the Watch and Ward's behest. Even Radclyffe Hall's groundbreaking lesbian novel, *The Well of Loneliness*, was deemed "not actionable" by the Watch and Ward. The book had been banned in England, after a sensational trial at which luminaries like Virginia Woolf and E. M. Forster tried (and failed) to testify for the defense, and came perilously close to being suppressed in more "liberal" New York City. But it was permitted to be sold in Boston. The Boston Police Department and the Suffolk District Attorney's office were relatively quiet during this period as well.

There were a number of reasons to explain this. Anti-censorship agitation was rising, with the introduction of three different bills in the Massachusetts legislature aimed at liberalizing the commonwealth's obscenity law. The city was receiving a raft of bad publicity as the term "banned in Boston" increasingly became a subject of mockery among the country's educated classes. In *Harper's Monthly*, Elmer Davis observed that "the city which used to write most of American literature was now forbidden by the police to read most of American literature." In lyrical, melancholy prose, he described the gilded State House dome (and by extension, the city) as "flawless, complete, finished, static, dead; it lies before you in an autumnal sunset splendor, like Rome under the Ostrogoths." The title of Davis's article was "Boston: Notes on a Barbarian Invasion."

Business leaders began to express concern that censorship might hurt not only Boston's image, but also its business climate. In a December 1927 letter to the *Boston Evening Transcript*, department store magnate A. Lincoln Filene worried that the city might be in danger of losing out to "younger and more vigorous sectors." "Perhaps it's up to those businessmen who have been laughing at the book censorship to take it a little more seriously," he wrote. Bookseller Richard Fuller observed that a large number of Boston book buyers had flocked to other cities to make their 1927 Christmas purchases, in some cases opening up charge accounts at New York bookstores. Perhaps Boston's censors had decided that the time had come for a period of calm.

But the calm didn't last. In April 1929, two years after Theodore Dreiser's novel *An American Tragedy* was originally banned and its publisher, Donald S. Friede, found guilty under the obscenity law, Friede's appeal finally went to trial. Two months later, a magazine serialization of Ernest Hemingway's novel *A Farewell to Arms* was banned. In the fall, Eugene O'Neill's Pulitzer Prize–winning play *Strange Interlude* was prevented from opening in Boston. Earlier that year, a Boston customs inspector had banned Voltaire's classic 1759 novella *Candide* under tariff laws that forbade the importation of obscene books.

The appeal trial of *An American Tragedy* publisher Friede illustrated the limitations of the commonwealth's censorship law. In its decision in the *Three Weeks* case back in 1909, the Massachusetts Supreme Judicial Court made it clear that the overall theme or moral stance or "lesson" of a book was immaterial so long as the work contained specific scenes or sections that might be considered indecent, obscene, or "manifestly tending to corrupt the morals of youth." A single passage found to be objectionable was enough to doom the most "moral" of books. This was a law—as censorship opponents such as Upton Sinclair were fond of point-ing out—that could have resulted in the suppression of certain plays by Shakespeare, or even the Bible. It was this narrow view of obscenity that the bills before the legislature at the time were attempting to change.

On the same day that the *American Tragedy* appeal opened, the Mas-sachusetts Senate rejected an effort to change the Massachusetts censor-ship law, insisting that a book's language be considered in connection with its entire context or theme. The bill, known as the "Massachusetts Library Club Bill" and supported by the Boston Bookseller's Committee, was defeated by a vote of 15 to 13. At a hearing a few months previously, the Watch and Ward president, the Reverend Raymond Calkins, was among those who testified against it.

The *American Tragedy* trial began on April 16, 1929, in Boston Superior Court, just two years and a day after Friede had been found guilty of sell-ing a copy of the 900 page novel, printed in two volumes, to Lieutenant Daniel J. Hines of the vice squad. Friede's legal team was led by Arthur Garfield Hays, who had defended Mencken in Boston three years earlier, and Clarence Darrow, the most famous criminal lawyer in the country and who had been lead defense counsel in the Scopes "monkey" trial. Defense witnesses were to include the author Dreiser himself and Rich-ard Fuller of the Boston Booksellers Committee. Friede and his attorneys were optimistic—at least until jury selection brought them back to reality. The jury, all-male and predominately Irish Catholic, was composed of "a janitor, a hatter, a shipper, an auto washer, a house painter, two machin-ists, two salesman, two clerks, and a treasurer," as Karl Schriftgiesser noted in the *New Republic*. This may have represented a fair cross-section of Boston's male citizenry, but it did not bode well for the defense.

On the first day of the trial, Assistant District Attorney Frederick T. Doyle read various pages from the book that his office had marked as ob-scene—a scene where Clyde Griffiths, the book's central character, visits a house of prostitution, a section concerning his girlfriend's pregnancy, and their fruitless efforts to obtain an abortion. The sections dealing with contraception and abortion were read to the jury, "with dramatic emphasis," according to Schriftgiesser. Prosecutor Doyle described the book as containing "the most disgusting, the most filthy, the most vi-cious, the most devilish language that a human being could think of."

Every time that defense attorney Arthur Garfield Hays tried to object or to introduce a different section of the novel to read aloud to put the allegedly obscene passages in the context of the entire book, the judge,

G. W. H. Hayes, blocked him. The judge was following the letter of the law: only the passages marked as obscene or indecent by the district attorney (all in volume one of the novel) could be entered as evidence, he ruled; no other passages or chapters were admissible. As the defendant, Friede, described it, "Hays [his attorney] had been jumping up and down all morning, objecting, arguing, questioning—and getting exactly no place. . . . [T]he judge refused to permit volume two to be introduced in evidence, refused to permit the whole of volume one from being introduced in evidence, refused Hays permission to read the first twenty-five pages of the book, in fact refused to do anything but make the jury consider the charges on the basis of the excerpts from volume one which had been read to them by the district attorney."

When the defense attorneys called Friede to the stand to give an outline of the book, they got nowhere. "Objection," shouted the district attorney. "Sustained," replied the judge. "Exception," said defense attorney Hays. Round and round they went. Hays put Dreiser himself on the stand and tried the same tactics, and a similar comedy ensued, with the book's author forbidden to explain what his book was about. Bookseller Fuller was permitted to say only that he had sold the book to mature individuals. And when Clarence Darrow took the stand as a defense witness, the judge dismissed the jury before permitting Darrow to speak. The attorney delivered an eloquent speech on the book as a moral lesson, with only the judge present to hear him; even reporters were ordered not to write about this part of the trial on penalty of contempt. In the end, the judge relented somewhat and allowed Darrow to read some sections of the book to the jury, but that was the extent of the trial lawyer's participation.

The courtroom proceedings were not going well for the defense, but even more damaging was a free speech/anti-censorship gathering held on the evening of the second day of the trial at Boston's Ford Hall Forum. Dubbed the "Ford Hall Frolic," the event was attended by 700 people and hosted by "Chief Roastmaster and Master of Rebelry," Harvard history professor Arthur Schlesinger. The evening featured birth control crusader Margaret Sanger with a gag on her mouth (public advocacy of birth control had been banned in Boston under Mayor James Michael Curley and continued under the current mayor, Malcolm Nichols), author Percy Marks in handcuffs (his novel The Plastic Age had been among the first novels suppressed in the censorship frenzy), and a skit called "The Suppressed Bookshop," which kept the audience in stitches for half an hour. The balcony was festooned with placards featuring titles of books that had been banned in Boston with words like "verboten" and "taboo" written under them. Students wearing costumes to resemble characters from banned novels wandered the hall. Clarence Darrow received a rapturous reception. A letter of support from H. L. Mencken was read, as was another from Upton Sinclair that went characteristically, "I would rather be banned in Boston than read anywhere else because when you are banned in Boston, you are read everywhere else." Arthur Garfield Hays read a mock letter supposedly sent by the Daughters of the Russian Revolution to the famously ultraconservative Daughters of the American Revolution, suggesting that both shared the same ideals—to prevent anyone from gaining any liberty.

The "frolic" was a lively and memorable one, and the bookshop skit —including a test necessary to be passed to buy the rhymes of Mother Goose—was the hit of the evening. But while the participants may have enjoyed themselves, the event backfired. The next day's newspapers were filled with angry letters condemning what readers called a bunch of elitists, many of them from other parts of the country, poking fun at Boston. Many saw the entire evening as an exercise in condescension, citing one woman in the bookshop skit who, when asked why she wanted to buy a specific title, replied, "I want to be intelligent, even if I do live in Boston."

Above all, the public reaction to the frolic sealed the fate of the American Tragedy appeal. For one thing, the presence of Margaret Sanger at the Ford Hall event unintentionally linked the book with birth control, precisely what the prosecutor was trying to do at the trial. The next day Darrow and Hays left town, thinking it better to leave the case in the hands of local attorney Thomas Lavelle. Lavelle asked for a new trial, telling the judge, "Mr. Friede is the victim of his friends, or if not, is the victim of those people at Ford Hall." The judge denied his request.

In his courtroom summation, Assistant District Attorney Doyle told the jury that he didn't know where the book's "imported attorneys" who had come to "our little village" got their ideas of obscenity. "I know not, sirs, from whence they derive their sociology or philosophy by which they determine what is obscene and what is not; I know not whether they are going to bring you to the jungles of Africa," he told the jurors. "But I got my notions, and I know you got yours, sirs, at your mother's knee when she prayed that you would be pure in thought, pure in word, pure in actions."

Friede lost his appeal and was offered the choice of ninety days in jail or a $300 fine. For a while, Friede toyed with becoming a martyr, reckoning that a stay in jail would give him a chance to catch up on his reading. "I was particularly anxious to read Proust slowly and without interruption," he wrote. But he opted to pay the fine instead. His further appeal to the Massachusetts Supreme Judicial Court failed the following year. Meanwhile, Lieutenant Hines never got the $5 he paid for *An American Tragedy* refunded by the police department. He was told that he was authorized to purchase narcotics or obscene postcards to secure evidence, but nowhere in the department's regulations did it say that he could purchase a book.

Anti-censorship forces were losing momentum, both in court and in the legislature, and two months later, another major novel fell to the censor's ax. On June 15, an emboldened Crowley asked Watch and Ward Secretary Bodwell to review the June issue of *Scribner's Magazine*. The magazine was serializing Ernest Hemingway's *A Farewell to Arms*, a World War I love story between an American ambulance driver on the Italian front and an English nurse; today, the book is viewed as one of Hemingway's finest novels. The June issue was the second installment and featured a scene in which the couple makes love for the first time, although the only hint of it is in the hero's own words, expressed in typical Hemingway style—"The wildness was gone and I felt finer than I had ever felt." Crowley believed that the chapter was "actionable"; Bodwell agreed. (Hemingway's first novel, *The Sun Also Rises*, had been banned in Boston in 1927.)

At Crowley's request, the New England News Company withdrew the issue from sale, although, as the *New York Times* noted, the action "was similar to locking the stable door after the horse had been stolen"—the magazine had been on the newsstands for three weeks at that point. A week later, the July issue, featuring the third installment of the novel, was also banned and withdrawn from newsstands and bookstores.

In a statement, Charles Scribner's Sons—publisher of both the book and the magazine—took very much the same line of argument used unsuccessfully against the suppression of *An American Tragedy*. It contended that the ban was an "improper use of censorship which bases its objections upon certain passages without taking into account the effect and purpose of the story as a whole." Arguing that the book was, in its effect, "distinctly moral," the statement continued, "If good can come from evil, if the fine can grow from the gross, how is a writer effectually to depict the progress of this evolution if he cannot describe the conditions from which the good evolved? If white is to be contrasted with black, thereby emphasizing its whiteness, the picture cannot be all white." The publishing house announced that installments of the novel would continue to run in *Scribner's*, and they did so for the next few months.

At this, all the frustrated *Boston Herald* could do was to throw up its hands: there was almost no point in expressing outrage any longer. The present censorship law, the newspaper editorialized, was "so unreasonable as to be farcical." But the law was the law, it noted, and the only opinions that counted were those of the police department, which had the final word. "Certain it is that far worse pages have been freely sold on our newsstands and plays depicting situations fully as offensive have been witnessed here in the not very remote past," the newspaper wrote. "But—there is the law such as it is, and there are enforcement agencies, and what are we to do about it?"

For the national press, the ban was further evidence that Boston's censors were running amuck. The liberal magazine the *New Republic* called it "a piece of stupid clowning which is sufficiently explained by saying that it took place in Boston." The *New York Herald Tribune* took a more arch view in an editorial headlined "Thanks to Chief Crowley." "Until Chief Crowley acted, many readers had doubtless missed Mr. Hemingway's powerful story, and they will be grateful to the chief [Crowley] for calling attention to it," the newspaper wrote.

Shortly after, another player—Mayor Malcolm Nichols—joined the censorship fray. In Boston, at the time, a theatrical license was granted at the pleasure of the mayor. According to law, if a play was considered not fit for public consumption, it could be stopped after being viewed by the mayor, the police superintendent, and the chief justice of the Municipal Court. So when Eugene O'Neill's play *Strange Interlude* was set to open in Boston in September 1929, it was Mayor Nichols who called a halt, making nationwide headlines and giving Boston yet another cultural black eye. In this decision, he was aided by the city's unofficial censor, John M. Casey (aka "Little Rollo"). Casey, a former drummer in burlesque pit bands and kettledrummer for the Boston Symphony Orchestra, had been appointed chief of the licensing division of the mayor's office back in 1904. His drumming career was cut short by an accident that required the amputation of his right arm, so his friends got him a job at City Hall. His theatrical standards were summed up in his statement: "Nothing should be placed upon the stage of any theatre anywhere to which you could not take your mother, sweetheart, wife, or sister." In his view, *Strange Interlude* did not fit the bill.

This was not Mayor Nichols's first foray into theatrical censorship. Eight months before, in December 1928, across the river in Cambridge, the Harvard Dramatic Club had put on Michael Gold's never-before-performed play *Fiesta*. Three performances were scheduled at Harvard's Brattle Hall, and the play would then move to Boston for a performance at John Hancock Hall. The work of a writer known for his left-wing politics—and for his fictionalized autobiography *Jews Without Money*, published two years later—*Fiesta* was a comedy with music set during a Mexican revolution against dictator Porfirio Diaz. Among the things that made the play noteworthy was that it required a parrot that swore in Spanish. (After a fruitless search throughout Boston for a Spanish-speaking parrot, a Harvard sophomore trained an English-speaking parrot to swear in fluent Spanish.) The parrot's lines remained, but a wary Harvard Dramatic Club went over the play several times and cut any other lines that might be offensive to good taste.

After the first performance, Cambridge Police Chief J. J. McBride received a complaint from a local lawyer. The chief sent two police sergeants and a policewoman to attend the next performance, and they found some of the dialogue "extremely objectionable" and the entire play thus "unfit for presentation." (It is not clear whether the parrot's lines were among those they deemed offensive.) The play was allowed to continue its run in Cambridge. However, that was not the case across the Charles. After receiving the police report and conferring with censor Casey and the corporation counsel, Mayor Nichols acted swiftly to ban the performance in Boston.

Eugene O'Neill's *Strange Interlude*, the winner of the 1928 Pulitzer Prize for drama, was a work of quite different magnitude. Produced by the prestigious Theatre Guild, it was a highly experimental play—a psychological examination of the mind of a woman from youth through middle age featuring characters who spoke their thoughts aloud in stream-of-consciousness asides that were more like a novel by James Joyce or Virginia Woolf. By the time it was scheduled to open in Boston, it had been seen by an estimated one-and-a-half-million people across the country. It had played for eighteen months in New York—resulting in the greatest financial profit ever made by a Theatre Guild production—and in state theaters in Stockholm, Vienna, and Budapest, with London and Berlin productions planned. The *Boston Globe* noted, "It is generally conceded by literary and dramatic critics that the play is Eugene O'Neill's masterpiece and called by some the greatest play ever written by an American." Fifty-five years later, New York Times theater critic Frank Rich described it as "a thunderous psychodrama that ushered Joycean modernism and Freudian theory into the American theater." The play became so ingrained in popular culture that Groucho Marx parodied it in a recurring gag in the film Animal Crackers. "Pardon me, while I have a strange interlude," Groucho says, looking straight at the camera and launching into a philosophical digression.

The play was also notable for being five hours long. Typically, performances began at 5:30 in the afternoon, continued without a break until 9:30, when there was an intermission so the audience could have supper, and then the play resumed, ending sometime around 11:00.

The touring company was to begin its Boston production on September 30, 1929. The Theatre Guild had been advertising it since May and had sold 7,000 advance tickets. The renowned actress Judith Anderson was scheduled to play the leading role. On September 16, two weeks before its scheduled opening, city censor Casey, acting on orders from Mayor Nichols, informed the Hollis Theatre that Strange Interlude would not be permitted to be performed in Boston. (Three years earlier, O'Neill's Desire Under the Elms had suffered a similar fate when censor Casey gave Mayor Curley a report proposing a complete revision of the play; at that point, the producers withdrew it.)

Nichols, a Republican, Harvard-educated lawyer and former federal tax collector, was hardly a moral paragon. Under his administration, graft was rampant at City Hall, according to Curley biographer Jack Beatty. Although Nichols, elected under a reform banner, was perhaps not personally dishonest, says Beatty, the mayor delayed action on land takings for a subway tunnel across the harbor to East Boston so his cronies could buy up the land and enrich themselves. In his autobiography, Mayor Curley puts it even more colorfully. Nichols was an "amateur," in Curley's view, and although a "highly reputable accountant [he] experienced considerable difficulty in accounting for some of the co-curricular activities of his department heads and palace guard."

The decision to ban the play, just two weeks before it was scheduled to open, shocked everyone. The Watch and Ward Society had actually approved the printed version as "not actionable," and the text could be purchased in Boston bookstores. The Theatre Guild promised to fight the suppression, and the local press was horrified. The Herald warned that the banning of Strange Interlude "will make the city a subject of national and international contempt and ridicule." The aristocratic Evening Tran-

script lamented, "Our city is a lasting loser in honor and general standing by the continuance of this nonsense." In a bitingly satiric editorial, the *Globe* suggested that City Hall's great objective was to enhance Boston's reputation for carrying the "banner" of "Banned in Boston." "Till the last Hottentot and the ultimate Eskimo have heard, till the denizens of farthest Siberia and Terra Del Fuego are familiar with the stimulating slogan [of Banned in Boston], we must not rest," lampooned the newspaper. "We must, like Columbus, go on and on, and on."

However, the mayor, who had the support of a number of Boston ministers, would not relent. After a meeting with representatives of the Theatre Guild, he announced that the play presented a "disgusting spectacle of immorality" and advocated atheism and infidelity. When the Theatre Guild offered to make some changes and eliminate some objectionable passages, the mayor emphasized that he objected to the entire theme of the play.

A week later, the Theatre Guild changed course. It decided to open the play in Quincy, a depressed industrial city of 70,000 located just south of Boston. The city, best known as the birthplace of John Adams and John Quincy Adams, was easily reachable by train. Thomas J. McGrath, the city's bachelor mayor, welcomed the play enthusiastically as a way to enhance his city's standing and boost its economy. "If the play is all right, the people will patronize it," he said. "If it's not, they won't tolerate it." However, Quincy was hardly known as a haven for liberal ideas, and McGrath appointed an informal jury of twenty-five clergymen and public officials to view the play on opening night. The theater where it would be performed, the Quincy Theater, was an old vaudeville house, whose main virtue was that it contained 1,400 seats.

On opening night, the Old Colony Railroad, which linked Quincy and Boston, put on extra trains. "The theater took on the air of a Hollywood premiere by late afternoon, as onlookers gawked at gowned and top-hatted socialites arriving in limousines, not entirely sure if the show would last beyond opening night," wrote the Quincy-based *Patriot Ledger* in an article memorializing the event years later. One critic of the time estimated that the audience that night was "ninety-nine and some tenths percent pure Bostonian."

When the performance finally concluded at 11:00 p.m., it received fourteen curtain calls. In the lobby afterwards, surrounded by well-wishers that included the governor's daughter, the mayor proclaimed it "a wonderful play, better than a hundred sermons." His hand-picked jury of local dignitaries backed him up. *Strange Interlude* continued in Quincy for another month, closing two days after the stock market crashed on October 24, ushering in the Great Depression. It was replaced the night after it ended by a vaudeville review called "On with the Show."

One spinoff effect was the success of a restaurant just across the street from the theater, where theatergoers repaired for a nine thirty p.m. supper during the five-hour play's intermission. The local restaurant, called Howard Johnson's, gained so much notoriety—and so many customers—during the run of *Strange Interlude* that it soon emerged as a restaurant and hotel chain ubiquitous across the American landscape. Boston censorship had created yet another success story.

CHAPTER 13

The Dunster Bookshop Fiasco, 1929

IN EARLY OCTOBER 1929, at a farmhouse in Madison, New Jersey, agents of the New York Society for the Suppression of Vice raided the Golden Hind Press. In the raid, the agents discovered order forms from the previous August for five copies of D. H. Lawrence's *Lady Chatterley's Lover*. The forms bore the name and address of Mr. James A. DeLacey at the Dunster House Bookshop in Cambridge, Massachusetts. Lawrence's erotic masterpiece about a married aristocratic woman who has an affair with her gamekeeper, described by the British author himself as "the most improper novel ever written," had been privately printed in Florence the year before; pirate editions were soon available in Paris and New York. John Sumner, the secretary of the New York anti-vice group, no slouch himself when it came to efforts at censorship (James Joyce's *Ulysses* and D. H. Lawrence's *Women in Love* were among his targets), immediately informed Charles Bodwell at the Watch and Ward of the Cambridge connection.

After staying away from most of the censorship excesses of the late 1920s, the Watch and Ward was still trying to find its footing after J. Frank Chase's death. Still, the society could not be counted out entirely. It had an endowment of close to $200,000 and many devoted contributors, and its vice presidents and directors included some of the most notable names in Brahmin Boston—among them the Episcopal and Methodist Episcopal bishops, the president of Boston University, and the headmaster of the Groton School. It had successfully blocked an effort to change the censorship law in early 1929. In the eyes of most of the country, Boston censorship still equaled the Watch and Ward. And the Watch and Ward was determined to live up to that reputation.

The result was the biggest blunder in the society's history, a blunder that came very close to destroying it utterly, and from which it never totally recovered.

Cambridge's Dunster House Bookshop was no ordinary bookstore. Located on Mt. Auburn Street (then called South Street), a few blocks from the center of Harvard Square in a small frame building that would later house the legendary undergraduate eating place, Elsie's, the Dunster House had a clientele primarily consisting of Harvard students and faculty. Its owner, James A. DeLacey, was a respected bibliophile who had been an assistant to the reference librarian at Yale. Three of the people for whom he had ordered Lady Chatterley were Harvard professors, one was a lawyer, and another was a book collector. DeLacey was the favorite bookseller of Harvard intellectuals.

On October 15, a Watch and Ward agent, John Tait Slaymaker, visited the bookshop and informed the manager and clerk, a young man named Joseph Sullivan, that he was interested in obtaining a copy of Lady Chatterley. Sullivan told him that they did not stock the book. If he wanted to order it, however, the bookshop could do so upon payment of $15. The agent returned the next day, when owner DeLacey was present, and placed an order for the book. When asked his name, the fifty-seven-year-old Slaymaker replied, "John Tait," which in fact represented only his first and middle names. The agent telephoned and then returned for a third time, on October 30, to pick up the book, a secondhand copy that DeLacey had obtained from a Harvard student. (Free-speech activist and author Christopher M. Finan suggests that the "student" may have in fact been yet another Watch and Ward agent.) DeLacey later stated that he had told Slaymaker he did not believe the book was fit to sell, although that did not stop him from doing so. On this visit, Slaymaker was accompanied by Watch and Ward secretary Charles Bodwell.

The Watch and Ward immediately began legal proceedings against DeLacey and Sullivan. On November 25, in Cambridge District Court, Judge Arthur P. Stone found both men guilty under the Massachusetts obscenity statute. Lady Chatterley's Lover, said the judge, was the most vicious piece of literature he had ever read in his life and the vilest he had seen in his twenty-five years on the bench. The same judge had convicted a Harvard Square news dealer for selling H. L. Mencken's *American Mercury* three years before. "Have this book wrapped up, sealed, and impounded," Judge Stone ordered his subordinates, "and keep it until you receive an order from the district attorney or the superior court." When the defense attorney, Richard C. Evarts, questioned the Watch and Ward's methods, Judge Stone threatened him with contempt. The sentences and fines imposed were extraordinarily heavy, even unprecedented, for a case of this nature. The judge sentenced DeLacey to four months in the House of Correction and fined him $800; Sullivan received two weeks in jail and a $200 fine.

DeLacey and Sullivan appealed the case to the Superior Court of Middlesex County. The case—especially the entrapment tactics employed by the Watch and Ward—immediately became a cause célèbre, arousing "the Harvard elements of Boston and Cambridge to an even greater extent than the banning of 'Strange Interlude,'" as Gardner Jackson wrote in the *Nation*. "It was the common tea-table and dinner talk in all Boston intellectual circles." Harvard students initiated a subscription fund to pay DeLacey's fine and assist him during his incarceration.

Boston newspapers, still exercised and embarrassed over the banning of *Strange Interlude* a few months earlier, showed no mercy to the Watch and Ward. In an editorial, the *Herald* went so far as to ask the question, rarely asked among Boston educated classes: Is the Watch and Ward Society "a necessity"? The newspaper answered its own question: "We hesitate to say. . . . If the Society is necessary, it is, as one well informed man has described it, a necessary and half-acceptable evil." It went on, attacking Watch and Ward tactics. "Its agents are given to excess," the newspaper wrote. "They acquire the professional, fanatical touch. They out-police the police. . . . Setting themselves up as guardians of morals, they resort to practices which fair-minded men loathe. . . . We cannot believe that all the officers approve of such methods as those used in the Dunster bookshop case, which, incidentally is not dissimilar from the procedure followed in a great many cases." The newspaper went on to list the officers of the society by name, in a kind of public flogging.

Then, on December 14, just a few days before the appeal trial was to begin, the first of what would soon be a long list of the society's directors resigned, in this case Harvard mathematics professor Julian L. Coolidge. Coolidge was slated to become the housemaster of Lowell House the following fall, and reports circulated that many students were refusing to live there because of his association with the Watch and Ward. "The fact that many Harvard men are thoroughly out of sympathy with the aims and methods of the Watch and Ward Society," wrote the *Harvard Crimson*, "makes it doubly desirable that University officials keep themselves from mixing in the many controversial questions with which the Society busies itself."

The appeal that began in Middlesex Superior Court on December 19, 1929, was, in many respects, as much a trial of the Watch and Ward and its tactics as it was a retrial of DeLacey and Sullivan. The courtroom was filled with "college men and women, [and] others bearing outward signs of 'the intelligentsia,'" according to the *Boston Globe*. Slaymaker and Bodwell testified, as did DeLacey. The bookseller's character witnesses included a historian, a Harvard English professor, and the Harvard librarian. The defense contended that the Watch and Ward had essentially induced the defendants to commit a crime, and it was particularly critical of Slaymaker for not using his real name in ordering the book. Watch and Ward agents were "procurers of crime, miserable false pretenders posing as the guardians of public morals," in the words of defense counsel Herbert Parker, former attorney general of Massachusetts.

Parker's harsh words might have been anticipated. What was not anticipated was the attitude of Middlesex County district attorney Robert T. Bushnell, the prosecutor in the case. A Harvard graduate with political ambitions himself (shortly after the trial, he announced his candidacy for the Republican nomination for lieutenant governor, and later he would serve as Massachusetts attorney general), Bushnell was focusing on the task in front of him: convicting DeLacey and Sullivan. To his mind, *Lady Chatterley's Lover* was "the work of a filthy degenerate, the product of a sewer brain," as he characterized the book in court. But he also made no bones about how he felt about the Watch and Ward Society, the very organization at whose behest he prosecuted the case. "I want the public to understand that the district attorney does not endorse the policy of the Watch and Ward Society," he said, in his summing up in court. Then, turning directly to Secretary Bodwell, seated only a few feet away from him, he stated bluntly, "I serve warning now that as long as I am district attorney of this district, and their agents go to a bookstore of good reputation and induce and procure the commission of a crime, I will proceed against them for conspiracy."

Going even further, Bushnell denounced the contributors and supporters of the Watch and Ward, alluding to the nation's increasingly dire economic situation—the stock market had crashed just two months before. "It is ironical to me," he said, "when misery and want fill the streets of every large city, that contributors, instead of bestowing their wealth for the benefit of the poor and unfortunate, consider it their duty to contribute to a private organization which hires paid snoopers to watch over the morals of the general public."

Bushnell's devastating courtroom comments demonstrated how low the Watch and Ward had fallen in the esteem of even law enforcement officials, who should have been its natural supporters. The judge in the case, Frederick W. Fosdick, was only slightly more charitable. "I do think," he said, "that the way in which the defendant was induced to sell the book calls for every part of the condemnation that has been placed on it by counsel for either side. . . . The court entertains no cordiality for the society."

The criticisms of the Watch and Ward made no difference in the final verdict, however. Judge Fosdick found that the book was obscene and that the state had convincingly proven that DeLacey and Sullivan had sold it. Poison was still poison, in the judge's view. He did somewhat mitigate the harsh sentences of the lower court, reducing DeLacey's prison time from four months to one month and his fine from $800 to $500. Sullivan's case was simply placed "on file."

Interestingly, the words "Lady Chatterley's Lover" were never spoken in the courtroom, by agreement of all parties, lest this might encourage members of the public to try and obtain the book. The *Boston Globe* never mentioned it in its coverage, although the *Boston Herald* and the *New York Times* did. When Robert T. Hillyer, assistant professor of English at Harvard, testifying for DeLacey, defended Lawrence as one of the most interesting modern authors, he was asked by District Attorney Bushnell, "You would not think of teaching that book in your classes?" Hillyer replied, "I shouldn't even mention it."

Realizing that perhaps incalculable damage had been done to its reputation, Watch and Ward secretary Bodwell and president Calkins quickly issued a statement just three days after the verdict, defending the society's tactics. After having received information that a book dealer had sold five copies of the book, "What, under such circumstances, should we do?" the statement demanded. "Should we have ignored such a situation? When our investigator went to interview this book dealer, should he have introduced himself as an agent of this society? When he found that this book was not on the shelves, should he have gone away? No efficient state detective would have done any such thing."

But the statement failed to contain the damage. One after another, some of the most prominent of the Watch and Ward directors and vice presidents decided that the society was not an organization with which they wished to be associated. Professor Coolidge, who had resigned even before the trial, was the first to go. Then came Bishop William Lawrence of the Episcopal Church, one of the most highly respected of the "proper Bostonians"; Bishop William F. Anderson of the Methodist Episcopal Church; Dean Henry B. Washburn of the Episcopal Theological School; and David D. Scannell, a prominent Boston surgeon. "I'm out, I'm free, and I'm glad to be out," was all that Dr. Scannell would say when questioned by the press. None of them condemned the society publicly, though. Daniel L. Marsh, the president of Boston University, held on until the following June, saying in a letter to Calkins that he had wanted to sever his connection with the organization for a long time but had remained on board "so that my withdrawal would not be any injury to the society." When Calkins sent him a letter pleading with him to reconsider, however, he refused.

In an additional attempt to keep things from deteriorating further, in that same month, the Watch and Ward asked William Henry Cardinal O'Connell if he might be interested in becoming an honorary vice president of the society. The invitation to the Roman Catholic prelate of Boston to join the leadership of the almost entirely Protestant Watch and Ward was a remarkable development, especially because the cardinal was a staunch proponent of keeping Catholics aloof from Protestants—going so far as to warn congregants never to attend Protestant services and ceremonies (including marriages and funerals) and even telling Catholic children not to join the Boy Scouts out of fear that they might be subjected to anti-Catholic attitudes. So the invitation to the cardinal was perhaps as indicative of the organization's desperation as anything else. While the Watch and Ward had frequently worked with Catholic police chiefs and public officials, it had never publicly cooperated with the cardinal on any issues over the years. In any event, Cardinal O'Connell rebuffed the Watch and Ward's overture; he was not about to get on board what appeared to be a sinking ship.

Equally significant was the loss of individual members who represented the bulwark of the organization. Typical was the response of Frederick Winsor, headmaster of the elite Middlesex School in suburban Concord, who had donated a total of $50 to the Watch and Ward from 1925 to 1928. When asked for his end-of-year donation, he refused. "Since

I am not in the least in sympathy with the prosecution in that case [Dunster House] or with the method of obtaining conviction by persuading individuals to commit crime," he wrote in a January 4, 1930, letter, "I do not desire to continue to support the work of the Watch & Ward Society." Mrs. E. W. Crew of Marlborough Street in Boston, who had given $180 over the years since 1909, had a similar reaction. In a letter to the society on December 21, 1929, the day after DeLacey's conviction, she wrote, "The methods of the Society in the Dunster House case cannot meet the approval of right minded people. I appreciate the good work done in the past and am sorry to discontinue my subscription." Mrs. A. Martin Pierce of New Bedford, who had given a total of $108 starting in 1916, was more succinct—and more brutal. "Gentlemen—Please remove my name from your list of donors—and never again send me any appeals," she wrote in a December 19, 1929, response to her donation request.

The Watch and Ward annual reports reported a drop in contributions from $6,800 in February 1929 to $4,278 in February 1931 and $3,180 in February 1932. Part of that drop could be credited to the Great Depression, but clearly the Dunster House Bookshop affair had hurt the society's finances as well.

Although the Watch and Ward publicly promised to investigate itself, Secretary Bodwell was privately unrepentant. In a letter thanking John Sumner, his counterpart in New York, for his support, Bodwell found other reasons for the society's troubles. "All the wets [liquor interests] are against us because our work has brought us into conflict with some disreputable hotels and cafés," he wrote Sumner. "A big drive against 'censorship' was on that added to the reasons why the papers should attack us just at that time." And he added, "We are going about our business just as unconcernedly as the Coast Guard is." (The latter comment was a reference to an incident in which an angry crowd tore down and trampled posters at a Coast Guard recruiting station on the Boston Common in early January, after the Coast Guard killed three rum-runners in the waters off Newport.)

The tactics employed by the Watch and Ward in the Dunster House Bookshop case were not significantly different from those the society's agents had used in the past, as the Herald editorial had pointed out. The society had employed undercover agents to ferret out crime and so-called indecent literature many times over the years. However, this time the target was Harvard—or at least an establishment dear to Harvard's hearts. Boston's educated classes were clearly fed up with the reputation that strict censorship laws and obscenity prosecutions were giving to the city that prided itself as the "Athens of America." Many were beginning to feel that the Watch and Ward had outlived its usefulness.

One of those people was Middlesex District Attorney Bushnell. In late January 1930, a month after the Dunster House trial, the district attorney called for the abolition of the Watch and Ward. The legislature had to power to abolish the organization entirely, he said, and "it would be a good thing."

Bushnell was speaking before a State House hearing on the liberalization of the Massachusetts obscenity law, a hearing attended by some 400 people. "I am sick to death of having Boston and Massachusetts represented as backwoods sections populated by yokels without backbone and spirit, who are compelled to look to others for permission to read, think, speak, or see," he said. At the hearing, a Watch and Ward director, Bernard J. Rothwell, spoke out against any change in the law, but his was a lone voice.

In fact, one of the consequences of the Dunster Bookshop fiasco was the renewed energy that it gave to supporters of obscenity law reform. The vote in the Senate the year before on liberalizing the law had been close, and pressure had been building for some time. After the hearing at which Bushnell spoke so passionately, the legislature's Joint Committee on Legal Affairs unanimously reported the bill favorably to the Senate. In mid-March, the Senate passed the bill, and then the House did the same, in the latter case by a 121–89 margin, with most of the Boston representatives opposed. The governor signed the new law shortly after its passage.

The new law hardly meant the end of censorship in Massachusetts, however. It removed some of the original obscenity language—that a book "containing obscene, indecent, or impure language or manifestly tending to corrupt the morals of youth" could be banned. Instead, a book could be banned if it was "obscene" in and of itself. (The new legal language read simply "which is obscene.") Language about taking into consideration "the book as a whole" was deleted as a compromise, to the dismay of censorship opponents. But the final effect was more or less the same. Obscene language or passages in themselves were not enough to ban a book; they would have to be viewed in the context of the entire work. That made it more difficult to ban a book like An American Tragedy or A Farewell to Arms, although probably not Lady Chatterley's Lover. (In March

1930, in the wake of the banning of Voltaire's *Candide* by customs agents, the U.S. Congress followed the same path, requiring customs officials to consider the work "as a whole" when determining whether to allow a book into the United States; foreign classics and books of "literary and scientific merit" were now permitted. This change helped pave the way to the lifting of the ban on the importation of James Joyce's *Ulysses* in 1933.)

The Watch and Ward tried to put the best face on the new law, stating in its 1930–31 annual report that the revision "met the entire approval of the Society" and "does not in any sense facilitate the distribution of indecent literature." In fact, the society noted, the new law relieved librarians and booksellers of "certain embarrassments."

Later that year, after the Massachusetts Supreme Court denied Dunster House bookseller DeLacey's appeal in June 1930, District Attorney Bushnell revoked DeLacey's prison sentence. (His fine was paid by contributions from the Harvard community.) In the days after his sentence was revoked, the *Harvard Crimson* reported that the bookseller had received more than 200 congratulatory letters and telegrams from all over the country, and "more messages are arriving at his office hourly." Almost every one of these messages denounced the Watch and Ward. But DeLacey did not triumph in the end. His bookshop went out of business, his wife left him, and he reportedly died of alcoholism some years later. The Watch and Ward, though significantly weakened, lived on to fight another day.

CHAPTER 14

Depression Days, 1930–1938

SINCE THE MENCKEN AFFAIR, nothing seemed to have gone right for the Watch and Ward. The timing of the Dunster House prosecution couldn't have been worse—on the heels of the *Strange Interlude* controversy, which made many Bostonians even less inclined to censorship of any sort, and two months after the stock market crash. The Great Depression that followed redirected everyone's attention from moral issues, and it also affected the pocketbooks of Watch and Ward contributors. Donations, which had plunged in the aftermath of Dunster House, continued their downward trajectory; throughout the 1930s, they remained at well under half of what they had been in 1929. Still, the society had substantial financial resources, with an endowment close to $200,000. And although some of its most distinguished higher-ups did resign in the wake of Dunster House, others remained (Godfrey Cabot and Groton School headmaster Endicott Peabody, to name two). The following year, when Calkins stepped down as president—remaining as a director—John C. L. Dowling, the widely respected former chairman of the state's "watchdog" Boston Finance Commission, was named to succeed him. Like the Coast Guard, as Secretary Bodwell put it, the Watch and Ward was determined to carry on.

Nonetheless, in response to all the criticism that it had received after the Dunster prosecution, the society made a tactical retreat. No longer would it bring cases on its own, independent of the police or other pros-

ecuting authorities. The "unofficial censoring" of books by the organization would come to an end, as well. "The Watch and Ward Society . . . no
longer gives its opinion in advance to those who ask for it, concerning
the legality of the sale of certain books under the law," stated the 1930–31
annual report. "We desire that this shall be distinctly understood. Officially, this Society does no more advance book censoring and cannot
justly be criticized in the future on this score." Neither of these vows
would last very long, and it isn't clear whether the new policy on book
censorship was ever put into practice.

Only two months after the Dunster House debacle, the Watch and
Ward was back in the business of banning books. In February 1930, the
society received a complaint from Superintendent Crowley about Michael
Gold's *Jews Without Money*, a fictionalized account of his life growing up
in the tenements of New York's Lower East Side that helped define the
proletarian movement in American literature of the 1930s. The Harvard
dramatic production of Gold's play *Fiesta* (including the swearing parrot) been banned in Boston a couple of years earlier. Secretary Bodwell
deemed *Jews Without Money* "actionable," and President Calkins described
it as "doubtful"; that information was sent to Crowley. It may have been
the book's radical politics, more than anything else, that doomed it in
Boston—it ends with a paean to the worldwide revolution, which the author, later a columnist for the Communist newspaper the *Daily Worker*,
announces to be "the true Messiah" that will transform the Lower East
Side into "a garden for the human spirit."

If the Watch and Ward retreated at all, it retreated to the tactics of the
"gentlemen's agreement" days. Georgia-born novelist Erskine Caldwell's
God's Little Acre, a story of a family of impoverished—and sexually avari-
cious—Southern farmers and millworkers, became a target both of the
New York Society for the Suppression of Vice and the Watch and Ward.
But while the New York Society's attempt to ban *God's Little Acre* in that
city wound up in a noisy courtroom (where the case was thrown out),
in Boston it was all done behind the scenes, in the old-style Watch and
Ward manner. In March 1933, after the society found *God's Little Acre* to be
"clearly actionable," the book was quietly removed from Boston bookstores by the Board of Trade of Boston Book Merchants, the successor
organization to the Boston Booksellers Committee.

The Watch and Ward also considered banning Caldwell's novel *Tobacco Road*, but in the end it changed its mind. The book was "extremely
dirty and revolting," in the view of the Reverend Raymond Calkins, yet

"the descriptions and characters were too realistic to be obscene." In July 1933, the Watch and Ward determined that the book was "not actionable."

Then there was the matter of Nathaniel West's novel *Miss Lonelyhearts*, an acclaimed black comedy about an advice-to-the-lovelorn columnist. The Watch and Ward had declared its disapproval of it in May 1933, but the Board of Trade's Fuller pleaded with the society to reconsider. The novel was making "quite a hit" in New York, he told Secretary Bodwell, and he doubted that they could win a legal case if the publisher went to court. However, the Watch and Ward held its ground, with Calkins arguing that the book should be banned not because of obscenity but because it was "blasphemous and extremely sacrilegious." This was not the first time that religion, not obscenity, was the proposed basis of a Boston banning, as cases of books ranging from *Elmer Gantry* to Bertrand Russell's *What I Believe* had proved in the past. Because these suppressions were done behind the scenes—and rarely had to be argued in court—books that were offensive to religion or religious institutions could be censored without any perceived connection to the state's obscenity statute. (If necessary, the state's blasphemy law could be invoked.) As for *Miss Lonelyhearts*, it is not clear whether the book was actually removed from Boston bookshelves.

In many other cases of lesser-known books, "gentle persuasion" of book dealers, either by the Watch and Ward or a local police chief, proved effective. For example, in December 1931, while Secretary Bodwell was in the western Massachusetts city of Pittsfield investigating the sale of lottery tickets, he borrowed a copy of the Dorothy Herzog novel *Some Like It Hot* from a local lending library. A Roxbury book dealer had already been convicted of selling it. The secretary spoke to the Pittsfield chief of police, and the chief said he would be glad to take care of the matter without a prosecution. On December 22 of that same year, a Watch and Ward agent checked Tiffany Thayer's best-selling novel *Thirteen Men* out of a lending library in Medford, a suburb of Boston. The book, which tells the life stories of twelve jurors and an accused killer, was notable for its experimental structure and what *Time* magazine described as a "gaudy, perfervid" quality. When, upon returning the book, the agent announced that he worked for the Watch and Ward, the abashed proprietor assured him that the book had been kept in circulation by mistake. He then led the agent into the basement of his shop and showed him several hundred books that had been withdrawn because they had been banned. He had faithfully adhered to the list sent out by the Board of Trade of Boston Book Merchants, he insisted. Again, no legal action appears to have been taken.

The decade also marked the Watch and Ward's first—and last—forays into the world of movie censorship, something it generally considered to be outside its scope. In October 1932, John Tait Slaymaker, late of the Dunster House matter, attended a showing of the film version of *Strange Interlude*, starring Clark Gable and Norman Shearer. The Watch and Ward had not objected to the play when Mayor Malcolm Nichols banned it, but now that it was a movie, the society apparently decided it was worthy of one of its crack investigators. Slaymaker wrote up a long report, in somewhat tortured prose, in which he found "the most devastating feature of the picture, as I could see it, was the display of the uncontrolled emotions and the selfishness of desire. In the course of the picture, references are very guardedly made to actions that are purposely reprehensible and none of these occurrences are reproduced on the screen." In short, there was no basis for action.

A few months later, in January 1933, the target was the movie version of Ernest Hemingway's novel *A Farewell to Arms*, which the Watch and Ward had played a role in banning as a magazine serial in 1929. (The movie, starring Gary Cooper and Helen Hayes, would eventually be nominated for an Oscar for Best Picture.) It was playing at two downtown Boston theaters, and newspaper advertisements touted the film with the tagline, "Let's Love Tonight . . . There May Be No Tomorrow." The Watch and Ward wrote a letter to the mayor's office complaining about the film's "objectionable features"—most likely, premarital sex and out-of-wedlock pregnancy. By the following week, the film had vanished from Boston theaters, but it is not clear whether that was the result of the Watch and Ward's complaint or the normal changes in movie schedules. In any event, Watch and Ward officials weren't the only ones unhappy with the film; Hemingway himself refused to see it because Hollywood gave his book a happy ending.

If the Watch and Ward was treading carefully in terms of books and movies, magazine censorship offered a more fertile field for action. Back in January 1929, at the society's invitation, fourteen magazine distributors from various cities in Massachusetts (plus one from Portland, Maine) met at the Boston City Club. They established an organization called New England Magazine Distributors, whose object was "to uphold the law regarding the sale of indecent literature in Massachusetts." A successor to the old Massachusetts Magazine Committee, it signaled a rejuvenated Watch and Ward role in this field. Wholesale magazine dealer Meyer J. Reiser was elected president, and Watch and Ward secretary Bodwell was made an ex officio member of the executive committee.

Many of those present at the meeting had actually been arrested previously as a result of Watch and Ward crackdowns. In Reiser's capacity as a magazine wholesale agent, he and others had distributed magazines to dealers without knowing which ones were legal and which weren't. "By handling magazines which are against the law, we found ourselves in a lot of trouble through different methods such as the police, and the Watch and Ward Society," Reiser said, "and quite a number of times retail dealers who were innocent of breaking the law were taken into court and had to pay a fine, also wholesalers."

In the wake of the meeting, an arrangement emerged that was very similar to the "gentlemen's agreement" regarding books. Magazine publishers would be asked to submit copies of their publications to the Watch and Ward, and telegrams would be sent to all member news dealers notifying them when any were disapproved. Although Scribner's Magazine would be targeted later that year for publishing A Farewell to Arms, most of the magazines in question were far less literary in nature, featuring names like Hollywood Nights, Paris Nights, Pep, Hot Dog, French Follies, Screen Art Studies, Broadway Nights, Snappy Stories, Ginger, and Spicy Stories. By 1930, Bodwell could state proudly that during the year, 122 issues of magazines had been submitted, with 54 of them deemed actionable and withdrawn from sale.

Reiser himself would insist, "I am not a member of the Watch and Ward Society. I am a wholesaler." But the New England Magazine Distributors was unquestionably a Watch and Ward operation, which distributors joined not out of any moral zeal but more out of a desire to protect themselves from prosecution.

The campaign against questionable magazines quickly expanded into the other New England states. In the spring of 1930, Bodwell, visiting New London, Connecticut, found copies of Hollywood Nights, Spicy Stories, Hot Dog, and Paris Nights on sale on newsstands on the main street. New London was a town with a rough-and-tumble maritime history and, in the nineteenth century, it had been the biggest whaling port in the country after Nantucket and New Bedford; it also had a flourishing red-light district. However, when Bodwell took his information to the local prosecutor, Max Boyer, he found him "the least willing to cooperate" of all the public officials he had approached in New England.

"What are you down in Connecticut for?" Boyer demanded. "Don't you have enough [to do] in Massachusetts?"

Bodwell replied, somewhat smugly, that prosecutions in Massachusetts had all but eliminated such magazines.

This line of argument failed to win over Boyer. *Hollywood Nights*, *Hot Dog*, and other magazines of their type remained openly for sale in New London, even as officials in Bridgeport, Danbury, New Britain, and Waterbury promised to remove them in those Connecticut cities.

Despite some setbacks, the Watch and Ward's battle against such magazines continued. In 1935, Bodwell was writing to his colleague, the Reverend Henry Pringle of the International Reform Federation in Washington, D.C., that newsstands in Boston, Providence, Springfield, and Manchester, New Hampshire, were "reasonably clean." The same could be said for Bangor and Portland, Maine, and Burlington, Vermont. The two most troublesome cities were Rutland, Vermont, and Portsmouth, New Hampshire. New London was not mentioned.

As a magazine censor, the Watch and Ward remained influential through much of the 1930s. Midwest Distributors, the Minneapolis-based dealer of magazines of somewhat dubious respectability, including *True Confessions*, *Radio Land*, *Golfer and Sportsman*, *Hooey*, and *Whiz Bang*, communicated directly with Bodwell on a monthly basis. In the case of popular but often raunchy humor magazine *Whiz Bang*, established in 1919 by Captain Wilford H. Fawcett, the company actually published a special edition for Massachusetts readers based on Bodwell's objections. (At its height, just after World War I, *Whiz Bang* claimed a circulation of nearly a million, but by the 1930s, its readership was declining because of the Depression and competition with the more sophisticated *Esquire*.)

Usually Bodwell and Robert Haig, the circulation manager in Minneapolis, communicated by telegram. So when the May 31, 1935, issue of *Whiz Bang* was approved, Bodwell's telegram said, "JULY WHIZ BANG DEEMED NOT ACTIONABLE." The previous month, however, the magazine required some changes before Bodwell would allow the issue to be sold in Massachusetts. His telegram read: "WITHOUT ARTICLE PROBABLY MISSED HER CUE PAGE FIFTY WHIZ BANG JUNE DEEMED NOT ACTIONABLE." A similar exchange that month took place regarding the June issue of the humor magazine *Hooey* (a precursor of *Mad*).

Haig's telegram, dated April 24, said: "IF PAGES THREE NINETEEN
TWENTY TWENTY ONE REMOVED JUNE HOOEY WILL YOU WITH-
DRAW OBJECTION TO NE DISTRIBUTION." Bodwell replied the same
day: "WITHOUT THREE NINETEEN TWENTY TWENTY ONE HOOEY
JUNE WOULD BE DEEMED NOT ACTIONABLE." In such snappy fash-
ion proceeded magazine censorship in 1930s Boston.

Whiz Bang's competition, the increasingly popular Esquire, also came
under the Watch and Ward's scrutiny, but the society's ability to influence
its content is less evident. In April 28, 1936, Endicott Peabody, headmaster of the Groton School, wrote Bodwell to ask, "Has the Watch and Ward
ever taken up the magazine called 'Esquire' with a view to their making
it decent or driving it out of existence?" Peabody had discovered a student
reading the May issue, which the headmaster found "not only vulgar but
blasphemous." Since Peabody was a vice president of the Watch and Ward,
a pillar of Boston society, and the most revered private school headmaster in the country, Bodwell replied quickly in a May 1 letter. The previous
January, he explained, the Watch and Ward had conferred with Boston
wholesalers about the magazine, and they in turn had conferred with Esquire's publishers. The result was "the elimination of the worst features
in succeeding issues." But Bodwell admitted to Peabody, "It certainly is
far from uplifting now and is highly objectionable. The new complaint
gives me good reason for further going over the matter with the people
concerned." However, nothing further seems to have happened.

The most publicized censorship controversies of the decade involved neither books nor magazines—they involved the theater. There, the Watch
and Ward's jurisdiction was limited because of the law giving the Board
of Censors—made up of the mayor, the police commissioner, and the
chief justice of the municipal court—ultimate authority in such matters.
Boston had its own strict code of theatrical morality, promulgated in 1915
under Mayor James Michael Curley and revised in 1934. Among other pro-
hibitions, the revised code banned "the appearance of female performers
without proper covering for the body," language that was "obscene or lascivious," and profanity. It also forbade the portrayals of "a dope fiend" or
"a moral pervert or sex degenerate."

The original code had not banned the use of profanity outright. However, in 1924, Mayor Curley issued a special edict prohibiting profanity of
all kinds on stage, including "damn," "hell," and "My God." (This was

codified in the 1934 revision.) In an article about the announcement, the *Boston Herald* mocked the mayor with a short poem, meant to be in the mayor's own voice:

> *You must never use a big, big D—*
> *You must never, never say, "My G!"*
> *That's my public ultimatum.*
> *They are bad words, and I hate 'em.*
> *Yes, and H—is also barred by me.*

With the revised code as the legal basis, 1935 became a momentous year for theatrical censorship in Boston. Three plays by major playwrights faced the censors' wrath. Two of them—eminent Irish playwright Sean O'Casey's *Within the Gates* and Lillian Hellman's *The Children's Hour*—were never permitted to open, while the opening performance of a third play —Clifford Odets's *Waiting for Lefty*—culminated in the arrest of four members of the cast. In the case of *Within the Gates*, in an ironic twist, the Watch and Ward wound up siding with the play, not the censors.

Within the Gates marked the first time that high Roman Catholic officials had publicly become involved in Boston theatrical censorship. O'Casey's play, set in London's Hyde Park, is a dark allegory of a bishop's illegitimate daughter who becomes a prostitute and dies in a poet's arms. The bishop's religion isn't specified, although the general assumption was that he was Roman Catholic. When it opened in New York in October 1934, *New York Times* drama critic Brooks Atkinson called *Within the Gates* "a great play," adding, "Nothing so grand has risen in our impoverished theatre since this reporter first began writing of plays." However, Father Russell M. Sullivan, a Jesuit priest and the head of the statewide Boston College Council of Catholic Organizations, saw it very differently. With the play slated to open in Boston in early January 1935, Father Sullivan, who was also active in the Legion of Decency (the Catholic censorship board that monitored and rated movies), launched a campaign to ban it, attacking the "sympathetic portrayal of the immoralities described"— prostitution, for one. As much as anything, he objected to "the clear setting forth of the futility of religion as an effective force in meeting the problems of life."

Boston's mayor at the time was Frederick W. Mansfield, a politician famously described by a newspaper reporter as "spectacular as a four-day-old codfish and as colorful as a lump of mud." A Catholic who would later serve as legal counsel to William Henry Cardinal O'Connell—many assumed that he had the cardinal's backing in his first, unsuccessful run for mayor against his arch-rival Curley some years before—Mansfield at first approved the play, with a few minor changes of language. However, under pressure from Sullivan and others, he sent City Censor Herbert L. McNary—John M. Casey's successor—to view the play in New York, where it had been running for two months. McNary returned convinced that the play should never see the light of day in Boston, and the mayor agreed, adding that he would personally take steps to prevent the sale of the printed edition as well. Within the Gates, said Mayor Mansfield, was "nothing but a dirty book full of commonplace smut."

Then, unexpectedly, the Watch and Ward entered the fray. "I doubt if it is bad enough to be banned," the society's new president Frank Chouteau Brown told the newspapers. Like the mayor, he hadn't seen the play and based his opinion on that of friends who had. The Watch and Ward also found the book version of Within the Gates to be "not actionable."

It was a curious and perhaps unprecedented moment: The Watch and Ward stood on one side, and the mayor, the city censor, and a number of religious groups—Catholic, Methodist, and Universalist—on the other. In an article the previous March, the New York Times had hailed Brown's ascent to the Watch and Ward presidency, describing Brown—an architect who had served as the head of Boston University's department of art and architecture and was a member of the Watch and Ward's board of directors—as "an open-minded, enlightened man who has frequented the playhouses all his life, who is well disposed toward the stage and the public." It went on, "Consequently, [there is] a general belief that, so far as it busies itself with the theatre, the Watch and Ward will pursue a more civilized course than has been its habit." The Times added that, "better still," the censorship of the "austere Mansfield" shows "signs of intelligent relaxation." In the latter prediction, the Times was wrong.

The Board of Censors, headed by the mayor, barred the play from opening, calling it "drenched in sex," and the Shubert Theatre was forced to refund thousands of dollars in advance ticket sales. By order of the new police superintendent (Crowley had died in 1933), the printed edition of the play was also banned. Letters poured into Boston's newspapers, mostly attacking the censors. Professor Henry Wadsworth Longfellow Dana, grandson of the poet and known for his left-wing political activism (he had lived for long stretches of time in the Soviet Union), announced he was going to do a public reading of the play at Tremont Temple downtown. The title of the play, after all, had come from one of his grandfather's poems. Dana was denied a permit, so he had to read the play at a private home instead; the city fathers were determined that Bostonians would not be exposed to Within the Gates in any public setting.

However, Boston theatergoers proved resourceful. A few days later, forty-six of them, including drama critics from four of the city's newspapers, made an excursion to New York to see the play there, most travelling in a streamlined railroad coach named for the occasion "The O'Casey Special." The trip, organized by the play's producers, included transportation, hotel accommodations, and an orchestra seat to Within the Gates, all for the relatively modest price of $16.50. "After all Boston's talk, it was extraordinary to come in and see a normal audience sitting there and enjoying it," said Edwin F. Melvin, drama critic for the Transcript. The New York Times account couldn't resist a poke at Boston censorship, headlining its article, "46 BOSTON REBELS ELUDE CENSOR HERE."

After the suppression of Within the Gates, Mayor Mansfield announced that in the future, any play would be allowed at least one performance in Boston before a ban could be imposed. So Clifford Odets's social protest drama, Waiting for Lefty, was permitted to open on April 5, 1935, at the Dudley Street Opera House before 500 people. It was no ordinary opening, however. Waiting for Lefty was a passionate play about a taxi strike, with revolutionary overtones. Members of the Boston police's "Red Squad," whose job was to keep tabs on radical elements, surrounded the theater. Sitting in the audience were City Censor McNary, a police captain, and a police sergeant. At the end of the play, on orders from McNary, police arrested four of the nine cast members and charged them with using profanity in a public assemblage. The play was ordered to close.

Waiting for Lefty's dialogue was filled with exclamations like "damn," "goddamn," and "Christ," language characteristic perhaps of New York City taxi drivers but a violation of Boston's moral code. However, there was widespread speculation that the real reason for Lefty's closure was not so much its language but its unabashedly radical politics. In fact, playwright Odets had been so sure that his play would be banned for that reason that he had issued a statement condemning its closing two days before it opened, even though neither the police nor the city had taken any action. " 'Waiting for Lefty' has been closed by the Boston Police," Odets's statement said. " 'Expressive of un American activity' is the charge. Americanism depends upon your point of view. If you are afraid of the deepest truths of the class conflicts of our times, all liberal or radical activity may be so labeled." He couldn't resist a jab at the locals, adding, "According to the Boston gentry, the legal murder of Sacco and Vanzetti was a decided American activity."

In the end, the official charge was profanity, and in that sense the Boston censors had outfoxed Odets. But Odets was the playwright of the moment (his plays *Awake and Sing* and *Till the Day I Die* had just been produced in New York, as had *Waiting for Lefty*), and Boston was under some pressure to permit a toned-down version of *Lefty*. A week later, the New Theatre League, the Boston producer, agreed to delete all profanity from the play, and it was allowed to open. At the court hearing, one actor, charged with profanity, was acquitted, while another was fined $1 as "a suspicious person." Oddly enough, the Western Union Telegraph Company ended up bearing a larger share of the financial hardship. The company was fined $500 for transmitting and delivering messages protesting the arrest of the actors. The messages had charged a "frame-up" and demanded the release of the men.

The Watch and Ward played no role in *Waiting for Lefty's* problems. A letter from Secretary Bodwell to Asher Lans, representing a group of students protesting a production of the play at Dartmouth College the following month, indicated that the society was favorably disposed towards *Lefty*, at least the "cleaned-up version." Bodwell admitted that the play contained vulgarity and profanity that "skated" near the edge of the obscenity law. However, he then proceeded to characterize Odets's play in sympathetic terms. "In essence the play is a protest against economic injustices or oppression, either real or fancied," he wrote. "I recall nothing in it that could be called seditious. It would seem to this mind that a kindly, persuasive presentation of the matter, either directly through the office of the University's Secretary or President, might secure modifications of the play to leave it unobjectionable."

In a curious sidebar, *Waiting for Lefty* did have one more Boston performance—an unauthorized one. It all had to do with another play about a strike, Paul Peters and George Sklar's *Stevedore*, a drama about black dockworkers in New Orleans who attempt to unionize after one is falsely accused of rape. *Stevedore* had opened in Boston in late September 1935 with the approval of Censor McNary and under the watchful eye of the police "Red Squad." The play's all-black cast was on the payroll of a drama project funded through the New Deal's Emergency Relief Appropriations Act (ERA), which, among other things, gave work to unemployed actors; actors on its payroll were permitted to do additional commercial work

like *Stevedore*. However, on the Saturday of the play's first week, ERA officials ordered the entire cast instead to Saugus, a town north of Boston, to
perform *Macbeth* at a time that conflicted with the performance of *Stevedore*. The play's producers, the New Theatre Players, were convinced that
the Red Squad had persuaded federal officials to schedule the conflict-
ing performance to sabotage *Stevedore* and force it to close. According to
them, the police had been harassing the production all week.

So the producers came up with a last-minute scheme. While the actors
were rushing through Shakespeare in Saugus, a "filibuster" would take
place at the Boston theater until the cast could make it back. That filibuster was highlighted by an unscheduled performance of *Waiting for Lefty*,
by yet another group of actors, interrupted by updates on the progress
of the cast's return from Saugus. When *Lefty* was finished, writer Albert
Maltz (later a member of the blacklisted Hollywood Ten) gave a speech
on censorship. At exactly 9:50 p.m., "after a breathtaking ride from Saugus," the cast finally arrived, having "doffed Shakespeare costumes and
donned waterfront motley," as the *New York Times* account described it.
With the Red Squad watching closely, the curtain went up on *Stevedore*.
"Censorship has been smashed in Boston or at least it has been reduced
to the final absurdity," proclaimed Frank L. Asher, executive secretary of
the New Theatre Players.

However, there was more absurdity to come. It involved Lillian
Hellman's play *The Children's Hour*, scheduled to open at Boston's Shubert
Theater on January 6, 1936. The critically acclaimed play, already running in New York City for thirteen months at that point, concerns two
boarding school headmistresses who are accused of having a lesbian relationship by a troublemaking ten-year-old student; the untrue accusation ruins their lives, closes the school down, and drives one of them to
commit suicide. Censor McNary was once again dispatched to New York
to see the production, and he reported back to the mayor unfavorably.
The homosexual aspect of the theme would bring it to the attention of
the board of censors automatically, he noted. Mayor Mansfield informed
the play's producers that he had read the play and that, as a member of the
board of censors, he was "unalterably opposed" to it. Producer Herman
Shumlin then offered to bring the entire cast of sixteen to Boston, plus
the set, for a private screening before the board. The mayor respectfully
declined the offer.

While the producers were considering opening the play in a Boston
suburb, as had been done with *Strange Interlude*, author Lillian Hellman

issued a statement suggesting that she might turn the matter into a "test case." She added, "But you might tell Mayor Mansfield that his righteous citizens will get to see it anyway. I've just returned from Hollywood, where I sold the movie rights to the play."

For his part, producer Shumlin was determined to fight. He petitioned the federal district court to enjoin the city from blocking the production. Next, he filed suit against the mayor and the city censor, demanding $250,000 in damages and accusing them of slandering and libeling his play. Leading lady Anne Revere sued the same two officials for $50,000 to protect her own reputation from the accusation of appearing in an indecent play. At the hearing on the injunction, Censor McNary told the judge that what bothered him the most about the play was the scene in which the little girl tells her grandmother that her two headmistresses engaged in "unnatural relations" and then whispers into her grandmother's ear exactly what occurred. The mayor also testified, invoking the Moral Code prohibition against any portrayal of a "moral pervert or sex degenerate." He also insisted that he hadn't actually banned the production; he had only told the producers that they would have to go before the censorship board. Judge George Sweeney sided with the city and refused to grant the injunction. The suits against Mansfield and McNary failed as well.

The Boston censors had the last laugh on The Children's Hour in another sense. As playwright Hellman had haughtily told the press, the play was indeed made into a movie a year later, directed by William Wyler with a screenplay by Hellman. But the title was changed to We Three, and the accusation of a lesbian love affair was transformed into a heterosexual one involving one of the teachers and the fiancé of her colleague. On orders of the Hays Office—Hollywood's censorship bureau—Hellman was given no screen credit and the advertisements never mentioned that the movie was based on the play. (In 1961, a second movie based on The Children's Hour was made, using its own name, giving Hellman credit, and starring Audrey Hepburn and Shirley MacLaine.) Hellman always maintained that her play was not about lesbianism but about "a lie."

The censorship follies of 1935 and, in particular, the banning of The Children's Hour led to a loosening of the Massachusetts law on which the city of Boston's theatrical moral code was based. Introduced by State Representative (later Governor) Christian Herter and backed by a petition signed by 1,000 prominent Bostonians, the new law stated that no play could be banned without first having a public hearing. Also, the composition of the three-person Board of Censors would be changed to replace the chief justice of the municipal court with a member of the city's arts commission. The new law didn't represent the end of theatrical censorship in Boston, but at least matters would be conducted somewhat more openly than in the past.

In the aftermath of the storm over the 1935 plays, *Tobacco Road*, the stage version of the Erskine Caldwell novel, a play that no one imagined would be allowed to open in Boston (it ran seven-and-a-half years on Broadway), actually did go on in April 1936. The city censor attended the opening performance. Mayor Mansfield, who had seen a performance of the play during a trip to Chicago, didn't like it, but he allowed it to go on nevertheless. Both as a novel and a play, *Tobacco Road* managed to evade Boston's censors. On stage, however, there was a caveat: the strongest oaths that could be uttered were "by Gad" and "by Judas."

For its part, the Watch and Ward tried to distance itself from theatrical censorship altogether. As Secretary Bodwell wrote in a 1938 reply to a letter from a woman in Berkeley, California, "While there has been some agitation in Boston against certain dramas, such as 'Strange Interlude,' 'Within the Gates,' and 'The Children's Hour,' this agitation has not originated with us, but with a man known as the city censor in the Licensing Division of the mayor's office in Boston." He added that the Watch and Ward's theatrical activities had been "almost totally confined to burlesque shows."

CHAPTER 15

This Was Burlesque, 1931–1953

DECEMBER 1931 WAS A TYPICAL MONTH for the Watch and Ward as the society attempted to remake itself in the early 1930s. It featured some of the usual preoccupations: an attempt to ban a book, in this case Boccaccio's *Decameron*—a longtime Watch and Ward bête noire—that was quashed by the Booksellers' Committee's Fuller; gambling, specifically a tip from a Watch and Ward investigator resulting in a police raid on an East Cambridge store where a gambling machine was seized; and the lottery, this time a campaign in Pittsfield to gather evidence regarding the sale of the illegal tickets, another longtime Watch and Ward target.

That month, however, another subject took center stage. Watch and Ward investigators were visiting a variety of burlesque shows in Boston—*The Big Revue* and *Facts and Figures* at the Old Howard in Scollay Square on December 2 and 9; *The Merry Whirl* at the Waldron Casino on Boston's Hanover Street on December 15; and *Rumba Girls* at the Old Howard on December 22. The last one, *Rumba Girls*, was the only show deemed actionable. The Reverend Raymond Calkins wrote a letter of complaint to Boston City Censor John M. Casey the very next day. Meanwhile, in Worcester, society agents investigated a burlesque theater called the Fox Plaza, where the show was "worse than any that are allowed in Boston," according to Secretary Bodwell. The next day, Bodwell conferred with "several influential Worcester people" in an attempt to shut it down.

Burlesque had had a long heyday in Boston, particularly at the Old
Howard, the oldest and most celebrated burlesque palace in the city. Located in Scollay Square, the downtown "entertainment district" that was
the site of various speakeasies, billiard halls, and tattoo parlors, the Old
Howard—officially known as the Howard Athenaeum, perhaps to make it
appear as if it were the site of elevating lectures—was established in 1845
as a legitimate theater where actors like Charlotte Cushman and John
Wilkes Booth performed. An imposing Gothic structure, with three tall
stained-glass windows, it resembled a church, as Ann Corio, a burlesque
headliner of the 1930s and 1940s, noted in her book *This Was Burlesque*.
She surmised it was built that way to fool the good citizens of Boston,
many of whom considered the theater to be an instrument of the devil.
In the 1870s, the Old Howard became a variety house, featuring acrobats,
jugglers, minstrel shows, pantomimes, and, most famously, the Human
Fly, who walked on the theater's ceiling. By the 1890s, burlesque made its
debut, with an emphasis on comedy—exploding bottles of soda water,
baggy pants, and props like eyeglasses with windshield wipers (the better to eat grapefruit with). In the early twentieth century, W. C. Fields, the
Marx Brothers, Fanny Brice, Sophie Tucker, (later) Abbott and Costello,
and Phil Silvers, all performed at the Old Howard.

However, burlesque wasn't all comedy. Starting in the 1890s, it added
a new feature—"cooch dancing" or the "hoochy-coochy" essentially
what we know today as belly dancing. By the 1920s, burlesque was fall-
ing on hard times, facing competition from that newly popular form
of mass entertainment—the movies. The Minsky brothers in New York
City added a runway to their National Winter Garden theater, extending
the stage out into the audience, in the manner of the Follies Bergère in
Paris. Soon the "cooch" became the "shimmy," done to jazz rhythms, and
eventually the striptease. From then on, comedy was less important—
and what comedy there was was bawdier than it had been in the past
—and burlesque became synonymous with the striptease. In the 1930s,
with the onset of the Great Depression, the popularity of burlesque un-
derwent a brief revival: "the poor man's theatre," as it was dubbed, represented inexpensive entertainment in a society that desperately craved
distraction from economic woes. There were plenty of out-of-work chorus girls prepared to take off their clothes if necessary to make a living.
By the 1930s, Boston's Old Howard, with its motto "Always something
doing from 1 to 11," was already a legend—attracting patrons rang-

ing from out-of-town businessmen to poet T. S. Eliot, future president John F. Kennedy, and Mayor James Michael Curley himself.

In fact, Harvard undergraduates, like Kennedy, were a major part of the Old Howard's clientele, as Ann Corio recalled in her book. "My favorite audience was from the educational institution along the Charles River," she wrote. "Friday's midnight performance was Harvard's show of shows. How those boys would howl." At the Friday midnight shows, Corio would edge closer and closer to the side of the stage where Harvard students filled the box seats. When she was nearly undressed, she would have the spotlight thrown on the upper boxes. "And there would be the Harvard boys hanging by their toes to get a good look at my bosom." In her book, Corio entitled the chapter about The Old Howard "You Can't Graduate Until You've Seen Ann Corio." Many students referred to the Old Howard as the "Old Harvard."

From the early years of its existence, the Watch and Ward had been concerned about the kinds of "indecent theatricals" Bostonians were exposed to at a time when the cooch, not the striptease, was seen as a threat to public morals. The society's unsuccessful attempt to prosecute cooch dancers La Belle Freida and Phil Hamberg back in 1897 was an example of this. In 1914, Watch and Ward agents visited ninety-six performances in Boston, finding the standards in burlesque theaters to be "very low" and their shows "frequently indecent" and "often positively lascivious," as J. Frank Chase noted in the 1914–15 annual report. On the burlesque stage, "It is cheaper to hire legs than brains, ribald drollery than genial humor, smut rather than wit," Chase added.

Shortly after the publication of that year's annual report, Mayor Curley proclaimed the city's code of theatrical morality. He made his announcement on May 29, 1915, at a meeting of forty theatrical managers in his office as a group of ministers waited expectantly outside. The code included the following:

- no suggestive jokes or songs, especially parodies;
- no "muscle," "coochy," "apache," or other risqué dances;
- no wearing of one-piece costumes by women where the outline of the figure is distinctly shown;
- no portrayal of a moral pervert or dope fiend;
- no women performers to mingle with the audience; and
- no more vulgarity or improper suggestions in performances.

The story goes that as the grim-looking theater managers exited Curley's office, the Reverend Raymond Calkins, Watch and Ward vice president and head of the assembled group of clergy, handed Mayor Curley a long list of salacious jokes that Watch and Ward agents had jotted down during their theatrical inspections. Curley handed the list back to the minister, telling him, "Read it yourself, it's too filthy for me." Calkins proceeded to do just that. Curley's reply: "Reverend, you must have enjoyed putting that collection together."

The Moral Code—plus its later amplifications and revisions—offered the Watch and Ward ammunition to try and persuade the Board of Censors to shut down or at the very least tame the burlesque houses. A year after the code was first promulgated, the Watch and Ward could report an "improvement" in the city's burlesque shows. But the society continued keeping tabs on the Old Howard and other burlesque palaces in Boston, Worcester, Springfield, and Providence. By the early 1930s, with burlesque becoming even racier and the Watch and Ward searching for an issue that might rally its supporters, burlesque became an appealing target.

There may have been another reason why the Watch and Ward was so eager to focus on burlesque. In early 1932, state representative William Corbett of Somerville called for a legislative investigation of the Watch and Ward's activities. The society took this seriously enough to compile a series of testimonials from the top police officials around the state, including Superintendent Michael H. Crowley and A. E. Foote, the commonwealth's Commissioner of Public Safety. Like District Attorney Robert T. Bushnell's call two years earlier for the abolition of the Watch and Ward, this idea went nowhere. But clearly the Watch and Ward was feeling increasing pressure to prove its importance to the moral life of Boston.

In any event, starting at the end of 1931 and through the entire year of 1932, Watch and Ward investigators made weekly visits to burlesque shows in Boston, Worcester, and Springfield, documenting each performance in detailed reports. On October 3, 1932, the ubiquitous John Tait Slaymaker was present at the State Theatre in Springfield, observing an evening performance of *Girls from Dixie*. "All the females in the show," he wrote in his report, appeared "with legs bare and, at all times, with more or less generous exposure of uncovered abdomens." One of them, Bee (Bubbles) Keller, "a platinum blonde of the Amazon type," was "the most pronounced in her contortioning and appeared to have a body that simply couldn't refrain from wriggling and squirming. She had pliable hips, oscillating buttocks, and breasts that seemed forever quivering." On October 18, Slaymaker's assignment was the Palais d'Or restaurant on Boston's Huntington Avenue, where a certain "Miss Blair" appeared "with a white lace garment and presented an interpretive Greek, or Egyptian dance carrying a brazier in which incense was burning."

At the Old Howard, where *Facts and Figures of 1932* played on November 15, another Watch and Ward investigator found the show "distinctly more vicious than the show of last week," noting that its "viciousness depended more on its homosexuality than on its obscenity." Throughout the entire show, actors played the roles of two men passionately in love with each other, "even to the point of kissing and fondling." Also at the Old Howard, at a performance of *Legs and Laughter* on November 21, the investigator's report called attention to one dancer's "diaphanous triangular breast coverings and a triangular cincture made conspicuous by varicolored sparkling glass. Through her breast covering, her nipples were plainly discernible." The next day, at the noon cabaret show at the Moulin Rouge on the corner of Tremont and Stuart streets in Boston, the ever-vigilant Slaymaker found a show of "eleven colored girls," three of whom "proved to be past masters of the art of vulgar body contortioning. . . . All the girls were bare-legged, but wore trunks and sufficiently concealing brassieres, leaving a none-too-pronounced expanse of uncovered abdomens."

In addition to the bare leg or uncovered abdomen, Watch and Ward investigators were always on the lookout for profanity, banned under Mayor Curley's 1924 edict. At the Shubert Theatre on December 9, investigator Lester F. Hiltz reported, "In the first act of 'Face the Music,' Mary Boland says, 'I've got the God damndest surprise for you.' The entire show is replete with 'hell' and 'damn.'" He also noted, "As the show began with profanity—so it ended—with Miss Boland saying or singing the words, 'I say it's spinach. The hell with it!'" Hiltz could not resist the role of drama critic, however, noting that the costumes were "adequate."

By the end of 1932, the Watch and Ward had compiled enough evidence to bring to the Board of Censors a case against the Old Howard, complaining of "disrobing acts," "obscene dialogues," and "vulgar contortions of the body." The next month, at the society's request, a hearing took place before the board, made up at that time of Mayor Curley, Chief Justice Wilfred Bolster of the Municipal Court, and Police Commissioner Eugene Hultman. The Old Howard's manager, Major Rufus Somerby, and his attorney were present; the Watch and Ward was represented by its president, John C. L. Dowling, as well as its legal counsel and three of its investigators. At one point, agent Slaymaker, described by the *Boston Post* as "a dignified little man with gray hair, gray mustache, and bone-rimmed spectacles" (he was close to sixty years old at the time), testified to the suggestive "sinuosity" of the dancers at the Old Howard. Curley asked Slaymaker to provide more details, but the agent had difficulty doing so. The mayor then suggested that Slaymaker impersonate one of the dancers. However, Slaymaker, determined to keep some shred of dignity, refused. The most prominent witness at the hearing was the redoubtable Ann Corio herself, testifying on behalf of the Old Howard. "My work is art," she told the group. "If the public considers me beautiful enough to look at, I fail to see what is wrong."

Once the hearing was over, the Board of Censors took only ten minutes to make its decision. It found "persistent, flagrant violation" and ordered the Old Howard's license suspended for thirty days, marking only the third time in Boston's history that a theater had actually been closed down. The shutdown of the burlesque palace, after eighty-seven years of operation, was the leading story in the city's newspapers. "30 DAYS IN DARK FOR OLD HOWARD," headlined the *Globe.* The article began: "Silence and darkness descend today on the Old Howard, theatre of Shakespearean drama, grand opera, and legitimate plays turned, of late years, into a circuit burlesque house with 'something always doing from 1 to 11.'"

Mayor Curley's role in the whole affair was ambiguous. The mayor was well known as a regular patron of the Old Howard. Ann Corio wrote that she never played a week at the burlesque palace "without at least one ceremonial visit" from Curley, his wife, and his staff. "The show would be underway and suddenly I'd spot a commotion in the back of the theatre," she noted. "Down the aisles would come ushers with folding chairs, and set them up right in front of the stage in the aisle space. Then, the Mayor and his retinue would roll down the aisle for a glimpse of burlesque heaven." In addition, Curley had no love lost for the Watch and Ward. As he wrote in his autobiography, "I was continually badgered by the eager, lip-pursing members of the Watch and Ward Society, who combined the fervor of bird feeders and disciples of the Anti-Vivisection society. For some time, a group of shocked ladies had been urging me to close the Howard Athenaeum, better known as the 'Old Howard.' 'I would like to honor your petition,' I told the ladies, 'but do you realize the historical significance of the Howard Athenaeum? You may think Harvard is well known, but the Old Howard is known in every port in the world. It is one of Boston's great institutions.'" But the mayor apparently felt he had no choice but to go along with the enemies of the "great institution" this time around.

The Old Howard reopened a month after its closing with a new show called Scrambled Legs. For a while, at least, the performances were relatively tame. One chorus girl is said to have complained backstage after a reopening rehearsal, "We should have brought our red flannels with us."

The Watch and Ward kept up the pressure, however, ordering its investigators back to the Old Howard over and over again. At the same time, it sent a barrage of complaints to the mayor about the shows at Minsky's Park Theatre (owned by the New York burlesque promoters) on Washington Street. Finally, in late February 1934, with Curley gone and Mayor Frederick W. Mansfield in the mayor's office, the city shut down the Park for a three-week period. Two or three days later, a large sign appeared in the theater lobby. It read: "Reserved seats now on sale for the grand opening, Monday, March 19. Burlesque. Bigger and better than ever! Due to agitation by the Watch and Ward Society, this theatre was closed until Monday, March 19, and one hundred people thrown out of work and left destitute. We will do our utmost to employ all those now out of work." Coming as it did at the height of the Depression, this was a potent argument.

Encouraged by the two temporary shutdowns, the Watch and Ward tried again in January 1935, when President Frank Chouteau Brown and Secretary Bodwell met with Mayor Mansfield and City Censor McNary. They brought with them recent evidence against the Old Howard and the Park Theatre. At that meeting, however, McNary praised the Old Howard's management and gave the Watch and Ward a dressing-down for wasting time on burlesque instead of paying attention to obscenity in plays and movies. Clearly, McNary was less than enamored of the Watch and Ward at this point, after President Brown had undercut him on Within the Gates the month before. Mayor Mansfield, more conciliatory, told Bodwell he would consider the situation. In fact, nothing was done.

In the 1934–35 annual report, President Brown contrasted the city's ban on O'Casey's Within the Gates—"one of the best and most interesting productions of the [New York] season," as he described it—with its inaction on burlesque, which he described as "far more objectionable and debasing." He noted that Within the Gates had been booked into Boston for only a week's performances, while burlesque shows were being performed seven times each day in Boston.

Boston was not the only city where there were attempts to crack down on burlesque; a few months later, in April 1935, New York City police, under the newly elected mayor Fiorello LaGuardia, raided Minsky's Republic Theatre, resulting in the arrest of three dancers and the revocation of the theater's license. In 1937, LaGuardia revoked the theater licenses of burlesque houses, going so far as to ban the name "Minsky" or the word "burlesque" from entertainment advertising. The LaGuardia administration kept up its "war against burlesque," and by the early 1940s, burlesque was entirely gone from New York City.

The Watch and Ward continued to monitor the Old Howard even through the 1940s, lobbying various mayors to close the theater without success. Finally, in 1953, after a complaint to the city vice squad, detectives sneaked into the Old Howard, cameras concealed under their coats, and captured on film the risqué performance of a dancer called "Irma The Body." The Old Howard's license was suspended indefinitely as a result. It is not clear from whom the complaint originated, but in his book about Scollay Square called Always Something Doing, David Kruh quotes a member of the vice squad at that time who says the complaint came "from a church group or maybe the Watch and Ward Society." In any event, the Old Howard was shuttered on November 9, 1953, and the building remained empty for eight years. On June 20, 1961, as preservationists were fighting to save it, a fire broke out in the theater and it was demolished on the same day. Later, the entire Scollay Square area was razed as part of an urban renewal project to pave the way for the new Government Center in Boston. Today, the site of the Old Howard's stage is marked by a concrete bench with a plaque behind the One Center Plaza building.

Over the years, despite the diligence of Slaymaker and other investigators, it isn't clear how effective Watch and Ward monitoring of burlesque really was. After all, burlesque persisted in straitlaced Boston long after it was forced out of New York City. Although Corio described Boston as a "rabbit warren of censors," a city in which "almost every citizen believed he was a voluntary member of the Watch and Ward Society," she insisted that the management of the Old Howard knew who the society's agents were and took precautions. (This was something that the Watch and Ward admitted as well.) It was the ticket-taker's job, wrote Corio, to "recognize every censor," and he never failed. As soon as the ticket-taker saw a censor coming, he would press his foot on a pedal and a red light would go on.

On stage, Corio noted, a stripper might be "giving her all for mankind, shimmying and grinding," with clothes flying in all directions, and the crowd yelling "take it off!" But once the red light would start blinking in the footlights, hips would cease grinding, clothes would appear as if by magic, and the musicians would break into a waltz. "And," she wrote, "by the time the censor reached the top of the stairs and looked down at the stage he would see—not a hip-swinging, hair-tossing, half-naked tigress—but a nun on a casual stroll through a most unlikely convent."

CHAPTER 16

The Forties, 1941–1948

In MARCH 1941, when William Henry Cardinal O'Connell, the Roman Catholic prelate of Boston, was returning from his annual winter vacation at his Caribbean retreat, he was met by reporters who asked him his opinion of John P. Marquand's H. M. Pulham, Esquire, just published by the Boston firm of Little, Brown, and Company. Marquand was the author of The Late George Apley, the Pulitzer Prize–winning novel of Brahmin Boston, and Pulham had a similar theme—a blue-blooded Bostonian, who has lived "the only sort of life for which I was really fitted," looks backwards on the anniversary of his twenty-fifth Harvard class reunion. But the novel added another aspect: Harry Pulham's wife has an affair with his best friend, something which the protagonist refuses to admit to himself.

The cardinal, eighty-one years old at the time, was known for his lavish lifestyle—the Nassau retreat, a private golf course at his home in Brighton. But he was not known for his critical thinking—famously disparaging the theory of relativity by saying "I never yet met a man who understood in the least what Einstein was driving at"—and rarely waded into literary waters. This time, though, he made an exception. While he told reporters that he had liked The Late George Apley, he found the new book "neither interesting nor edifying." He added, "Of course, my experience is limited, but I sincerely hope that Bostonians, especially women, have not degenerated into the type he describes."

It took just two days for Maurice H. Sullivan, a member of the Boston City Council, to opine that he thought the police commissioner should ban the novel because it was "a decidedly dirty book" that slandered Boston womanhood. The entire council agreed in a unanimous resolution, even though three members later admitted that they hadn't read the book. However, the police commissioner refused to take action, and H. M. Pulham, Esquire remained on the shelves.

Little, Brown was elated. The city council vote sent sales "whooping upward," as the Boston Transcript noted, and lending libraries were flooded with customers lining up to reserve a copy of the book. The Old Corner Bookstore put clippings from the press in its window, asking readers in big, bold type: "WHAT DO YOU THINK?" For the publisher and the bookstores, it was a marketing dream come true: the book carried the label "banned in Boston," but it still was available in Boston.

The fate of Budd Schulberg's What Makes Sammy Run? his novel of a ruthless young man who rises from the tenements of New York to the upper echelons of Hollywood, was a less happy one. On the same day that the City Council was urging a ban on the Marquand book, the Board of Trade of Boston Book Merchants sent a notice to its members relaying the information that certain booksellers had removed What Makes Sammy Run? from their shelves. That was a widely understood code—a clear warning to other booksellers that if they didn't follow suit, the police would take action. Immediately, one Boston bookseller returned all its copies to the publisher.

What happened to these two books indicates the way that censorship was conducted in Boston at the beginning of the 1940s. With a weakened Watch and Ward, the initiative had largely passed to the booksellers themselves, who engaged in self-censorship (aka "private censorship") under the watchful eye of the police. Richard Fuller, still the president of the Board of Trade of Boston Book Merchants, in concert with the police commissioner, virtually controlled what could and could not be read in Boston. Fuller had been a key player in the old pre-1927 "gentlemen's agreement." But if Fuller was the "junior partner" in the old arrangement, he was in a much stronger position now.

In his column "The Easy Chair" in Harper's Magazine, the critic Bernard DeVoto explained the Boston way of censorship: "We have set up a committee of the Board of Trade of Boston Book Merchants. Whenever the committee thinks that a book may be prosecuted by the police, it notifies the booksellers that that book has been withdrawn from sale—

withdrawn, that is, by stores represented on the committee. That notification suffices. No Boston bookseller sells that book, knowing that if the police should prosecute him, the Board of Trade would not come to his defense."

DeVoto added, "Everyone is happy. The affair has been conducted in complete privacy, free of official dictation and social control. There has been no official censorship, no one has achieved any objectionable publicity, the police are tranquil and the booksellers safe, and if any freedom of any Bostonian or any author has been infringed, Boston does not give a damn."

It was an updated version of the old "gentlemen's agreement."

In early March 1944, Boston's Police Commissioner Thomas F. Sullivan, who had just ascended to the position a few months before, wandered into the Old Corner Bookstore and asked to see a copy of Lillian Smith's novel *Strange Fruit*. The language in *Strange Fruit* had elicited a complaint from a father who had bought the novel as a gift for his daughter serving in the WAVES, the all-women division of the U.S. Navy. So the commissioner himself went to the Old Corner to investigate. He was not pleased with what he read, especially the use of the word "fucking," which appeared twice in the book's 371 pages. After leafing through the novel, he handed it back to the clerk, mentioning that some of the passages were indecent. Then he left the store without saying anything more. He didn't have to. The Old Corner Bookstore, of course, was owned by Richard Fuller of the Board of Trade of Boston Book Merchants. As in the case of *What Makes Sammy Run?* three years earlier, Fuller sent out a warning to the other booksellers that a complaint had been registered with the police commissioner. Overnight the book disappeared from every bookstore in the city of Boston. It was simply unavailable. No legal action had been taken, so there could be no hearing.

But *Strange Fruit* would not go quietly. The author, Lillian Smith, was the editor of a highly respected quarterly magazine, *The South Today*, and *Strange Fruit* provided a sensitive look at race relations that was notable for its time. The book told the story of the relationship between a young white man and a black woman, who becomes pregnant. Eventually, after many plot turns, the woman's brother is lynched on a ball field in front of the entire town. *Strange Fruit* had been praised by First Lady Eleanor Roosevelt as "a very moving book and a very extraordinary one." Her comments were quoted in advertisements. In the *New York Times Sunday*

Book Review, William DuBois wrote, "It should be required reading in every deanery, every parsonage—and every legislature, on both sides of the Mason Dixon Line."

Such accolades aside, there was an irony here that was difficult to escape. As Bernard DeVoto noted, *Strange Fruit* was being sold freely in Atlanta and Birmingham, and "in those ominous little Southern towns which we Bostonians recognize as socially sick and from which we fear an American fascism may emerge sometime." But it was not being sold in educated, presumably enlightened Boston.

A week after the Board of Trade's decision to pull *Strange Fruit* from bookstores, the police across the river in Cambridge ordered booksellers in that city to follow suit. DeVoto, following in the path of H. L. Mencken and Donald S. Friede in the 1920s, decided to bring a "test case" there, this time with the help of the American Civil Liberties Union (ACLU). He was one of America's most distinguished literary critics (and a well-regarded historian of the American West), so publicity was sure to follow.

The police were informed in advance, and, on April 4, four officers followed DeVoto and an ACLU lawyer into the University Law Book Exchange, near Harvard University. DeVoto laid down $2.75 for the novel. As if by design, a copy of a hefty 438-page book called *Law of Crimes* tumbled off the shelf and hit one of the police officers on the head. The bookstore proprietor, Abraham A. Isenstadt, was arrested, along with DeVoto.

Later that month, on April 26, 1944, East Cambridge District Court Judge Arthur P. Stone ruled *Strange Fruit* obscene. Judge Stone, who was by now in his seventies, had doled out harsh penalties to the booksellers in the Dunster House case back in 1929. This time, during arguments, the judge commented to Alfred A. Albert, the young ACLU attorney who argued for the defense, "If one single rhyme in Mother Goose were lascivious, then in my mind that copy of Mother Goose would be obscene." The judge fined Isenstadt $200 for possessing and selling the book, a lesser penalty than he had meted out in the Dunster House case. He dismissed charges against DeVoto, however, saying there was no law against purchasing an obscene book. Isenstadt's lawyers appealed the case.

Within a few weeks of the Cambridge decision, the attempt to ban *Strange Fruit* reached a national level. On the morning of May 16, the book's publisher, Reynal and Hitchcock, received notification from the U.S. Post Office that the book was now barred from the mails. Then, two hours later, without explanation, the Post Office suspended the ban and informed the firm that the book could be mailed "at the publisher's risk." The risk in question was prosecution under Section 598 of the Postal Laws and Regulations prohibiting the mailing of lewd books, pictures, advertisements and other matter—the old Comstock Law, dating from 1873. Postal authorities had cracked down on the mailing of various books during the 1940s, including such highly regarded works as Ernest Hemingway's For Whom the Bell Tolls and John O'Hara's Appointment in Samarra, in the name of fighting obscenity. A postal ban had little effect, however, since most books were shipped by freight and not the mails. That evening, Strange Fruit's publisher announced it would take its chances and continue sending the novel through the mails.

More than a year later, on September 17, 1945, the Massachusetts Supreme Judicial Court ruled by a 6-to-1 majority that Strange Fruit was obscene and upheld the Cambridge bookseller's conviction. In a seventeen-page majority opinion written by Justice Stanley E. Qua, the majority of the court labeled the book as "salacious," noting, "There are distributed fairly evenly throughout the book approximately fifty instances where the author introduces into the story such episodes as indecent assault upon little girls, an instance of, and a soliloquy on, masturbation of boys, and references to acts of excretion, to 'bobbing' or 'pointed breasts' to 'nice little rumps.'"

The majority opinion did concede the literary merits of the book. But literary quality only made the problem worse, in the justices' opinion. "Indeed obscenity may sometimes be made even more alluring and suggestive by the zeal which comes from sincerity and by the added force of artistic presentation," continued the decision.

The ban in Massachusetts was now in force, but even before that, the entire controversy over Strange Fruit had had extraordinary effects on the sales of the book. On the day the U.S. Post Office announced—and then withdrew—its ban, the book had already sold 200,000 copies and was number one on the New York Times fiction best-seller list. By year's end, 475,000 copies had been sold, and many stores were already out of stock of the book by Christmas. In Publishers' Weekly's ranking of the leading national best sellers of 1944, Strange Fruit ranked second. A Boston ban had catapulted a serious, sensitive novel that otherwise would probably have enjoyed only modest sales into a raging, national best seller.

Ironically, just a month after the Massachusetts high court had declared the book obscene, John J. Spencer, Boston's city censor, ruled that the theatrical version of *Strange Fruit* could be performed in Boston for its pre-Broadway "try out." Spencer had seen the play in Montreal and asked the producers to eliminate "certain profane uses of the name of God." The producers said that they would comply. Spencer also said he did not find in the play the objectionable scenes and actions that led to the Supreme Judicial Court ruling. The book remained banned, but the play was on.

When the stage version of *Strange Fruit* opened at the Plymouth Theatre in Boston at the end of October 1945, the Watch and Ward Society was less than pleased. Louis Croteau, a former Watch and Ward agent who had become secretary upon the death of Charles Bodwell in 1941, was in attendance, noting that although the play contained no obscene dialogue, "it fairly reeked with vile and vulgar expletives which bordered on obscenity." Like the book, "the play certainly lacked moral tone and considered as a whole was in very bad taste."

The next morning, Croteau marched into City Censor Spencer's office to complain. But Spencer was unmoved. The city censor informed him that there was nothing in the play to harm the morals of Bostonians. "The Secretary seriously disagrees," Croteau wrote, in his October 1945 secretary's report, "and firmly believes that in granting the showing of this play in Boston we have opened a precedent for the showing of vile and vulgar theatrical productions."

In keeping with its approach to censorship—and perhaps its waning power—the Watch and Ward Society had taken a low profile during most of the *Strange Fruit* affair. Still, the Cambridge police kept the society informed about DeVoto's test case. On March 23, as the Cambridge police were sending out warnings to booksellers against selling *Strange Fruit*, Croteau conferred with Cambridge police chief Leahy and with Middlesex County district attorney Robert Bradford. On the same day, the secretary met with Attorney General Robert Bushnell, longtime critic of the Watch and Ward, who advised him to refrain from making any comments on the matter to the newspapers. "He [Bushnell] further stated," wrote Secretary Croteau, "it would be best to let the police bring about a prosecution of the book, adding, we had gone a long way in the past ten years by obtaining the good-will of some officials and the public at large. He stated that it would be unfortunate if we were to lose all the headway that we had made just for the sake of a dirty book."

Essentially, the authorities were telling the society not to employ one of its agents to try to buy a copy of the book in Cambridge, upsetting the test case. It was much more helpful for everyone if the Watch and Ward sat this one out. The Watch and Ward had no choice but to agree.

But the society wasn't going to be kept quiet for long. Louis Croteau, who became secretary at the age of thirty-seven, was a tough and aggressive character. He was the first secretary who was not an ordained minister, and also the first secretary to come up through the organization's ranks, previously serving as an investigator and a chief investigator. And he was the first Roman Catholic to serve in the position. Since becoming head of the Watch and Ward, he had led hundreds of investigations of prostitution and gambling—twelve of the latter in 1943 in one unnamed large city, near Boston, a year that Croteau claimed was "our busiest year in the past decade." Under Croteau, the society's expenses for investigations jumped from $1,877 in 1941–1942 to $6,114 in 1943–1944, with a conviction rate in gambling cases of 98.2 percent.

Croteau also led a crackdown on homosexual activity. In January 1944, for example, a Watch and Ward complaint resulted in the arrest and conviction of nine gay men for "unnatural acts." A year later, as a result of a painstaking investigation by Croteau, the Boston police department's vice squad raided a "love-nest" of homosexuals, arresting sixteen men and two women. All were convicted but put on probation, leading Croteau to write, "It is unfortunate that our judges cannot or will not impose substantial fines and sentences upon these perverts."

In the 1943–44 annual report, Croteau proudly proclaimed the Watch and Ward, in capital letters, "A QUASI GOVERNMENTAL LAW ENFORCEMENT AGENCY." He was more like a police officer than a Sunday moralist, and far more in the mold of J. Frank Chase than the other relatively genteel Watch and Ward secretaries. By the autumn of 1944, the society returned to the censorship fray with a vengeance.

Forever Amber, Kathleen Winsor's bawdy historical romance set in Restoration England, was going to be the Gone with the Wind of 1944, pure and simple—Gone with the Wind with plenty of sex thrown in. It was published by Macmillan, the firm that had published Margaret Mitchell's Civil War blockbuster eight years earlier. The book's first printing was an impressive 50,000 copies, the publisher set aside an equally impressive (for the time) $20,000 for advance publicity, and there was an immediate scramble for movie rights. It was the height of the wartime book boom. "More than ever, in the stress & strain of war, people were reading to be entertained, to

escape from their everyday worries," wrote *Time*, which was even predict-
ing the "start of a new cultural era." Winsor, who would turn twenty-five
years old on the date of the book's publication, had never written a book
before. Her entire literary output consisted of a series of articles for the
Oakland Tribune on the subject of football from a woman's point of view.

During her student days at Berkeley, Winsor had married Robert John
Herwig, an All-American football center. While her husband was working on a class paper on the death of seventeenth-century English monarch
Charles II, she browsed through his books and became intrigued by the
Restoration period, famous for its dissolute character and relaxed sexual
mores. She read 356 books on the subject before starting her own, a 972-
page novel. Featuring 250 characters—half real, the rest imagined—the
book took her five years and 4,967 hours to complete. (She kept a me-
ticulous record of every time she sat down at the typewriter.) When her
husband went into the Marines, Winsor followed him to boot camp,
her two-and-a-half-million-word manuscript under her arm—or more
likely in a large suitcase.

Although it was hardly the first of its breed, *Forever Amber* became the
prototype of romantic historical fiction. Winsor's heroine marries three
times and has a string of lovers, including a highwayman, an earl, a lawyer's clerk, a captain in the Horse Guards, the Duke of Buckingham, and
(why not?) King Charles II. Experts found Winsor's historical research on
the Restoration to be superb.

If the publishing world was entranced at the prospect of blockbuster
sales—"Gold from Amber?" as a *New York Times* headline mused—literary critics were more equivocal. *Time* magazine panned it: "Many readers may never finish so poor a book." While Orville Prescott in the *New
York Times* at least partially dismissed the novel as "vulgar and trivial"
and three times as long as it needed to be, he did concede that "its easy
readability, its brisk pace from one melodramatic adventure to another,
its exuberant sexuality will insure that it will be read and that it will be
discussed . . . Kathleen Winsor has hit the bull's eye."

But Prescott observed something else about the book. Winsor had
re-created the Restoration period "with such gusto, such repetitious enthusiasm, that her book seems more like a glorification of Amber's way
of life than a serious interpretation of it." Others shared Prescott's concern. Before the book was even published, Joseph Breen, head of Hollywood's Production Code responsible for censorship in movies, promised
a ban on filming it; the novel was "utterly and completely unacceptable,"

he said, "a saga of illicit sex . . . bastardy, perversion, impotency, pregnancy, abortion, murder, and marriage without even the slightest suggestion of compensating moral values." Twentieth Century-Fox bought the film rights anyway.

And the Watch and Ward Society, still smarting from being sidelined in the Strange Fruit affair, decided to seize the moment. It contacted Hale and Dorr, the law firm that represented Macmillan, Amber's publisher, in Boston, and threatened criminal proceedings. The publisher panicked and agreed to withdraw the book in Boston. The following day, October 19, 1944, Secretary Croteau himself proclaimed the book's banning, a coup of sorts for the Watch and Ward. Ironically, the announcement came just three days after Kathleen Winsor—looking "more like a cover girl than a hard-working historical novelist," in the words of Mary McGrory of the Boston Herald—had wowed the audience on the first day of the Boston Book Fair.

With Forever Amber, once again the Boston way of censorship had triumphed—no hearing, no trial, simply the disappearance of an objectionable book. Boston booksellers could not have been pleased, however, at the loss of a book that the Herald noted "had enjoyed a brisk sale in the short time it was available." The Watch and Ward was emboldened. After being so quiet on the book censorship front for so long, the society had knocked out the most ballyhooed book in the country, run it out of town, and the publisher and the bookshops didn't put up a fight. Just in case anyone was tempted to go to nearby Fitchburg or Worcester or Springfield to track down a copy, Watch and Ward agents fanned out to bookstores in those cities, inquiring if they had copies of Amber. But the lady was completely gone.

Croteau, who had always thought that going after gambling or tracking down prostitutes and "perverts" was far more interesting and important than suppressing books, was suddenly having fun. The Watch and Ward's next target was Tragic Ground, a new novel by Erskine Caldwell. The Watch and Ward had tangled with Caldwell before, in March 1933, when it prevailed upon Boston booksellers to remove his God's Little Acre from their shelves.

Tragic Ground tells the story of an impoverished group of Southern whites, marooned in a Gulf Coast city during World War II after being lured from their beloved hill country by offers of bourbon for the men and black lace panties for the women. When the plant they had been working at shuts down, the rural transplants find themselves jobless, homesick, and hopeless, the men obsessed by sex with thirteen-year-olds while at the same time terrified their daughters will wind up as prostitutes. The book was generally not considered one of Caldwell's best. *Time* wrote that "Caldwell's characters, as usual, outrage every decent instinct and stir every other kind." However, it did have its admirers—the *New York Times Sunday Book Review* critic found it "a more significant novel" than the author's previous work—and today, its rich sociological look at urban squalor in the wartime South remains unexpectedly fascinating.

However, the Watch and Ward saw only the loose morals (and there were plenty of them) portrayed in the book. Just a few weeks after driving *Forever Amber* from Boston, the society marked out twenty paragraphs in *Tragic Ground* as obscene. In mid-December 1944, Watch and Ward agent Wilfred E. Pratt and Boston police detective Edward F. Blake went hunting for a copy to purchase. They wandered into the Dartmouth Street Bookstall in the fashionable Back Bay, where they were richly rewarded. Three days later, criminal complaints were lodged against the bookstore clerk, E. Margaret Anderson, who had rung up the sale, and the Dartmouth Street Bookstall itself. *Tragic Ground* quickly disappeared from the shelves of Boston bookstores.

The tactics here were very different from those employed in the *Strange Fruit* and *Forever Amber* cases, and even that of *What Makes Sammy Run?* a few years earlier. Instead of a polite "warning" to bookstores to remove a book from their shelves that originated with the Board of Trade or the police commissioner, this time the Watch and Ward reverted to the way of doing things that it had abandoned after the Dunster Street fiasco of 1929. Its agent bought a book that was perfectly legal to sell and then swore out a criminal complaint. Barbara Wright, the manager of the Dartmouth Bookstall, did not hesitate to denounce the Watch and Ward, characterizing the society as "a small group of private individuals not appointed or authorized by the government to act in the capacity of censors," a rare example of booksellers publicly criticizing the society's censorship activity.

The case came before Municipal Court judge Elijah Adlow on December 27, 1944, and from the outset the forty-eight-year-old judge showed little sympathy for the Watch and Ward and the police. "Must a book dealer read every book before he sells it?" the judge asked Wilfred Pratt, the Watch and Ward agent. "I want to know. You're the fellow who eradicates vice."

Pratt demurred. "That's a large question."

When Detective Blake, the arresting officer in the case, called the
court's attention to passages in *Tragic Ground* that mentioned houses of
prostitution, the judge asked him if he had read *Gone with the Wind* or
Hervey Allen's *Anthony Adverse*, both of which had made mention of such
establishments. When Blake shook his head, Judge Adlow replied with a
broad grin, "That's the trouble. They haven't got a big enough library at
police headquarters."

A frustrated Blake tried one final gambit, asking to court read a passage that described a woman reclining on a couch, her nightgown fall-
ing from her shoulders and revealing one of her breasts. "What's wrong
with that, for anyone over twelve years old?" the judge demanded. "Do
you think that's obscene?"

"Well," a red-faced Blake replied, "the Police Department didn't think
that particular part was so bad."

"But the Watch and Ward didn't like it?" asked the judge.

"That's true," Blake conceded.

The judge continued, "I'm not interested in these crusades against literature. I'm getting tired of books being banned. It has reached the point
where the court's business is divided between booksellers and bookmakers. It's not for me or for you to try to establish the literary tastes of the
community."

Pronouncing the book "dull—one you would have to chain yourself
to a chair to read," Judge Adlow dismissed the case.

When the trial was over, in a conversation with reporters, the police
commissioner found it necessary to defend the department's library. It
was primarily devoted to statutes and law books, he told them.

Erskine Caldwell might not have appreciated the judge's dismissal of
his book as "dull," but for the guardians of Boston's morals, it had been a
particularly humiliating experience. As *Time* noted, the Watch and Ward
had "suffered one of the worst defeats in 66 years of protecting Boston
from naughty thoughts."

While all this was going on, *Forever Amber* was becoming the most successful book in the country, eventually selling 3 million copies. A month after
its publication, it was number one on the *New York Times* and *New York Herald
Tribune* best-seller lists. A survey of the taste of the American reading public
during the first six months of 1945 found that 95 percent of those polled
had read the Bible during this period, followed by 84 percent who had
read *Forever Amber*. *Amber* probably should have been number one, though;

a large percentage of Bible readers read only a few verses in church or had read it before at some time in their lives. *Amber* was also breaking records in sales of war bonds—savings bonds offered to the public to fund the war effort. At a Westchester County, New York, sale, an autographed first edition of *Amber* went for $150,000 in war bonds. At a Waco, Texas, army airfield rally, where Winsor herself spoke as a part of a group of authors, an autographed copy fetched the extraordinary sum of $1,750,000 for the war effort. Whatever the value of the loss of sales in Boston and Worcester and Springfield, there is no doubt that the Boston ban was doing nothing to hurt the book—quite the contrary, in fact.

Meanwhile, the commonwealth of Massachusetts was changing its obscenity laws. Despite "gentlemen's agreements" and self-censorship, for years Boston's booksellers had quietly chafed under the threat of prosecutions. The *Tragic Ground* case had only been the latest one in which booksellers had faced legal penalties. Boston booksellers had lost huge sums of money by their inability to sell *Forever Amber*. Librarians, too, had been unhappy with the situation. So Hiller Wellman, head of the Springfield Public Library and longtime opponent of censorship, conceived the new law and persuaded the Massachusetts Library Association to sponsor it. Richard Fuller, who had done his best to accommodate Boston booksellers to censorship over the years, led the legislative lobbying effort.

By this time, even Fuller seemed fed up with censorship. "Strange as it may seem in view of what has happened, the booksellers themselves hate such so-called private censorships," he told *Publishers' Weekly*. When the Watch and Ward approached Fuller in 1945 regarding Walter Karig's naturalistic novel of working-class Staten Island, *Lower Than Angels*, which Croteau labeled as "definitely borderline," Fuller was unsympathetic, if not hostile. "It would seem," noted Croteau, "that Mr. Fuller on the one hand did not want to withdraw the book from sale but on the other threatened the Secretary with a lawsuit if we presented it to the Court for examination without first obtaining his permission."

The new law, enacted in late 1945, was intended to bring some order and fairness to the process. Now, court action would be taken against books, not booksellers. The new law established that a bookseller could be prosecuted for selling a book only if the book had been legally ruled obscene and if the person to whom he sold it was under the age of eighteen. That would have thrown out any prosecutions against *Tragic Ground* and wouldn't have applied to *Forever Amber*, either—neither book had been declared obscene by a court. Equally important, only a district attorney or the attorney general could bring suit to prevent the sale of a book. That eliminated direct legal action by the police or a private group like the Watch and Ward. It also reduced the power of threats, which had been responsible for many of Boston's banned books, as in the Forever Amber case. (Of course, a private group could still persuade a district attorney or attorney general to launch an effort to ban a book.) And the merits of a book as literature or scholarship were now permitted to be presented as evidence in court, which gave opponents of censorship a new weapon.

Clearly the ground was shifting, and no one realized it more than the Watch and Ward Society. In January 1946, Secretary Croteau had reviewed ten novels and found five of them—Daisy Kenyon, Kitty, Bubu of Montparnasse, We Always Come Back, and The Glittering Hill, all of them forgotten today—to be obscene. However, he realized that under the new law, it would be difficult to bring about successful court action on any of them. There was going to be a test case of the new obscenity law, but now Croteau was convinced that someone other than the Watch and Ward should be involved. "It is his [the Secretary's] belief that the book publishers and dealers are just awaiting to have a 'roman holiday' at our expense on certain novels, and they are hoping that the society will be an instigating factor in the complaints," he wrote in his January 1946 secretary's report.

It turned out that the test case under the new law was none other than Forever Amber, which had never officially been declared legally obscene and was probably the one book that every Boston bookseller was particularly eager to display in his or her shop window. However, Amber's rehabilitation got off to a shaky start when a Hampden County (Springfield) Superior Court judge issued an interlocutory decree in July 1946 that prohibited the sale of the book. In this case, the complaint had been brought by the attorney general of the commonwealth. The judge's decision was binding until final adjudication in court.

Eight months later, in March 1947, Judge Frank J. Donahue of Suffolk Superior Court overturned the decree after a three-day trial and in a six-page decision ruled that Forever Amber was not obscene, indecent, or impure. The judge, who admitted in court that he had fallen asleep reading the book, stated in his decision, "There is much more to the book than sexual episodes. . . . The book is by its very repetitions of Amber's adventures in sex acts like a soporific rather than an aphrodisiac. While conducive to sleep, it is not conducive to a desire to sleep with a member of the opposite sex." Ironically, it was the tediousness of the 972-page book that a variety of witnesses pointed to in defending its sale. Howard Mumford Jones, a Harvard professor of English literature, said the book left him cold and bored his wife. The assistant attorney general struck back, describing the book as "utter trash and filth." He reported that he had counted seventy references to sexual intercourse, thirty-nine illegitimate pregnancies, seven abortions, and ten descriptions of women undressing in front of men. But that did not convince Judge Donahue. Once again a book's perceived "dullness" had saved the day. The New York Times headline read: " 'FOREVER AMBER' PUT TRIAL JUDGE TO SLEEP."

Interestingly, in the Amber case, for the first time the Board of Trade of Boston Book Merchants played an active role in defending a book instead of throwing it to the wolves. Its brief to the court noted that booksellers had to keep abreast of changing trends in reader interest, something that the police and organizations like the Watch and Ward tended not to do. "The law enforcement agencies, official and unofficial, became unable to adjust their standards to the changes in the habits of thought of the people as a whole," the brief noted. There developed, the booksellers noted, "a condition known as 'Boston Censorship' in which books never actually judged indecent were kept off shop counters and some publishers made great profits out of the catch phrase 'Banned in Boston.' " The brief warned against the "setting up of too narrow and rigid a standard" under the new law and urged the law should not be interpreted so strictly as to cover "such innocuous books as 'Forever Amber.' " It was a stunning about-face for booksellers, who had been so complicit in the old system.

After Judge Donahue's decision, Amber was finally back on the bookstore shelves in Massachusetts, but its trials were not quite over. There was now the matter of the movie, directed by Otto Preminger and starring Linda Darnell in the title role, which opened in October 1947. The film version had been sanitized right from the beginning, but the final product still faced passionate opposition from Roman Catholic prelates like New York's Francis Cardinal Spellman and Philadelphia's Dennis Cardinal Dougherty, and above all from the Catholic Legion of Decency, which gave it a "C"—condemned—rating, making it a mortal sin for Catholics to see it.

In Boston, Archbishop Richard Cushing, the successor to Cardinal O'Connell, ordered priests to inform their congregations at Mass that they could not see the film "without grave scandal." The Pilot, the archdiocesan newspaper, called the movie "debased entertainment," and said the novel upon which it was based was "preeminent for two qualities—a

ditch-water dullness and a ditch-water filthiness." The newspaper criticized Hollywood for even attempting to "convert a sow's ear into a silk
purse." The Pilot's conclusion: "It is still a sow's ear."

Nonetheless, Mayor John B. Hynes decided to let it be shown in Boston, where the crowds were so huge that that a jewelry store located near
where Amber was playing sued for damages because customers were unable to get near its front door. There was only one caveat: the movie could
not be shown on Sundays.

Amber's last encounter with the Massachusetts judicial system came on October 11, 1948. On that date, the Massachusetts Supreme Judicial Court,
the same court that had ruled Strange Fruit obscene, upheld Judge Donahue's decision that Forever Amber could be sold in Massachusetts. If the
court had ruled that artistic purpose was irrelevant in determining obscenity in the Strange Fruit decision, in this case it seemed to imply that historic
purpose was relevant. There was little erotic allurement for the reader, in
part because the author's description of the world of Amber was deliber-
ately made so unappealing. "As to the individual characters, the reader is
left with an estimate of an unattractive, hedonistic group, whose course of
conduct is abhorrent and whose mode of living can be neither emulated
nor envied," the decision stated.

It was a curious distinction, but, in any event, Amber's judicial trials
had finally come to an end.

That same year, 1948, Watch and Ward secretary Louis Croteau died
at the age of forty-four. His death was the result of a beating by gangsters
that had occurred the previous year. Two men were charged with assault
and battery in the case and convicted. Croteau had made a lot of enemies
over the course of his twenty-year service to the Watch and Ward, particularly because of his crusades against gambling. Just the month before
he died, he had testified before a legislative committee considering the
legalization of bookmaking in the commonwealth, relating the story of
a Mattapan man who had been assaulted after he refused to accept $500
for the $5,000 he had won in a gambling pool. The words that Delcevare
King had spoken after the death of former secretary J. Frank Chase—"his
was the most difficult and disagreeable job in all New England"—seemed
even more apt this time around. With Croteau's death, the Watch and
Ward would chart a course very different from the past.

CHAPTER 17

A Kinder, Gentler Watch and Ward, 1948–1967

WITH THE DEATH OF LOUIS CROTEAU IN 1948, the old Watch and Ward essentially came to an end. The way the society conducted its affairs had always been heavily influenced by the personalities of its secretaries—the genteel ministers Henry Chase and Charles Bodwell, the pugnacious "soldier of the Lord" J. Frank Chase, and the crime-busting Croteau. Now, with Croteau's passing, a new secretary took the helm—Dwight Strong, a social worker, boys' club leader, and director of activities at the YMCA in the Hyde Park section of Boston. Under Strong's leadership, the Watch and Ward ceased its role in censorship of any kind. By 1957, it was no longer the Watch and Ward at all; it had changed its name to the New England Citizens Crime Commission, a name that did not carry the baggage of the past.

Croteau had been aware that the Watch and Ward's days in the censorship business were numbered. The society's reputation had sunk to a new low after the *Tragic Ground* prosecution and the trial judge's public criticisms of the society. The Board of Trade of Boston Book Merchants' Fuller had turned against his erstwhile allies. When the occasion came to bring a "test case" under the revised obscenity law in 1945, Croteau recognized that any Watch and Ward role would be counterproductive.

There were other problems, too. Each year throughout the 1940s, the society was running large deficits—$10,607 in 1946 and $8,857 in 1947, for instance—something that hadn't happened even in the darkest days of the Depression. Its endowment—still more than $200,000, half of it from the Martha Hunt bequest of forty years earlier—kept the Watch and Ward afloat, but the existing situation could not continue much longer.

When Strong took over in late 1948, he radically changed the society's approach. The board of directors approved a five-point program that emphasized "community cooperation, education, and prevention," as the 1950–51 annual report described it. The society promised to work with law enforcement by securing information about organized rackets, vice, and gambling. It wasn't going to act as if it *were* law enforcement. It would work for "the rehabilitation of offenders, juvenile and adult, into abiding citizens"; study problem areas causing "breakdowns in personal, family, and community life"; seek the advice of community leaders "regarding current trends in delinquency"; and join with churches, schools, and Parent-Teacher Associations (PTAs) to develop "a great sense of responsibility for civic affairs and legislation." This was a kind of language that the Watch and Ward had never used before. There was nothing about obscenity or indecent literature, no mention of the word "morality." In many respects, it could have been the platform of any civic organization.

The changes in the society caught the notice of the press, receiving front-page coverage from the *Boston Globe* in two articles on April 4 and 5, 1951, the first headlined "WATCH AND WARD CHANGES ITS SPOTS." "Most of the things that were true of the old one [Watch and Ward], it appears, are not true of the new one," noted reporter Joseph F. Dinneen. "There is nothing of the pompous or prudish Pecksniff about those in its Mt. Vernon St. headquarters today. . . . It does not censor Boston's books. It does not censor Boston's plays. It does not haunt burlesque houses. It employs no snoopers to ensnare law violators by entrapment, soliciting them to commit a crime."

Some of the longtime, now aging, leaders of the Watch and Ward— Delcevare King, the Reverend Raymond Calkins, and the redoubtable Godfrey Cabot—remained. King and Calkins were members of the board of directors; Cabot, who turned ninety in 1951, was honorary president. But starting in 1952, there were striking innovations: three women sitting on the board of directors, as well as a women's auxiliary. At the first meeting of the auxiliary, held in late January 1951, the participants held a roundtable discussion on issues ranging from gambling, narcotics, and liquor licensing to unwed mothers.

If the new Watch and Ward was a kinder, gentler, and more inclusive organization, it still had some of its old-time moral zeal. In reinventing itself, it focused on the issue that had been a priority since its inception—gambling. The organization compiled information on bookmakers and gangsters, trying to present a clearer picture of organized crime in Boston. When the Kefauver Commission, the U.S. Senate's high-profile probe into organized crime nationwide chaired by the Tennessee senator Estes Kefauver, sent its chief investigator to Boston, one of the first groups he met with was the Watch and Ward. When the committee's investigator, Joseph Nellis, arrived at the society's Mount Vernon Street headquarters, he came "prepared to scoff and remained to praise," the *Globe* reported. Nellis told Secretary Strong, "This is as good as any crime committee in the country." Many of the men listed for questioning by the Kefauver Commission, including bookies and well-known gamblers throughout the city, noted the *Globe*, "might be surprised to know how much information about them, their habits, customs, business behavior and connections was discovered by the Watch and Ward Society investigators."

Meanwhile, the society campaigned against the establishment of a state lottery, defeated in a 1950 referendum but still a popular idea, and continued to work to outlaw betting at horse and dog racetracks, legal since the mid-1930s. The lottery, insisted Secretary Strong, was "a community cancer." The list of the Watch and Ward's 1951 investigations included 562 for gambling, 28 for "ill fame," 14 for narcotics, 1 for obscene pictures, and 1 for theater.

In 1961, Dwight Strong and the Watch and Ward (by then under its new name) actually achieved the kind of national attention—and praise—that eluded past secretaries. For ten years, Watch and Ward sleuths had kept their eyes on the Swartz Key Shop, located on Massachusetts Avenue two blocks from Boston's Symphony Hall and well known as a focal point for illegal off-track betting and numbers games. Over the years, Secretary Strong complained to the Boston police, to the state police, and the Massachusetts State Crime Commission. However, the establishment remained open. Finally, the secretary turned to the television program CBS *Reports*, known for its hard-hitting documentaries, to investigate the key shop and the issue of gambling in Boston in general.

On November 30, 1961, CBS aired "Biography of a Bookie Joint," an hour-long, nationally broadcast piece of investigative journalism, narrated by Walter Cronkite and using information generated by the Watch and Ward. Secretary Strong appeared on camera in the report. CBS had set up shop in a building across the street from the key shop—which it characterized as "probably the busiest key store in the world"—where its producer, Jay McMullen, counted 1,200 people entering the place in a single day, starting as early as 5:30 in the morning. Using a hidden 8-mm camera and microphone, inside the shop's back room McMullen surreptitiously filmed betting on horse and dog racing, with bets running as high as $100. Outside, constantly changing lines of cars were double-parked, and carbon copies of betting slips were being burned in a trash can in full public view. Even more significantly, McMullen's camera caught ten uniformed Boston police officers entering and leaving the shop.

The result was a sensation, revealing rampant corruption in the police department and questionable ethical conduct in the state legislature as well. The documentary was so incendiary that it couldn't even be shown in Boston because of ongoing court cases. It was clear from the broadcast that the Boston police department had protected the bookie joint for years. One state legislator stated on camera that at least four of his colleagues had defended bookies in their private law practices. In the aftermath, there was a major shakeup in the Boston police department and a variety of corruption investigations throughout state government. In the most startling development of all, Boston Police Commissioner Leo J. Sullivan was forced to resign under pressure from the governor.

For the Watch and Ward, this was its most highly publicized corruption-fighting achievement since the ouster of district attorneys Joseph Pelletier and Nathan Tufts in the 1920s. The organization had regained at least some of the respect that it had lost through years of overzealous prosecutions. In the course of the documentary, however, the society was always referred to by its new name, the New England Citizens Crime Commission adopted four years earlier. It was never called the Watch and Ward. Television viewers across the country, many of whom might have remembered the Watch and Ward for making the term "banned in Boston" a national catchphrase, never knew that that organization and the one that brought down the powerful Boston police commissioner were one and the same. The year of the Watch and Ward's last major accomplishment was also the year that Godfrey Cabot died at the age of 101. The last of the Puritans undoubtedly died with a smile on his face.

When Dwight Strong appeared before a legislative hearing in the early 1950s to argue against toughened censorship legislation, legislators were dumbfounded. "You *are* from the Watch and Ward, aren't you?" asked one mystified lawmaker. But if the Watch and Ward had withdrawn from the field of battle, censorship was still alive and in relatively good health in Boston and Massachusetts as a whole. In 1950, the Massachusetts Supreme Judicial Court took up the case of Erskine Caldwell's novel *God's Little Acre*, which the Watch and Ward had quietly banned back in 1933. It was the era of the postwar boom in cheap paperbacks, lurid covers, and drugstore "spin-it" racks—resulting in the widespread availability of sexually frank books—and so the attorney general asked the court to rule on the reissued paperback version of Caldwell's novel, which had become an international best seller. (By 1968, *Time* magazine's All-Time Fiction Best-Seller List featured *God's Little Acre* at number three, with over 8 million copies sold.) Under the new law, unless a book was declared obscene by a court, there was no way to stop sales; despite the Watch and Ward's 1933 ban, no Massachusetts court had ever ruled on *God's Little Acre*. The court quickly remedied the situation, unanimously finding *God's Little Acre* to be obscene. "It abounds in sexual episodes and some are portrayed with an abundance of realistic detail," said the court. That same year, however, the high court ruled in favor of another paperback reissue from the 1930s, crime writer James M. Cain's hard-boiled early novel *Serenade*.

In view of the provision in the new law that booksellers could be prosecuted for obscenity only if they sold a book to someone under the age of eighteen, the availability of obscene materials, particularly cheap paperbacks, to minors became a focal point for a series of moral crusades. In the fall of 1951, in Cambridge, Al Vellucci, later a political fixture in that city, launched his campaign for a seat on the local school committee, distributing a pamphlet called "Arouse Ye Citizens." It demanded that so-called immoral books be eradicated from newsstands where children might read them. The pamphlet was signed, "Al Vellucci, father of six." Immediately, Cambridge police removed a number of paperback books from Cambridge newsstands and drugstores, including John O'Hara's novel *A Rage to Live*. No charges were brought, and no court ordered their suppression; the Cambridge School Committee, including its newest member, Vellucci, promptly passed a resolution praising the police commissioner for his actions.

A couple of years earlier, Attorney General Francis E. Kelly had established the Massachusetts Advisory Committee on Juvenile Reading, representing groups ranging from the PTA to the Knights of Columbus. In the first three years of its existence, the group recommended that 250 paperbacks, comic books, and lurid magazines be taken off the shelves.

Meanwhile, the Holy Name Society, a Catholic men's organization, was carrying on a campaign of its own, pressuring booksellers and drugstore owners to eliminate cheap paperbacks, comics, and magazines.

Much of this was related to a nationwide effort by the National Organization for Decent Literature (NODL), a Catholic group established in 1938 that attempted to monitor books in the same way the Legion of Decency monitored movies. By the early 1950s, paperbacks had become a key NODL target, as Christopher M. Finan observes in his book *From the Palmer Raids to the Patriot Act*. The NODL featured a list of some 300 paperback titles, including books by Erskine Caldwell, John O'Hara, Ernest Hemingway, and William Faulkner, that the organization pushed to have removed from bookstores and drugstores around the country. The NODL also published a "white list" of stores that removed such books; this list, notes Finan, was read in Catholic churches and published in parish publications. Many of the books removed in the Boston area during this period appeared on the list of books condemned by the NODL.

In 1952, with the Communist "Red Scare" at its height, the daily *Boston Post*, under its new owner John Fox, led a campaign to remove Communist publications (including the Soviet newspapers *Pravda* and *Izvestia*) from the Boston Public Library. Eventually, after much controversy, the library trustees voted 3-2 to keep such literature on display.

One bright spot for opponents of censorship occurred in the fall of 1956, when Eugene O'Neill's late masterpiece *Long Day's Journey Into Night* had its world premiere at Boston's Wilbur Theatre. The city's censors, of course, had banned O'Neill's *Strange Interlude* outright and blocked the openings of other O'Neill plays like *Desire Under the Elms* and *The Iceman Cometh*, demanding unacceptable changes and rewrites. This time, the play was officially welcomed by Governor Christian Herter, who expressed confidence that *Long Day's Journey* would be received with "great enthusiasm and exceptional interest" in Boston. A *New York Times* article on the subject began, "This city, which once banned Eugene O'Neill's plays as if they were contagious diseases, has granted the late playwright high praise and has welcomed his last work."

However, Boston still had a city censor, a former Associated Press reporter, Richard J. Sinnott, with a strangely appropriate name (Sin Not). Taking over the job in 1960, Sinnott demanded that sixty lines be deleted from Edward Albee's play *Who's Afraid of Virginia Woolf?* when it was scheduled to open in Boston three years later. In the end, nine "irreverent references to the Deity" were excised, and the play went on. In the 1970s, Sinnott demanded that a scene in which the American flag was desecrated be removed from the musical *Hair*. The musical opened without the desecration, but it was closed when the Supreme Judicial Court banned a nude scene. Finally, appeals to the federal courts, including the U.S. Supreme Court, allowed the show to go on. Sinnott spent most of his last years keeping tabs on rock concerts. The post of city censor was abolished in 1982, effectively ending theatrical censorship in Boston.

By the late 1960s, thanks to a series of federal and state court decisions, Bostonians were generally free to purchase almost any book they wished. A 1957 U.S. Supreme Court decision written by Justice William Brennan clearly distinguished sex from obscenity, stating that "the portrayal of sex, e.g., in art, literature, and scientific works, is not itself sufficient reason to deny . . . constitutional protection." So long as a book or publication had some degree of "redeeming social importance," it was protected under the First Amendment, the court ruled. In the past, books that had talked about sex with any frankness were viewed as legally outside the protections of free speech. What the high court offered, for the first time, was a broad definition of First Amendment protection and a narrow definition of obscenity.

Once that wall had been breached, a series of far-reaching legal decisions followed. In 1959, the U.S. District Court for the Southern District of New York ordered the Post Office to permit copies of *Lady Chatterley's Lover* to be sent through the mail on the grounds of free speech, a momentous ruling that overturned the 1873 Comstock Law. In 1963, the Massachusetts Supreme Judicial Court overturned a lower-court ban on Henry Miller's *Tropic of Cancer*. Even though the novel was "dull, dreary, and offensive," in the court's view, the justices ruled that it deserved First Amendment protection. In 1966, the same court ruled that William Burroughs's *Naked Lunch* could be sold in Massachusetts. That year, the U.S. Supreme Court also overruled a previous decision by the Massachusetts high court and allowed the eighteenth-century erotic novel *Fanny Hill* to be sold in Massachusetts. Justice William J. Brennan said that the Massachusetts ban could not stand because the state court itself had conceded that the book had "a modicum of literary and historical value."

All these books were extremely explicit, certainly compared to the books that caused such controversy thirty or forty years earlier. Although censorship and free speech issues did not go away—far from it—much of the work that the Watch and Ward and its counterparts in other cities had fought so hard for so many years to perform had lost any legal basis.

As Finan put it, "Although 'hard-core pornography' remained illegal, the Supreme Court had finally set literature free."

As for the Watch and Ward itself, Dwight Strong retired in 1967, and, in that year, the society's successor, the New England Citizens Crime Commission, became the Massachusetts Council on Crime and Correction. In 1975, the council merged with another organization to form the Crime and Justice Foundation. The original Watch and Ward endowment rolled over from transition to transition. In 1999, this organization was renamed Community Resources for Justice, a social service and advocacy organization that focuses on criminal justice system reform, problems faced by prisoners once they leave jail, and running residential homes for mentally retarded and developmentally disabled adults. John J. Larivee, the CEO of the organization, says he sometimes mischievously introduces himself at meetings as representing the New England Society for the Suppression of Vice. "That wakes them up," he says. He does see some continuity, however. While the old Watch and Ward was concerned with public safety and public order, "We're concerned about that in a different way—to reform individuals caught up in that behavior." The reformist strain of the Watch and Ward, so much of a part of its activities in its early days, had won out. After death, the society had returned to its progressive roots.

EPILOGUE

THE WATCH AND WARD is frequently blamed for every act of censorship that occurred in Boston in the last hundred years. In reality, the most egregious examples of "the censorship decade" of the 1920s—the bans on *Elmer Gantry*, *An American Tragedy*, *Oil!* and *Strange Interlude*—had little, if anything, to do with the society directly. The suppression of *Strange Fruit* in the 1940s was not a Watch and Ward operation, as much as Secretary Louis Croteau later tried to jump on the bandwagon. The Watch and Ward rarely involved itself in theatrical censorship after the early part of the century; it even defended Sean O'Casey's play *Within the Gates* during the period of *perestroika* under Frank Chouteau Brown. The ban on "hell" and "damn" on the Boston stage emanated not from the Watch and Ward but from Mayor James Michael Curley. But to most of America's educated classes, Boston censorship equaled the Watch and Ward, and the Watch and Ward equaled Boston censorship.

It has been argued that given the city's potent mix of Puritanism and conservative Catholicism, censorship in Boston would have happened anyway, and that in the days when the Watch and Ward ruled absolutely—the period of the "gentlemen's agreement"—it did a relatively decent job of deciding what Bostonians could and could not read. That was certainly a widespread feeling when it lost control of book censorship in Boston in the late 1920s, and the arrival on the scene of district attorneys, police commissioners, and freelancing ministers launched a period of Watch and Ward "nostalgia," even among some of the most fervent opponents of censorship.

Still, it is extremely difficult to defend an organization that spent its early years trying to ban Whitman, Balzac, Boccaccio, and Rabelais, managed to prevent Bostonians from reading books by D. H. Lawrence, Aldous Huxley, Sherwood Anderson, and Ernest Hemingway, and finished its career crusading against relatively harmless targets like *Forever Amber* and the Old Howard. Even in cases of censorship from which it remained aloof, the Watch and Ward has to take some responsibility. It was the inspiration and created the atmosphere and the model for everything to come over the years.

Undoubtedly, the Watch and Ward outlived its time. It even outlived its name. Its zealous execution of its role as self-appointed censor and its sense of noblesse oblige were relics of an earlier day. At various points, the society was a quasi-vigilante organization, a private police force, and a junior varsity vice squad that squandered time and resources on burlesque shows and bingo games and workmen playing poker on their lunch hour.

H. L. Mencken said of Watch and Ward progenitor Anthony Comstock that he had done more than any other man to ruin Puritanism in the United States. Could the same be said of the Watch and Ward itself? Certainly the society turned the phrase "banned in Boston" into a national joke, fattening the coffers of publishers that it professed to despise, elevated self-promoters like Upton Sinclair and Mrs. Glyn, undermined Boston businesses by forcing the city's large book-buying public to spend their money at New York bookstores and Grand Central Station newsstands. Its often misplaced zeal ruined the life of James DeLacey of the Dunster House Bookshop and the lives of many others as well.

With the assistance of the Roman Catholic hierarchy and certain public officials, it created a stultifying intellectual climate in Boston, sending the city's artists and writers fleeing to New York and other places, from which they "looked back on Boston for the rest of their lives with a mixture of amused vexation and amused regret," as journalist Elmer Davis observed. If New England was the dominant literary center of the country before the Civil War, "the Great Silence," as Davis called it, descended after that period. This may not have been totally the Watch and Ward's doing—there were economic and other forces at work—but Watch and Ward repression was unquestionably a factor.

Absolute power—which the Watch and Ward possessed during the J. Frank Chase era—corrupts absolutely. The society's secrecy, overreaching, questionable tactics, arrogance, and fanaticism did much to undercut its own efforts. The Dunster House episode of 1929 was followed by the first revision of the Massachusetts obscenity law, limiting the definition of obscenity—and the Watch and Ward's freedom of action. The botched prosecution of Erskine Caldwell's *Tragic Ground* in 1944 resulted in another liberalization. In many respects, the Watch and Ward turned out to be its own worst enemy. In addition, this kind of absolute power encouraged pettiness and vindictiveness, as in the Mencken affair, that only came back to haunt the Watch and Ward.

In areas like gambling, prostitution, and the drug trade, the Watch and Ward's legacy is more complicated. Its rabid opposition to a state lottery may seem archaic, but anyone who has stood in line in a convenience store, watching the most downtrodden members of society spend their dwindling money on lottery tickets, may well come to the conclusion that the Watch and Ward was not so wrong after all. While its raids on lunchtime poker games and church raffles were certainly overzealous, its passionate focus on the destructive effects of gambling seems prescient today, particularly as Massachusetts considers legalizing resort casinos at the end of the first decade of the twenty-first century. Its raids on houses of "ill fame" may seem prudish to many contemporary Americans, but in an era when young women moved to cities and were often forced into prostitution by economic circumstances, it was very much part of a progressive and reformist tradition. The society was among the first to call attention to the dangers of opium and cocaine and to the trafficking in women. And in cities throughout the commonwealth where corrupt local governments and police were sometimes in league with gamblers, gangsters, madams, and pimps—and there were a number of such jurisdictions—one could argue that there was a need for an extralegal authority to create some sense of law and order. The Watch and Ward, for better or worse, filled the bill.

The Watch and Ward could claim some positive accomplishments as well. As deplorable as its tactics could be, as much as the society seemed to take the law into its own hands in many situations—the bugging of District Attorney Pelletier's office by dictagraph comes to mind—it was often the only group with the will and the courage (and the financial means and social position) to challenge powerful figures in Boston and surrounding cities when the police were unable or unwilling to do so. The "Biography of a Bookie Joint" episode is a more contemporary example of the Watch and Ward vigilance when law enforcement agencies declined to act against, or were even in league with, those outside the law.

In the end, the moralism of the Watch and Ward has passed into history, at least in Boston, even as battles involving censorship continue to rage in other parts of the country. So much of what the organization accomplished or attempted to accomplish was a rearguard action against historical forces—the secularization of society, the increased frankness about sex and sexuality in literature and on the stage, the diversity of a city where the old families no longer controlled many key levers of power, where immigrants and their descendents made up a larger and larger percentage of the population. These were vast historical changes that Boston's ruling first families, despite their money and their influence, were ultimately helpless to fight. Many of the attempts at book and theatrical censorship in our own time stem from the same root causes as those that led to the founding of the Watch and Ward—fear of social and cultural change and an attempt to shore up traditional values. (Today, one can simply substitute gay parenting for heterosexual sex, and J. K. Rowling's sorcery for Sinclair Lewis's affronts to religion.) The Watch and Ward was unable to stop the sweep of history and of cultural change; while one can admire some of its goals and deplore others—and both wonder at and recoil from the audacity of its tactics—it was inevitably a quixotic venture.

If one wished to be charitable to the Watch and Ward, one could cite a letter to his son from an aging George Apley—himself a member of the fictional "Save Boston Society," closely based on the Watch and Ward—in John P. Marquand's novel of Boston's aristocracy, *The Late George Apley*: "I have stood for many things which I hope will not vanish from the earth. I am only one of many here who have done so. The world I have lived in may be in a certain sense restricted but it has been a good world and a just world. Much of it may have been built on a sense of security which is now disappearing but it has also been built on certain elements of the spirit which will also be secure: on honour and on courage and on truth." Still, there are many who would disagree.

ACKNOWLEDGMENTS

A NUMBER OF INDIVIDUALS AND INSTITUTIONS were invaluable in the research and writing of this book. I list some of them here: the Boston Athenaeum, Carl Beckman, the Boston Public Library Special Collections department, Michael Bronski, Michael Downing, Kathy Hirbour, Theresa Lang, John J. Larivee, Nan Levinson, the Massachusetts Historical Society, the New Bedford Public Library, Tim Orwig, Elizabeth Robeson, Lesley Schoenfeld and other staff members at the Harvard Law School Library's Special Collections department, Jonathan Strong, the Tisch Library at Tufts University, and Tom Unterberg.

I am greatly indebted to Brian Halley, who conceived the idea of this book while he was at Beacon Press; to Gayatri Patnaik for guiding the book through its early stages; and especially to Joanna Green, perceptive and trusted editor. I am grateful to Susan Lumenello, Sue McClung, and the Beacon Press production staff. Thanks also to my agent Todd Shuster and everyone at Zachary Shuster Harmsworth. Above all, I am deeply grateful to my partner, Paul Brouillette, for his encouragement, incisive comments and suggestions, and his love and support.

BIBLIOGRAPHIC ESSAY

Because this book spans a seventy- to eighty-year period, the research required a large and varied array of sources. Still, there were some major primary sources on which I relied:

- The New England Watch and Ward Society Records, 1918–1957. Located at the Harvard Law School Library in Cambridge, Massachusetts, these records include investigators' reports, Secretary's Reports, correspondence, and financial information. They are referred to throughout as "NEWWS Records," with the box and folder numbers included.
- The Godfrey Lowell Cabot Collection, Massachusetts Historical Society, Boston, Massachusetts. These include letters, news clippings, and Watch and Ward documents. I refer to these sources as the "GLC Collection," with box numbers only.
- Annual Reports of the New England Society for the Suppression of Vice, 1880–1890. These can be found at the Boston Public Library. I refer to them as "NESSV Annual Reports" throughout.
- Annual Reports of the New England Watch and Ward Society, 1891–1951. These reports include the society's activities for the year, lists of arrests and convictions, text of speeches made at the annual public meetings, and financial reports. I refer to them as "NEWWS Annual Reports" or simply "ARs" throughout.

SECONDARY SOURCES

In writing this book, I used the *Boston Globe*, the *Boston Herald*, the *Boston Evening Transcript*, the *Boston Post*, the *Boston Daily Advertiser*, the *Boston Telegram*, and *The Pilot*, as well as the *New York Times*, the *Providence Journal*, the *Harvard Crimson*, the *Patriot Ledger*, and *Time* magazine. Both the *New York Times* and *Time* covered Boston censorship extensively for many years, sometimes in more detail than the Boston press. I also used national magazines, including *Harper's, Atlantic Monthly, American Mercury, Publishers' Weekly,* the *Nation,* and the *New Republic.* In many cases, if the source and exact date are mentioned in the text, I don't reference them in this text. No other books devoted entirely to the Watch and Ward have been published thus far, but I found helpful a great many with chapters on or references to the Watch and Ward. Paul S. Boyer's *Purity in Print,* 2d ed. (Madison: University of Wisconsin Press, 2002), a rich, scholarly work that offers an excellent overall picture of the Watch and Ward's censorship activities from its founding through the Dunster House affair and its aftermath, was especially valuable. I refer to the book as "Boyer" throughout. On the topic of stage censorship, I am indebted to William Robert Reardon's "Banned in Boston: A Study of Theatrical Censorship in Boston From 1630 to 1950" (doctoral thesis in speech and drama, Stanford University, Stanford, Calif., November 1952). I refer to this manuscript as "Reardon."

PROLOGUE: THE BATTLE OF BRIMSTONE CORNER, APRIL 1926

Two biographies of H. L. Mencken—Terry Teachout's *The Skeptic* (New York: HarperCollins, 2002), and Marion Elizabeth Rogers's *Mencken: The American Iconoclast* (New York: Oxford University Press, 2005)—provide vivid accounts of the Mencken-Chase face-off. I also relied on the April 6, 1926, editions of the *Boston Globe, Boston Herald, Boston Evening Transcript,* and *New York Times.* See also "Hatrack," published in the April 19, 1926, edition of *Time.* Mencken's references to "preposterous Puritans," "malignant moralists," and "cannibals turned Christians" are cited in Mark Schorer's *Sinclair Lewis* (New York: McGraw-Hill, 1961), p. 482. The description of Mencken's physical appearance comes from British journalist (and later TV personality) Alistair Cooke, quoted in Teachout, p. 5.

CHAPTER 1: FOUNDING FATHERS, 1878

For the founding meeting of the Watch and Ward, I relied on the *Boston Daily Advertiser,* May 29, 1878. I am indebted to Margaret Lamberts Bendroth's *Fundamentalists in the City* (New York: Oxford University Press, 2005) for background on the Park Street Church. For background on Anthony Comstock, I relied on Heywood Broun and Margaret Leech's *Anthony Comstock: Roundsman of the Lord* (New York: Albert and Charles Boni, 1927), which is still the best biography of this vice crusader. The physical description of Comstock by Charles Gallaudet Trumbull is cited in Broun and Leech, p. 13; for the Shaw quote, see p. 18. Another helpful source on Comstock was Helen Lefkowitz Horowitz's *Rereading Sex* (New York: Alfred A. Knopf, 2002). H. L. Mencken's comments on Comstock and his legacy come from "Emperor of Wowsers," in Mencken's *Prejudices, Sixth Series* (New York: Alfred A. Knopf, 1927), pp. 116–17. For descriptions of pre–

Civil War Boston, I quoted from Edward Everett Hale's *A New England Boyhood* (Upper Saddle River, N.J.: Literature House, 1970), p. 1, originally published in 1893, as well S. Foster Damon's essay, "The Genesis of Boston," which appeared in the October 1935 issue of the *Atlantic Monthly*. An excellent source for historical background on post–Civil War Boston is Boston College historian Thomas H. O'Connor's *The Hub* (Boston: Northeastern University Press, 2001), pp. 137–82. The Oliver Wendell Holmes comment is repeated in O'Connor, p. 174. Stephen Puleo's *The Boston Italians* (Boston: Beacon Press, 2007) is another useful source on the changing Boston. Dr. Francis Peabody's address to the twentieth-anniversary meeting appears in the New England Watch and Ward Society Annual Report, 1897–98. For background on the early Watch and Ward leaders, I relied on Boyer, pp. 7–8, and also Nicola Beisel's interesting and well-researched *Imperiled Innocents* (Princeton: Princeton University Press, 1997) as well as her essay, "Class, Culture, and Campaigns Against Vice in Three American Cities, 1872–1892" (*American Sociological Review*, 1990, vol. 55). The phrase "old guard on guard" comes from Cleveland Amory's amusing but not always reliable *The Proper Bostonians* (New York: E. P. Dutton, 1947), pp. 312 and 328–31. The Reverend Frederick Baylies Allen's comments on fighting "evil and sin" can be found in the NEWWS Annual Report, 1902–1903. Historian Frederick Lewis Allen's memoir of his father, *Frederick Baylies Allen* (Cambridge: Riverside Press, 1929) brings to life one of the Watch and Ward's most enduring personalities. For the early activities of the society, I drew on the NESSV Annual Reports (1881–1890) and particularly the NEWWS Annual Report of 1897–98, which includes a very helpful twenty-year overview of the organization.

CHAPTER 2: FIRST FORAYS INTO CENSORSHIP, 1881–1898

I drew on a variety of sources in exploring the vice society's campaign against *Leaves of Grass*. Frederick P. Hebb's article, "When Boston Censored Walt Whitman" (*New York Times*, June 19, 1927), provides an excellent overview. For details on the Watch and Ward's involvement, see Beisel's treatment in *Imperiled Innocents*, pp. 164–67. The quotes from Comstock and Homer P. Sprague come from Beisel, pp. 164 and 166. I also used the NESSV Annual Report, 1881–82. The *Boston Globe* editorial appeared on May 28, 1882, while the *Transcript*'s view comes from its May 22, 1882 edition. I relied on the April 29, 1894, edition of the *Boston Globe*, for information on the Boston Public Library's "Inferno." The speeches of the Reverend Frederick Allen and the Reverend Endicott Peabody to the 1900 annual meeting were reprinted in the NEWWS Annual Report, 1899–1900. Allen's attack on European "corruption" appeared in the 1900–01 AR; Peabody's anti-French screed was reprinted in the 1899–1900 AR. Louis Auchincloss's caustic description of Peabody comes from the novel *The Rector of Justin* (Boston: Houghton Mifflin, 1956), p. 43. For the section about *The Clemenceau Case*, I drew on Reardon, the October 15 and 16, 1890, editions of the *Boston Globe*, and the October 16, 1890, edition of the *New York Times*. The *Globe* editorial appeared on October 16. The opening in Lynn was reported in the *Globe* on November 28, 1890, and the Boston reopening on December 12. The *New York Times's* opinion of the second version of the play appeared in its December 16 edition. For the Watch and Ward's view, see AR, 1890–91. The *Globe's* pre-Christmas theater roundup appeared in December 23, 1890. For the Watch and Ward's monitoring of theaters, see AR, 1897–98. For Comstock's horror at the Chicago World's Fair, see Broun and Leech, pp. 226–28. The story of La Belle Freida's courtroom performance appeared in the February 22, 1898, edition of the *Globe* under the headline "DANCED FOR THE JUDGE."

CHAPTER 3: POLITICS, POKER, AND THE "SOCIAL EVIL," 1884–1897

For the widespread nature of gambling in Boston, I relied on the NEWWS Annual Report of 1897–98, which includes the twenty-year retrospective. Henry Chase's "survey" of gambling in Boston appeared in the February 22, 1884, edition of the *New York Times*. Allen's comment comes from his speech before the Watch and Ward public meeting on February 20, 1898, reprinted in the 1897–98 NEWWS Annual Report. For Beisel's analysis of the importance of the gambling issue in the society's early days, see her article "Class, Culture, and Campaigns Against Vice in Three American Cities, 1872–1892." For the society's early conflicts with the police over gambling, I drew on the 1897–98 AR, as well as Beisel's work. The 1894–95 AR vividly depicts the raid on the last faro bank in Boston. Allen's "How Shall a Great City Deal with the Social Evil?" later published as a pamphlet, appears in the same annual report. For the increase in gambling and prostitution convictions, see AR 1895–96 and AR 1897–98. Allen's claim that no city could equal Boston's record on gambling appeared in his speech at the 1898 public meeting.

CHAPTER 4: MRS. GLYN AND SIN, 1903–1909

For the 1903 arrest for selling the *Decameron*, I relied on the November 28 and December 12, 1903, editions of the *Boston Globe*. See also a letter to the *Globe*, November 28, 1903, signed only "Clergyman, Boston." For the 1894 arrest and trial, I drew on the *Globe* coverage of March 23 and 30, 1894. Comstock's comparison of the *Decameron* to a "wild beast" appears in Broun and Leech's biography *Anthony Comstock: Roundsman of the Lord* (New York: Albert and Charles Boni, 1927), p. 241. Littlefield's comment appeared in the March 30, 1894, edition of the *Globe*. All excerpts from Elinor Glyn's *Three Weeks* come from the reissue of the book, with an introduction by Cecil Beaton (London: Duckworth, 1974). The *New York Times* review appeared on September 28, 1907. For information on the suppression of *Three Weeks*, I relied on Boyer, as well as the NEWWS Annual

Report, 1908–9. The *Boston Globe* review of the dramatization comes from the April 26, 1910, edition. For the origins of the "gentlemen's agreement," I am indebted to Boyer and the February 13, 1928, edition of the *Springfield* (Mass.) *Daily Republican*. In its February 13–18 editions, the *Republican* ran an extremely thorough five-part survey of censorship in Massachusetts from its beginnings. The anecdote about *Flaming Youth* comes from the February 14, 1928, edition of the *Republican*. I am grateful to Boyer for the details of the "gentlemen's agreement," the Robert Keable case, and the Richard Fuller quote that Massachusetts "stands as the cleanest state in the union," p. 173. F. Scott Fitzgerald's reference to *Simon Called Peter* appeared in *The Great Gatsby* (New York: Charles Scribner's Sons, 1925), p. 29.

CHAPTER 5: TOUGH GUYS AND "BLUE BLOODS," 1907–1925

For my portrait of J. Frank Chase, I used A. L. S. Wood's "Keeping the Puritans Pure," which appeared in the *American Mercury* in April 1926. A far more sympathetic portrayal—and the one I relied on for the experiences that shaped Chase's character—can be found in John W. Hawkins's profile "J. Frank Chase: The Clean-up Specialist" (*New Bedford Sunday Standard*, July 16, 1916). To put Chase's "tough-guy" image in a social context, I am indebted to E. Anthony Rotundo's *American Manhood* (New York: Basic Books, 1993), pp. 232–48, as well as James J. Connolly's *The Triumph of Urban Progressivism* (Cambridge: Harvard University Press, 1998), pp. 100–101. For the impact of Chase's ascendency to the post of secretary on the Watch and Ward itself, I used the NEWWS Annual Reports for 1907–8 and 1908–9. Allen's praise of Chase comes from the AR of 1909–10. Chase's speech on the "Dope Evil" appeared in the 1911–12 AR. An account of Chase's legal troubles appeared in the *Boston Globe* on April 30 and May 1, 1915. *Rob Roy's Pellets*, the source of the anonymous attack on Chase, can be found in the GLC Collection, Box 18. For my portrait of Godfrey Cabot, I relied on Leon Harris's biography, *Only to God: The Extraordinary Life of Godfrey Lowell Cabot* (New York: Atheneum, 1967). For Cabot's views on various books, see Harris, pp. 166–67 and p. 215. Harris's book was my source for Cabot's erotic letters to his wife, pp. 228–30. Chase's letter to Cabot on expenditures appears in the GLC Collection, Box 17. The account of Cabot's habits and quirks comes from a *Time* obituary, "Zest for Life," published in its November 9, 1962, edition. Thomas D. Cabot's comments about his father come from the younger Cabot's autobiography, *Beggar on Horseback* (Boston: David R. Godine, Boston, 1979), pp. 1–2. For the account of Martha R. Hunt's life, death, and bequest to the Watch and Ward, I relied on the April 10 and May 26, 1910, editions of the *Globe*. For the impact of the Hunt bequest on Watch and Ward expenditures and endowment, I relied on the 1913–14 and 1914–15 ARs.

CHAPTER 6: NEW BEDFORD, 1916

For the Watch and Ward raid and reactions to it, I relied extensively on the July 9, 1916, edition of the *New Bedford Sunday Standard*. Clippings of these articles can be found in the GLC Collection, Box 17. For the arrest of Thomas H. Kearns, I relied on the July 12 and 21, 1916, editions of the *Boston Globe*.

CHAPTER 7: THE BATTLE OF DIAMOND HILL, 1917–1918

Allen's August 2, 1917, letter outlining the War Department's aims appears in the GLC Collection, Box 17. For details on the raid on the "Farms," I drew from the April 22, 1917, edition of the *Springfield Union*, the NEWWS Annual Report, 1917–18, and a letter from Chase to Cabot dated May 1, 1917, found in the GLC Collection, Box 17. The raids in the immediate area of Camp Devens are also described in the 1917–18 report. For the national perspective, I relied on Allen M. Brandt's excellent social history of venereal disease in the United States, *No Magic Bullet* (New York: Oxford University Press, 1987). I also found Nancy K. Bristow's *Making Men Moral* (New York: New York University Press, 1997) to be quite helpful. I owe the quote about New Orleans as a "Gibraltar of commercialized vice" to Brandt, p. 75. Chase's comments on the danger of "a bad or diseased woman" are cited in Brandt, p. 73, and his view of the relationship between venereal disease and liquor comes from the Watch and Ward pamphlet "The First Corps of Moral Engineers," found in the GLC Collection, Box 17. The Gloucester raid is described in the May 6, 1918, edition of the *Gloucester Daily Times*; the New Bedford raid in the May 19 and 21, 1918, editions of the *New Bedford Times*; and the Taunton raid in the August 26 and 28, 1918, editions of the *Taunton Gazette*. For these articles on various raids, I am indebted to the GLC Collection, Box 18. For the Cumberland, Rhode Island, raid, I drew on a number of sources, including the October 28, 1918, editions of the *Boston Globe*, *Boston Herald*, and *Providence Journal*. I also relied on J. Frank Chase's account, "The Challenge of Diamond Hill," found in the GLC Collection, Box 17.

CHAPTER 8: CAFÉ SOCIETY, 1917–1919

Allen's call for café partitions, made at the annual meeting held on March 29, 1916, is in the NEWWS Annual Report, 1915–16. For the mob attack on the Watch and Ward, I relied on the March 29 and 30 and April 5, 1916, editions of the *Boston Globe*. The trial at which the society's tactics were strongly condemned was reported in the *Globe* on April 11. The society's defense appeared in the *Boston Daily Advertiser* on April 19, 1916. I took Professor William T. Sedgwick's praise of informers from the 1915–16 AR. The report of agent #1 at the Florence Hotel café is found in the GLC Collection, Box 18. For the mass roundups on the streets of Boston, I relied on the *Globe*'s coverage, starting June 12, 1918, and continuing through the beginning of July. For the CTCA social worker's comment on the "charm and glamour" of the uniform, I am indebted to Brandt, p. 81. Major R. W. Pullman's comments to the police were reported in the *Boston Globe* on September 19, 1918. For the Revere House incident, I drew upon J. Frank Chase's letter to Godfrey Cabot, January 3, 1917, found in the GLC Collection, Box 17; the *Boston Post* reporting of November 29, 1917, found in the GLC Collection, Box 17; and *Boston Globe* coverage of the trial January 9–19, 1918. The judge's final decree was reported in the *Globe* on March 23, 1919. The *Globe* detailed the glamorous history of the Revere House in its August 3, 1919, issue.

CHAPTER 9: CORRUPTION FIGHTERS, 1913–1924

The downfalls of Joseph Pelletier, Nathan Tufts, and Daniel Coakley provided fodder for Boston's newspapers for many years. I took my account of the woman abused by the amorous Boston physician from Leon Harris's *Only to God* (New York: Atheneum, 1967), pp. 236–39. The Harris book also provided background on Tufts and Pelletier, pp. 239–41, as did Francis Russell's engaging *The Knave of Boston and Other Ambiguous Characters* (Boston: Quinlan Press, 1987), pp. 2–5. I took my description of the "badger game" from Russell, p. 5. For the Mishawam Manor case, I drew on David Yallop's biography of silent-film star Fatty Arbuckle, *The Day the Laughter Stopped* (New York: St. Martins, 1976), pp. 67–70, as well as Jack Beatty's definitive biography of James Michael Curley, *The Rascal King* (Reading, Mass.: Addison-Wesley, 1992), pp. 195–96. For the Emerson Motors case, I drew from Arthur Warner's article, "Blackmail à la Boston," in the *Nation*, November 2, 1921. Warner's article provides an informative overall guide to the Tufts and Pelletier cases. For Godfrey Cabot's campaign against Pelletier and Coakley and their counterattack, see *Only to God*, pp. 243–51. The wiring of Pelletier's office comes from the report of Operative #8 on October 30, 1917, found in the GLC Collection, Box 17. The *Globe* covered Pelletier's response in its November 15, 1919, edition. I took my coverage of the Cabot trial from the *Globe*, November 15, 1920, through January 27, 1921. The *Globe* was also the source for the Tufts trial in articles beginning on July 11, 1921; for Tufts's reaction to his sentence, see the October 2, 1921, edition of the *Boston Globe*. The populist nature of Pelletier's mayoral campaign is discussed in James. J. Connolly's *The Triumph of Urban Progressivism* (Cambridge: Harvard University Press, 1998), p. 176. For Pelletier's abortive run for mayor and for his trial, I relied on the *Globe*, starting on October 12, 1921, extending through January 22 and 24, 1922. Jack Beatty's *The Rascal King*, pp. 220–24, presents a vivid account of Pelletier's withdrawal from the race. For Pelletier's death, see the March 26, 1924, edition of the *Globe*. H. L. Mencken provides an interesting account of Pelletier's trial attorney in "James A. Reed of Missouri" (*American Mercury*, April 1929). For the story of Coakley's later years, I recommend Russell's *The Knave of Boston*, pp. 10–19; Russell also discusses rumors regarding Pelletier's death,

p. 10. Tufts's strangely incomplete obituary appeared in the *New York Times* on November 10, 1952. Godfrey Cabot's pride in the ousters of Pelletier and Tufts and his reaction to the Pelletier case are illuminated in the Harris biography, p. 251.

CHAPTER 10: MENCKEN VERSUS CHASE, ROUND 2, 1926

Much of the narrative in this chapter draws on Mencken's book *The Editor, the Bluenose, and the Prostitute: H. L. Mencken's History of the "Hatrack" Censorship Case*, edited by Carl Bode (Boulder, Colo.: Roberts Rinehart Publishers, 1988), a richly detailed, if unsurprisingly one-sided, account of the entire affair. The Walter Lippmann quote on Mencken's influence is cited in Teachout's *The Skeptic* (New York: HarperCollins, 2002), p. 9. The Hemingway quote appears in *The Sun Also Rises* (New York: Scribner, 1926), p. 49; Mencken's own comments on Puritans and Puritanism were cited in Teachout, p. 125, and in Schorer's *Sinclair Lewis* (New York: McGraw-Hill, 1961), p. 482. Descriptions of the hearing before Judge James P. Parmenter also come from the April 8, 1926, editions of the *Boston Globe*, *Boston Herald*, and *New York Times*. Mencken's dinner at the St. Botolph Club is related in *The Editor, the Bluenose, and the Prostitute*, pp. 68–69. For Mencken's appearance at Harvard, I relied on *Time* magazine's vivid April 19, 1926, "Hatrack" article. The depictions of Mencken and Chase's post-trial maneuvers are based on Mencken's book and newspaper accounts. The *Harvard Crimson's* April 14, 1926, story was the basis for my information on Chase's "New Puritanism" speech. Coverage of the police ban on "stunt arrests" comes from the *Globe* and *Herald* of April 22, 1926. The *Boston Telegram's* vitriolic series of attacks on Chase and on the Watch and Ward can be found in the newspaper's April 23–28 editions. For the Watch and Ward lawyers' end run around Chase, I relied on *The Editor, the Bluenose, and the Prostitute*, pp. 149–50. Chase's comment on the nature of reputation appeared in the profile "J. Frank Chase: The Cleanup Specialist" (*New Bedford Sunday Standard*, July 16, 1916). Mencken's "surmise" appeared in *The Editor, the Bluenose, and the Prostitute*, p. 151. Accounts of Chase's death come from the November 4, 1926, edition of the *Globe*. I drew on details of his funeral from the family Web site, the "Chase Chronicles," http://www.webnests.com/Chase/chronicles.htm.

CHAPTER 11: CENSORSHIP GOES WILD, 1927–1928

For my portrait of 1920s Boston, I drew on Charles H. Trout's *Boston: The Great Depression and the New Deal* (New York: Oxford University Press, 1977), pp. 3–26, and Jack Beatty's *The Rascal King* (Reading, Mass.: Addison-Wesley, 1992), pp. 272–73. The information on Oliver Garrett comes from the February 1, 1931, edition of the *Miami News*. Boyer was an invaluable guide in trying to understand the censorship machinations of this period; he has done the seminal research here. Upton Sinclair's joke about being banned in Boston comes from his biography, *Radical Innocent*, by Anthony Sinclair (New York: Random House, 2006). William Henry Cardinal O'Connell's background is related in James O'Toole's fair-minded *Militant and Triumphant: William Henry O'Connell and the Catholic Church in Boston, 1859–1944* (South Bend, Ind.: University of Notre Dame Press, 1992). Also recommended is Thomas H. O'Connor's *Boston Catholics* (Boston: Northeastern University Press, 1998). My information on Irish book banning comes from "Censorship in the Irish Free State," by Senia Paseta (*Past & Present*, no. 181, November 2003, pp. 193–218). See also "Boston Book Censorship in the Twenties," by Paul S. Boyer (*American Quarterly*, vol. 15, no. 1, Spring 1963, pp. 11–12). *The Plastic Age* was reviewed in the *New York Times* on February 3, 1924; *The Rebel Bird* on February 20, 1927; and *The Hard Boiled Virgin* on December 12, 1926. Michael H. Crowley's comments on censorship appeared in *Publishers' Weekly* on March 19, 1927. For the ban on *Elmer Gantry* and the collapse of the "gentlemen's agreement," the best source are the April 13 and 14, 1927, editions of the *Boston Herald*. See also *Publishers' Weekly*, April 16, 1927, and coverage in the *New York Times* during this same period. The background on Crowley comes from the October 17, 1913, and February 11 and 14, 1915, editions of the *Boston Globe*. For Crowley's views on sex in fiction, I quoted from Elmer Davis's "Boston: Notes on a Barbarian Invasion" (*Harper's Monthly*, January 1928). Publisher Donald S. Friede's background is detailed in his lively autobiography, *The Mechanical Angel* (New York: Alfred A. Knopf, 1948), and his obituary in the *New York Times*, published on May 31, 1965. For reactions to the book bans, I drew on the April 15 and 16, 1927, editions of the *Boston Herald*; the April 17 edition of the *New York Times*; and the April 23 and May 28, 1917, editions of *Publishers' Weekly*; see also Boyer here. The *Pilot* editorial was quoted in the *Herald* on April 16, 1927, and William J. Foley's speech before the Abstinence League comes from Davis's article in *Harpers*. The ban on *Oil!* was reported in the *New York Times* on May 28, June 1, and June 8. Sinclair's description of bookseller John Gritz as "a cherub" and himself as a "prize prude" appeared in his article "Poor Me and Pure Boston" (*Nation*, June 29, 1927). For the story of Sinclair's misadventures in Boston, his book *Money Writes* (published by the author, Station B, Long Beach, California, 1927) was a useful, if self-serving, guide; his interview with Crowley appears there, pp. 181–82. The comment about Boston as "our advertising department" comes from Boyer, p. 187. See also *New York Times* coverage of Sinclair on June 3, June 13, and June 22, 1927. The *New York Times* discussed Charles Sherman Bodwell's ascendency at the Watch and Ward in its July 3, 1927, issue. For Bodwell's re-entry into the censorship game and conflicts with the Reverend Paul Sterling and Crowley, I relied on Secretary's Reports of 1927 and 1928, in NEWWS Records, Box 16/3. Mary Lee's article on the Kafkaesque nature of Boston's book ban appeared in the *New York Times* on January 22, 1928; this was an attempt to grapple with the subject that no Boston newspaper attempted. I also highly recommend Paul S.

Boyer's "Boston Book Censorship in the Twenties" (*American Quarterly* 15, no. 1, Spring 1963), as well as P. C. Kemeny's "Power, Ridicule, and the Destruction of Religious Moral Reform Politics of the 1920s" in the anthology *The Secular Revolution*, edited by Christian Smith (Berkeley: University of California Press, 2003).

CHAPTER 12: BOSTON, 1929

The Watch and Ward's judgment on *The Well of Loneliness* comes from the December 1928 Secretary's Report, NEWWS Records, Box 16/3. Elmer Davis's observations on Boston come from his article "Boston: Notes on a Barbarian Invasion." The effect of censorship on Boston's commerce is discussed in Boyer. For the *American Tragedy* appeal trial, I drew on Friede's *The Mechanical Angel*, pp. 142–48; Karl Schriftgiesser's article, "Boston Stays Pure" (*The New Republic*, May 8, 1929); and W. A. Swanberg's biography, *Dreiser* (New York: Scribners, 1963), pp. 352–53. For the Ford Hall frolic, I relied on Boyer, pp. 193–94, and the April 17, 1929, edition of the *Globe*. Friede's book, p. 147, is the source of the quote, "I know not, sirs, from whence they derive their sociology . . ."; he also relates the woes of Lieutenant Daniel J. Hines. The Watch and Ward's involvement in the *A Farewell to Arms* ban is made clear in NEWWS Records, Box 6/12. The *New York Times* coverage of the episode, including the Scribner's statement, comes from its June 21, 1929, edition. The *Boston Herald* editorial, *New Republic* comment, and *New York Herald Tribune* editorial are all included in "Ernest Hemingway's *A Farewell to Arms*: A Documentary Volume," edited by Charles M. Oliver in the *Dictionary of Literary Biography*, Volume 308 (Detroit: Thomas Gale Publishing, 2005). The background on Boston's city censor comes from Karl Schriftgiesser's "How Little Rollo Came to Rule the Mind of Boston," published in the September 21, 1929, issue of *Boston Transcript* magazine. I took John M. Casey's famous statement about theatrical standards from John H. Houchin's *Censorship in the American Theatre in the Twentieth Century* (Cambridge, UK: Cambridge University Press, 2003), p. 112. My information on the *Fiesta* episode comes from the December 10, 13, and 16, 1928, editions of the *New York Times*, as well as the December 1 and 15 editions of the *Harvard Crimson*. For the *Strange Interlude* ban, I drew on the *Globe*, *Herald*, and *Transcript* coverage starting on September 17, 1929. The *Transcript* editorial was published on September 17, 1929, and the *Globe* editorial on September 18. Frank Rich's view of *Strange Interlude* appeared in the February 22, 1985, edition of the *New York Times*. For Mayor Malcolm Nichols's background, I used Jack Beatty's *The Rascal King*, p. 273. Curley's view of Nichols comes from his autobiography, *I'd Do It Again* (Englewood Cliffs, N.J.: Prentice Hall, 1957), p. 190. For a retrospective look at *Strange Interlude* opening in Quincy and its effect on the city, I recommend "Banned in Boston, OK in Quincy," published in the *Patriot Ledger* on November 13, 2007.

CHAPTER 13: THE DUNSTER BOOKSHOP FIASCO, 1929

The description of the raid on the Golden Hind Press appears in Jay A. Gertz-man's *Bookleggers and Smuthounds* (Philadelphia: University of Pennsylvania Press, 1999). My account of the Dunster House entrapment comes from the ap-peal trial testimony of John Tait Slaymaker, James A. DeLacey, and others, as reported in the *Boston Globe* on December 20, 1929. Gardner Jackson's account, "My Brother's Peeper" (*Nation*, January 15, 1930), was helpful as well. The pos-sibility that the "student" who sold DeLacey a secondhand copy of *Lady Chatter-ley's Lover* might have been a Watch and Ward agent is reported in Christopher M. Finan's *From the Palmer Raids to the Patriot Act* (Boston: Beacon Press, 2007), p. 103. The details of the trial in Cambridge district court trial were reported in the *Harvard Crimson* on November 26, 1929. The *Boston Herald* editorial flogging the Watch and Ward appeared on December 21, 1929. The December 24, 1929, edition of the *Crimson* relates the reluctance of Harvard undergraduates to live under Professor Julian Coolidge's tutelage. For coverage of the appeal trial, I consulted the *Boston Globe*, *Boston Herald*, and *New York Times* editions of Decem-ber 19–21, 1929. The Watch and Ward's defense of its conduct is from NEWWS Records, December 14, 1929, Box 12/1. David D. Scannell's comment appeared in the *Globe* on January 14, 1930. The Reverend Raymond Calkins's letter plead-ing with President Daniel L. Marsh to stay on, dated June 30, 1930, is in NEWWS Records, Box 8/1. The invitation to Cardinal O'Connell, dated June 2, 1930, also appears in NEWWS Records, Box 9/4. The cardinal's attitudes towards "mingling" with Protestants are described in Thomas H. O'Connor's *Boston Catholics* (Boston: Northeastern University Press, 1998), p. 216. NEWWS Re-cords, Box 12/1, is the source of letters from disillusioned members. The drop in contributions is evident from NEWWS Annual Reports, 1928–29 through 1931–32. Secretary Bodwell's letter to John Sumner blaming the "wets" on January 22, 1930, is in NEWWS Records, Box 10/1. District Attorney Rob-ert T. Bushnell's attack on the Watch and Ward was reported in the *New York Times* on January 23, 1930. I took my account of the passage of the liberalized censorship law from Boyer, p. 205; for more detail on the legislative maneuver-ings, see *The Gentleman Mr. Shattuck* by John T. Galvin (Boston: Tontine Press, 1996), pp. 243–45. For more on new restrictions on book banning by U.S. Cus-toms, see Finan, pp. 103–7. Congratulatory messages to DeLacey are described in the *Harvard Crimson* on June 10, 1930. DeLacey's fate is recounted in Boyer, p. 198.

CHAPTER 14: DEPRESSION DAYS, 1930–1938

The society's book censorship activities during this period appear in the Sec-retary's Reports in the NEWWS Records, Box 16/3. *Time* magazine's evaluation of *Thirteen Men* appears in "Shoe Box Notes," in its September 27, 1937 edition.

Attempts at movie censorship can be found in NEWWS Records 13/5 and 13/6. For magazine censorship and Meyer J. Reiser's comments, see the "Minutes of the New England Magazine Distributors," November 18, 1930, found in the NEWWS Records, Box 16/3. Secretary Bodwell describes his difficulties in New London in an October 14, 1930, letter to the Reverend J. Beveridge Lee, found in the NEWWS Records, Box 5/1. For information on the newsstands in other cities, I used Bodwell's letter of June 18, 1935, found in the NEWWS Records, Box 5/12. For background on Whiz Bang, I recommend William Coyle's informative "From Scatology to Social History: Captain Billy's Whiz Bag" (www.compedit .com/whiz/bang). Telegrams between Bodwell and Robert Haig can be found in NEWWS Records, Box 8. The correspondence between Peabody and Bodwell regarding Esquire is in the NEWWS Records, Box 10/11. The revised Moral Code appears in the NEWWS Records, Box 13/8. The Herald parody of Curley is cited in Reardon, p. 129. For the travails of Within the Gates, I am indebted to Reardon and to "Boston v. O'Casey," published in Time on January 28, 1935. Brooks Atkinson's review of the play can be found in his book Sean O'Casey: From Times Past (Totowa, N.J.: Barnes and Noble Books, 1982), pp. 60–61. Father Russell M. Sullivan's objections are detailed in "Boston v. O'Casey" (Time, January 28, 1935). The reporter's description of Mayor Frederick W. Mansfield is gleefully recounted in Curley's I'd Do It Again (Englewood Cliffs, N.J.: Prentice Hall, 1957), p. 192. Mansfield's view of Within the Gates was reported in the Time article of January 28, 1935, while Frank Chouteau Brown's opinion appeared in the New York Times on January 17, 1935. The impression of Brown as "open-minded" comes from "Notes of the Back Bay Region" (New York Times, January 29, 1935). For an interesting look at Henry Wadsworth Longfellow Dana, I recommend Douglass Shand-Tucci's The Crimson Letter (New York: St. Martin's Press, 2003), pp. 129–37. The trip of the forty-six Boston "rebels" to New York was reported in the Times on February 3, 1935. On Waiting for Lefty, I drew upon Reardon's description, pp. 198–99, and the New York Times reporting of April 7 and 15 and July 20, 1935. The saga of Stevedore was covered extensively in the Boston Globe on September 21 and 22, 1935, and in the Times on September 23. For the controversy over The Children's Hour, I relied on Globe and Times coverage starting December 14, 1935, and continuing through the rest of the month. The testimony before Judge George Sweeney is related in Houchin's Censorship in the American Theatre in the Twentieth Century (New York: Cambridge University Press, 2003), pp. 124–25; see also New York Times, January 30, 1936. For the background on the two movie versions of the play, see Brett Eliza Westbrook's intriguing essay, "Second Chances: The Remake of Lillian Hellman's 'The Children's Hour'" (www.brightlightsfilm.com). I relied on Reardon, pp. 204–7, for most of my information on the loosening of the theatrical censorship law. I recommend Reardon, as well, on the opening of Tobacco Road (p. 208). The oaths "by Gad" and "by Judas" are noted in the article "Infinity via

Tobacco Road," *New York Times*, March 10, 1940. Secretary Bodwell's comments on theater censorship can be found in his letter to Ruth Haney dated October 28, 1938, in the NEWWS Records, Box 4/12.

CHAPTER 15: THIS WAS BURLESQUE, 1931–1953

The Watch and Ward's activities on censorship, gambling, and burlesque for December 1931 can be found in the Secretary's Report of that date, found in the NEWWS Records, Box 16/3. For background on the Old Howard, I drew on David Kruh's book about Boston's Scollay Square, *Always Something Doing* (Boston: Northeastern University Press, 1989); Theresa Lang's "Interred in Concrete: The Censorship of Boston's Old Howard Theatre" (doctoral thesis in drama, Tufts University, Medford, Mass., 2004); and Ann Corio and Joseph DiMona's highly entertaining but not always reliable *This Was Burlesque* (New York: Grosset and Dunlap, 1968). For background on burlesque, I relied on Robert C. Allen's *Horrible Prettiness: Burlesque and American Culture* (Chapel Hill: University of North Carolina Press, 1991). The Ann Corio quotations come from *This Was Burlesque*, pp. 154–56 and 175. The original Boston Moral Code is cited in Reardon, pp. 123–24. I owe the anecdote about Calkins and Curley to Reardon, p. 124. Information about the William Corbett investigation and the Watch and Ward testimonials from police chiefs can be found in the NEWWS Records, Box 7/8. The Watch and Ward investigative reports on various burlesque shows can be found in the NEWWS Records, Box 13/5. The letter to the Board of Censors complaining about the Old Howard appears in the NEWWS Records, Box 13/6. I am indebted to Kruh for the description of investigator Slaymaker, pp. 67–68. Ann Corio's comment before the Board of Censors hearing is quoted in Reardon, p. 192. The *Globe's* coverage of the closing of the Old Howard dates from January 18, 1933. Curley's view of the Watch and Ward comes from *I'd Do It Again*, pp. 255–56. Kruh's book, p. 69, is the source of the "red flannels" anecdote. The shutdown of the Minsky's Park Theatre and its ramifications are described in the NEWWS Annual Report, 1933–34. The meeting of society president Brown with Mayor Mansfield and the city censor is recounted in the Secretary's Report, January 1935, found in the NEWWS Records, Box 15/1. For Fiorello LaGuardia's war against burlesque, see Lang, p. 132. I relied on Kruh's depiction of the last days of the Old Howard, pp. 78–85.

CHAPTER 16: THE FORTIES, 1941–1948

Few historical accounts have touched upon the Watch and Ward's vigorous censorship activities of the 1940s. For Cardinal O'Connell's reaction to *Henry Pulham, Esquire* and subsequent attempts to ban it, I used the April 12, 1941, issue of *Publishers' Weekly*. I am indebted to the same article for the fate of *What Makes Sammy Run?* For the cardinal's view of Einstein, see the April 8 and 9,

1929, editions of the *New York Times*. Bernard DeVoto's view of Boston censorship and his comments on *Strange Fruit* appeared in "The Easy Chair" (*Harper's*, May 1944). For the ban on *Strange Fruit*, see the April 9, 1944, edition of the *New York Times* and the March 25, 1944, edition of *Publishers' Weekly*. Eleanor Roosevelt's laudatory comments on *Strange Fruit* can be found in the May 16, 1944, edition of the *New York Times*; the *Times* review appeared in March 5, 1944. *Time* magazine's "Ban on Fruit," an article published in the April 17, 1944, issue, offers an account of DeVoto's test case in typically lively style. For the first obscenity trial of *Strange Fruit*, see the April 27, 1944, edition of the *Boston Globe*. The Post Office ban on *Strange Fruit* is described in the *New York Times* on May 16, 1944; see Christopher Finan's *From the Palmer Raids to the Patriot Act* (Boston: Beacon Press, 2007), pp. 171–72, for a wider account of U.S. Post Office censorship. For the Supreme Judicial Court ruling on the book, I used Felice Flanery Lewis's *Literature, Obscenity, & Law* (Carbondale: Southern Illinois University Press, 1976). For *Strange Fruit* sales figures, see the November 25, December 9, and December 16, 1944, issues of *Publishers' Weekly*. For the theatrical version of *Strange Fruit* in Boston, I relied on the October 18, 1945, edition of the *New York Times*. Secretary Croteau's view of *Strange Fruit*, the play, can be found in the October 1945 Secretary's Report, found in the NEWWS Records, Box 17, while his maneuvers regarding the book are in his March 1944 Secretary's Report, also in Box 17. For background on Croteau, I am indebted to Lois Stryker's very helpful pamphlet on the history of the society, "Crime and Justice Foundation 1878–1975," found in the NEWWS Records, Box 13. Information on Croteau's anti-gay campaign comes from the Secretary's Reports dated January 24, 1944, and March 16, 1945, found in NEWWS Records, Box 17. For background on Kathleen Winsor, I relied on the September 18 and October 8, 1944, editions of the *New York Times*, and her obituary in the *Times* on May 28, 2003. I also drew on the article "Ods-Fish, Madame," which appeared in the December 18, 1944, issue of *Time*. *Time* magazine's report on book sales in wartime comes from its December 18, 1944, issue. Orville Prescott's review appeared in the *New York Times* on October 16, 1944, while the *Time* review came out on October 23, 1944. Hollywood's Joseph Breen's comments appear in Gregory D. Black's *The Catholic Crusade Against the Movies, 1940–75* (New York: Cambridge University Press, 1997), p. 56. For the Watch and Ward role in the *Forever Amber* ban, see the November 4, 1944, edition of *Publishers' Weekly*. Mary McGrory's article in the *Boston Herald* appeared on October 17, 1944. The *Herald's* report on *Amber's* sales comes from its October 20, 1944, issue. The Watch and Ward's efforts to track *Amber* in other cities are detailed in the Secretary's Report dated January 11, 1945. For the *Tragic Ground* case, I drew on the December 23, 1944, edition of *Publishers' Weekly* and the December 29, 1944, editions of the *Boston Globe* and *New York Times*. For *Time's* evaluation of the verdict, see "Setback," January 8,

1945. The tastes of the American reading public were documented in the *New York Times* on May 5, 1946. For *Amber*'s enormous success in raising money for war bonds, see the December 30, 1944, edition of *Publishers' Weekly*, and the January 5, 1945, edition of the *New York Times*. Revisions in the censorship law were discussed in the December 30, 1944, edition of *Publishers' Weekly* and the January 6, 1947, edition of the *New Republic*. Croteau's increasingly difficult relations with Fuller are discussed in his Secretary's Report dated March 1, 1945, found in the NEWWS Records, Box 17; his doubts about Watch and Ward involvement in any censorship test case appear in the January 1946 Secretary's Report, also from Box 17. For lower-court decisions in the *Forever Amber* case, see the July 6, 1946, and March 4 and 11, 1947, editions of the *New York Times*. I took the Boston bookseller's brief from the April 5, 1947, issue of *Publishers' Weekly*. The *Pilot*'s critical view of *Forever Amber* the movie appeared in its October 31, 1947, editorial; I owe the jewelry store anecdote to Black, p. 62. The Supreme Judicial Court decision appears in Edward de Grazia's *Censorship Landmarks* (New York: R. R. Bowker, 1969), p. 159. For the death of Croteau, I relied on Lois Stryker's historical overview, "Crime and Justice Foundation 1878–1975," found in the NEWWS Records, Box 13.

CHAPTER 17: A KINDER, GENTLER
WATCH AND WARD, 1948–1967

I drew much of my information about the reinvented Watch and Ward from the NEWWS Annual Report, 1951. Joseph Dinneen's articles "The Watch and Ward Changes Its Spots" and "Organized Crime Only Target of N.E. Group" appeared in the *Boston Globe* on April 4 and 5, 1951, respectively. The video of CBS *Reports's* "Biography of a Bookie Joint" can be viewed online at http://atlantis2 .cbsnews.com. For information about the postwar paperback boom, I recommend Dan B. Miller's *Erskine Caldwell* (New York: Alfred A. Knopf, 1994). *Time*'s "All-Time Fiction Bestseller List" appeared in the February 2, 1968, issue. For the court's ruling on *God's Little Acre*, see de Grazia, pp. 169–70. For Cambridge and Boston censorship efforts, I relied on the April 5, 1951, edition of the *Boston Globe* and the December 12, 1952, edition of the *Harvard Crimson*. For the "Red Scare" at the Boston Public Library, see the October 4, 1952, edition of the *New York Times* and the November 1, 1952, issue of the *Nation*. For information of the National Organization for Decent Literature and its attacks on paperback books nationwide, I used Finan, pp. 175–77. Boston's reaction to *Long Day's Journey Into Night* and the censorship of *Who's Afraid of Virginia Woolf?* is related in the *New York Times* on October 17, 1956, and September 4, 1963. For court decisions on obscenity in the 1960s, I relied on Finan, pp. 194–203, and Boyer, pp. 275–82. Also see the July 18, 1962; March 22, 1966; and May 23, 1970, editions of the *New York Times*. I also recommend Fred Kaplan, "The Day Obscenity Became

Art" (*New York Times*, July 21, 2009). Comments regarding the Watch and Ward's successor organization come from the author's interview with John J. Larivee on October 22, 2009.

EPILOGUE

Apley's comment appears in John P. Marquand's *The Late George Apley* (Boston: Little Brown and Company, 1937), p. 346.

INDEX